Transnational LGBT
Activism

TRANSNATIONAL LGBT ACTIVISM

Working for Sexual Rights Worldwide

RYAN R. THORESON

UNIVERSITY OF MINNESOTA PRESS
MINNEAPOLIS · LONDON

Chapter 5 was previously published as "Power, Panics, and Pronouns: The Information Politics of Transnational LGBT NGOs," *Journal of Language and Sexuality* 2, no. 1 (2013): 145–77. Reprinted with the kind permission of John Benjamins Publishing Company, Amsterdam/Philadelphia.

Published by the University of Minnesota Press
111 Third Avenue South, Suite 290
Minneapolis, MN 55401–2520
http://www.upress.umn.edu

Library of Congress Cataloging-in-Publication Data

Thoreson, Ryan R.
    Transnational LGBT activism : working for sexual rights worldwide / Ryan R. Thoreson.
    Includes bibliographical references and index.
    ISBN 978-0-8166-9271-2 (hc : alk. paper) — ISBN 978-0-8166-9274-3 (pb : alk. paper)
    1. Gay rights—Cross-cultural studies. 2. Human rights advocacy—Cross-cultural studies.
3. International Gay and Lesbian Human Rights Commission. I. Title.
    HQ76.5.T477 2014
    323.3'264—dc23

                                                                2014002045

for Kimberly Theidon

Contents

Abbreviations

AAA	American Anthropological Association
ACHPR	African Commission on Human and Peoples' Rights
ACT-UP	AIDS Coalition To Unleash Power
ADEFHO	L'Association pour la Défense des Droits des Homosexuels
ADP	Asylum Documentation Program
AFHRO	African Human Rights Organization
AI	Amnesty International
AIMLGC	Amnesty International Members for Lesbian and Gay Concerns
ALITT	Asociación Lucha por la Identitdad Travesti y Transexual
AMSHeR	African Men for Sexual Health and Rights
API	Asia and the Pacific Islands
AU	African Union
CAL	Coalition of African Lesbians
CAT	Convention Against Torture
CCM	Country Coordinating Mechanism
CEDAW	Convention on the Elimination of All Forms of Discrimination Against Women
CEDEP	Centre for the Development of People

CERD	Convention on the Elimination of All Forms of Racial Discrimination
CGE	Council for Global Equality
CHR	Commission on Human Rights
CHRR	Centre for Human Rights and Rehabilitation
CMHR	Charter of the Ministry of Human Rights
CRC	Convention on the Rights of the Child
CSW	Commission on the Status of Women
CUNY	City University of New York
EAC	East African Community
ECOSOC	Economic and Social Council
ERN	Emergency Response Network
FARUG	Freedom and Roam Uganda
FIERCE	Fabulously Independent Educated Radicals for Community Empowerment
GALCK	Gay and Lesbian Coalition of Kenya
GALESWA	Gays and Lesbians of Swaziland
GATE	Global Advocates for Trans Equality
HRC	Human Rights Council
HRF	Human Rights First
HRW	Human Rights Watch
HURCLED	Human Rights Clinic and Education Center
IAB	International Advisory Board
IACHR	Inter-American Commission on Human Rights
ICASA	International Conference on AIDS and STIs in Africa
ICCPR	International Covenant on Civil and Political Rights
ICESCR	International Covenant on Economic, Social, and Cultural Rights
ICJ	International Commission of Jurists
IDAHO	International Day Against Homophobia and Transphobia

IDUs	injection drug users
IGLHRC	International Gay and Lesbian Human Rights Commission
ILGA	International Lesbian, Gay, Bisexual, Trans, and Intersex Association
ILGA-Europe	European Region of the International Lesbian, Gay, Bisexual, Trans, and Intersex Association
KEMRI	Kenya Medical Research Institute
LAC	Latin America and the Caribbean
LBL	Landsforeningen for Bøsser og Lesbiske
LeAP	Lesbian Advocates Philippines
LEGABIBO	Lesbians, Gays, and Bisexuals of Botswana
LGBT	lesbian, gay, bisexual, and transgender
LSVD	Lesben und Schwulenverband in Deutschland
MARP	most-at-risk population
MENA	Middle East and North Africa
Mercosur	Common Market of the South
MSM	men who have sex with men
NAMBLA	North American Man/Boy Love Association
NSP	National Strategic Plan
NYU	New York University
OAS	Organization of American States
OCCUR	Japan Association for the Lesbian and Gay Movement
OHCHR	Office of the High Commissioner for Human Rights
OSI	Open Society Institute
PEPFAR	President's Emergency Plan for AIDS Relief
PRA	Political Research Associates
PSI	Population Services International
QEJ	Queers for Economic Justice
SASOD	Society Against Sexual Orientation Discrimination

SIDA	Swedish International Development Cooperation Agency
SMUG	Sexual Minorities Uganda
SOGI	sexual orientation and gender identity
SRLP	Sylvia Rivera Law Project
STRAP	Society of Transsexual Women of the Philippines
Third Committee	Social, Humanitarian, and Cultural Affairs Committee
UCT	University of Cape Town
UDHR	Universal Declaration of Human Rights
UN	United Nations
UNAIDS	Joint United Nations Programme on HIV/AIDS
UNDP	United Nations Development Programme
UNGA	United Nations General Assembly
UPR	Universal Periodic Review
UU-UNO	Unitarian Universalists' United Nations Office
WILPF	Women's International League for Peace and Freedom
WSW	women who have sex with women

Introduction

"Studying Up" and the Anthropology of Transnational LGBT Human Rights Advocacy

On a warm spring evening during my fieldwork, I sat in a lecture hall in Washington, D.C., listening to the keynote address at a conference on sexual transgression. At the podium, the speaker incisively critiqued the complicity of lesbian, gay, bisexual, and transgender (LGBT) organizations in perpetuating anti-immigrant stereotypes and practices in Germany, where Lesben und Schwulenverband in Deutschland (LSVD) had built on legislative victories with a series of campaigns to promote tolerance toward LGBT persons. Among other strategies, activists had endorsed acceptance of homosexuality as a criterion for immigration into the country; put posters in Turkish neighborhoods of Berlin depicting two men, two women, and a man and a woman kissing; and relocated LGBT parades and events to working-class and migrant areas.

The vivid anecdotes deftly illustrated how sexual politics intersect with the politics of race, ethnicity, citizenship, religion, gender, and class. They also underscored why the agendas set by NGOs matter. By focusing on particular issues and adopting certain framings that shape suggested responses—for example, naming antigay violence as a problem and proposing hate crimes legislation as a solution—activists in Germany mobilized and asserted their political power in a way that affected a range of different communities. As the speaker pointed out, a hate crimes bill, if passed, would likely have a disproportionate impact on young, working-class, and migrant populations who were already the most targeted by the police in Germany. The passage of hate crimes legislation had nevertheless become imperative, the speaker concluded, as a transnational LGBT movement deemed it an essential marker of progress in any advanced democracy.

1

I paused, pen hovering over paper, at this final assertion. The speaker's critique of hate crimes legislation was not altogether novel; in the United States, progressive organizations like the Sylvia Rivera Law Project (SRLP) had offered similar justifications for declining to support the Matthew Shepard and James Byrd Jr. Hate Crimes Prevention Act.[1] Nor was it inconceivable that transnational NGOs might advance a culturally or politically insensitive agenda; LGBT human rights advocacy has often uncritically reproduced Euro-American assumptions and priorities.[2] Both of these objections were familiar and, to my mind, fairly persuasive.

Instead, I paused because hate crimes legislation had recently been a topic of internal debate at the International Gay and Lesbian Human Rights Commission (IGLHRC), the NGO where I was conducting fieldwork with LGBT human rights activists from September 2009 to September 2010. At a staff meeting, the regional coordinator for Asia and the Pacific Islands (API) had suggested that staff should clarify their institutional position on hate crimes legislation, noting that IGLHRC had no clear policy about asking "for criminalizing, what kind of criminalization, and for whom."[3] She had struggled with this ambiguity when she worked on a submission to the Special Rapporteur on the Right to Health regarding hate crimes laws in India, which some organizations in India endorsed.[4]

As IGLHRC's research and policy associate noted at the meeting, the discussion raised two questions: whether staff *generally* supported hate crimes legislation and whether staff would *specifically* support hate crimes legislation in particular contexts. The Middle East and North Africa (MENA) Program coordinator responded that a case-by-case approach would make more sense than an overarching policy. IGLHRC's local partners had different positions on the issue, and universal support for hate crimes laws would be counterproductive in contexts where discrete penalties and procedures for anti-LGBT violence bolstered the narrative that LGBT rights were "special rights." The program coordinator for Latin America and the Caribbean (LAC) agreed, noting that Brazil was the only country in his region with such a law. He attributed this not only to the historically high rate of crime targeting minorities but also to the ongoing debate over crime in Brazil generally. Most people in the region, including the staffer himself, were said to oppose such laws.

The meeting did not produce any conclusive position, for reasons that were logistical as well as theoretical. Some staff wanted to consult activists in their regions. The executive director was traveling, and his input was necessary to form a position. More mundanely, bandwidth problems in the office were scheduled to be fixed that afternoon, and multiple staffers were repeatedly dropped from Skype or unintelligible for portions of the call. The regional staff eventually agreed to submit position papers from their regions so the regional coordinator for API could compile them for further study.

Of course, the assertion that hate crimes legislation is part of a particular kind of LGBT agenda is not false. LGBT organizations in the United States made hate crimes legislation a perennial priority until a bill was finally signed into law by President Obama in 2009. Activists from South Africa to the Philippines have prioritized similar legislation in their own domestic advocacy.[5] International NGOs have also demanded hate crimes laws, including the European Region of the International Lesbian, Gay, Bisexual, Trans, and Intersex Association (ILGA-Europe), which works closely with LSVD.[6]

As the meeting at IGLHRC suggested, however, transnational activists can also complicate or resist the uncritical adoption of a hegemonic LGBT agenda. Staff at transnational NGOs typically consider a wide range of perspectives, moved both by the unique imperatives of global organizing and by their own convictions. Yet discussions of human rights, and particularly sexual rights, often become polarized, with defenders insisting on their universality and detractors dismissing them as Western inventions with little applicability elsewhere. During my time at IGLHRC, I was struck by two sources of ambiguity that exacerbated this polarity—first, the extent to which the category of LGBT human rights remains undefined and contested, and second, the degree to which the politics that shape that category are opaque to outsiders.

From an ethnographic perspective, these ambiguities counsel deeper engagement with LGBT human rights activists and the work they do. In practice, what *do* LGBT human rights encompass? And *how* is that category constructed, promoted, and institutionalized by transnational NGOs?[7] Although these three practices of human rights advocacy are often conflated, they can be usefully disaggregated, and staff at IGLHRC simultaneously engaged in all of them. Like many human rights activists, IGLHRC's staff *constructed* rights by delineating their scope, assigning responsibility for them, and demanding redress when they were violated. They *promoted* rights by publicizing them and drawing attention to instances where they were not respected. They *institutionalized* rights by encouraging NGOs, governments, and intergovernmental bodies to recognize them and incorporate them into their mandates. Exploring these processes requires attentiveness to the ways that human rights advocacy is undertaken and shaped, not merely in abstractions, but by groups of actual people with their own goals, backgrounds, and politics.

THE CONTESTABILITY OF LGBT HUMAN RIGHTS AS A CATEGORY IN FLUX

LGBT human rights have been among the most contentious topics in contemporary human rights debates. The terms "LGBT," "sexual orientation," and "gender identity" do not appear in the Universal Declaration of Human Rights (UDHR) or in any United Nations (UN) treaties—a point that their detractors regularly stress—but nevertheless have been read into agreements by treaty bodies and taken up by a variety of Special Procedures.[8] References to sexual orientation and gender identity have sparked acrimonious debates about Gender Equality Architecture Reform and the mandates of Special Procedures, and have repeatedly divided the UN's Economic and Social Council (ECOSOC); Social, Humanitarian, and Cultural Affairs Committee (Third Committee); and General Assembly (UNGA).

Despite fierce contestation,[9] activists have insisted that LGBT human rights are universal, inviolable, and nonnegotiable, and their efforts appear to be bearing fruit. In 2008, when a statement affirming the human rights of LGBT people was presented to the UNGA, approximately one-third of states voiced support, one-third issued a counterstatement objecting to the recognition of such rights, and one-third abstained or opted not to take a position.[10] On December 10, 2010, UN Secretary General Ban Ki-moon publicly and unequivocally expressed support for the recognition and protection of LGBT human rights at a groundbreaking event before the UNGA. Ban's statement followed years of increasing support for LGBT people at the UN, perhaps most consistently at the UN Commission on Human Rights (CHR) and then Human Rights Council (HRC) under High Commissioners for Human Rights Mary Robinson, Louise Arbour, and Navanethem Pillay. Support from a sitting secretary general was hailed as momentous by LGBT human rights activists. On March 22, 2011, another statement was presented to the UNGA, with an unprecedented eighty-five states voicing support.[11] On June 17, 2011, the HRC passed its first resolution expressing concern about violations on the basis of sexual orientation or gender identity.[12] The resolution narrowly passed amid heavy lobbying, with twenty-three members voting in favor, nineteen against, and three abstaining. These milestones point to real shifts in support, but they also illustrate that the recognition of LGBT human rights remains controversial.

LGBT human rights have also been contested domestically, where they are trumpeted or decried in assertions of national identity, sovereignty, and morality. As Martha Nussbaum has suggested, formulations of sex, gender, and the family are tightly yoked to understandings of tradition and culture, making contests around them potent sites of sociopolitical self-definition.[13] Homosexuality has been rejected outright by Iranian president Mahmoud Ahmadinejad;[14] labeled "un-African" by presidents Robert Mugabe of Zimbabwe, Sam Nujoma of Namibia, Yoweri Museveni of Uganda, Daniel arap Moi of Kenya, and Julius Nyerere of Tanzania;[15] and deemed contrary to "Asian Values" by the government of Singapore.[16] In the Americas, Australia, and parts of Europe, political leaders similarly invoke national and religious traditions in their opposition to homosexuality and LGBT marriage and adoption.[17] In the North and South alike, governments regularly use debates about sexuality to define national identity, whether through their insistence on the preservation of a heterosexual order or assertions of tolerance and diversity.[18]

Although the terms "gay" and "lesbian" and the politics associated with them originated in North America and Europe,[19] same-sex practices and identities have been documented virtually everywhere, and LGBT advocacy has taken root around the globe. Even in sub-Saharan Africa, where anti-LGBT animus has been heavily publicized, "gay rights organizations have been allowed to develop, if not to flourish, in many southern African countries in recent years—LEGABIBO in Botswana, GALESWA in Swaziland, Sister Namibia and the Rainbow Project in Namibia among them."[20] At present, many countries in sub-Saharan Africa not only have a national LGBT organization but also a multitude of groups with a range of distinctive identities, agendas, and priorities. The proliferation of these NGOs is accompanied by diversity among them as human rights approaches are complemented or supplanted by strategies focusing on gender, health, development, religion, and media.

In recent years, social scientists have begun exploring the unique demands and considerations of Southern LGBT advocacy.[21] They have highlighted the dilemmas that LGBT activists face in applying Northern frameworks to their own identities and struggles in a meaningful way, and the adaptation and hybridity necessary to do so.[22] These analyses have invited reflection on the globalization of sexual identities and politics, especially the diffusion of a "Global Gay" identity, and the processes by which particular sexual subjectivities circulate and become hegemonic as they travel around the globe.[23] The globalization of sexuality is usually attributed to the enormous political, economic, and cultural power of the "West" in general and the United States in particular.[24] The spread of networked technologies;[25] the circulation of mass media;[26] the reach of transnational NGOs;[27] the incorporation of gender sensitivity, family planning, and sexual health into development programs;[28] and the broader changes wrought by globalization all constitute mechanisms by which sexualities circulate globally.[29]

In the North and South alike, the universality and supposed finality of law, and particularly human rights law, have made it an especially attractive resource for LGBT activists. As Jean and John Comaroff have observed in postcolonial settings, law "has become the medium in which politics are played out, in which conflicts are dealt with across otherwise-incommensurable axes of difference, in which the workings of the 'free' market are assured, in which social order is ostensibly erected and the substance of citizenship made manifest."[30] In the United States and European Union, too, law has been a primary framework through which LGBT social movements have sought to advance their claims.[31] By adopting a human rights framework, activists appeal to principles that are both supranational and suprapositive;[32] they situate themselves in a global community and invoke universal values that are supposed to transcend local contexts. The human rights framework is also able to transform widespread exclusion and mistreatment into discrete problems with identifiable culprits and technical solutions. The popularity of hate crimes legislation, for example, arguably derives at least in part from law's promise to turn habitual anti-LGBT violence into a legal issue with a legal remedy.

Critics have often decried these features of transnational LGBT advocacy, arguing that transnational models ride roughshod over local specificity and variation. In textured descriptions of Southern LGBT identities and politics, however, the complexity of sexual identities and politics in the North and in transnational networks tends to be downplayed or ignored. A blizzard of adjectives dismissing human rights as necessarily individualist, neoliberal, juridical, secular, colonizing, or firmly grounded in identity politics that do not resonate in the South obscures the possibility that

"LGBT human rights" as a category might itself be heterogeneous and unstable.

In practice, the multiplicity of LGBT groups internationally, the information and resources with which they operate, and their particular constituencies, funders, and sociolegal contexts have produced strikingly divergent understandings of what LGBT human rights might encompass. Amid a patchwork of statutes, rulings, and public statements, the category of LGBT human rights remains legally and normatively dynamic.

Rather than seeing LGBT human rights as a Northern framework that is imported wholesale, then, anthropologists need to more fully interrogate understandings of human rights, and where and how they are negotiated. Thus far, ethnographies of human rights have focused primarily on the ways in which rights are globalized, vernacularized, or resisted in particular contexts around the globe.[33] Anthropologists have also focused on spaces where human rights are developed, from the debates that shaped the UN Trafficking Protocol[34] to the operation of the Committee on the Elimination of Discrimination Against Women (CEDAW Committee)[35] to the work of NGOs like Amnesty International (AI)[36] and Human Rights Watch (HRW).[37] These studies explore what Mark Goodale calls "the practice of human rights," or how actors "talk about, advocate for, criticize, study, legally enact, vernacularize, and so on, the idea of human rights in its different forms."[38]

Focusing on the practice of human rights follows Richard Wilson's suggestion that scholars might productively set aside disputes about the universality of human rights to consider how actors deploy rights and the legal, normative, and discursive work that rights do.[39] On a daily basis, human rights activists construct, promote, and institutionalize particular understandings of human subjectivity and the rights and responsibilities that inhere within it, and thereby expand what the human rights regime protects. Wilson has more recently drawn attention to these processes of "legalization," observing that "to state it in legal terms, human rights organizations seek to make an ever-widening set of claims 'justiciable.'"[40] Exploring the practice of human rights does not occlude discussions of universality and relativism; to the contrary, it helpfully foregrounds the processes by which actors universalize claims to the legal and normative protections of human rights or relativize those claims to sap them of their legitimacy.

By recognizing these underappreciated dynamics of LGBT human rights, we uncover critical questions: Why do some human rights claims become controversial? What role does law, or the semblance of law, play in these debates? How is legitimacy sought by proponents of rights, and how are they delegitimized by their detractors? The insistence that LGBT human rights are universal has often precluded any acknowledgment that the boundaries of this category remain contested, or that human actors are influential in defining its scope. As one of the most controversial topics in contemporary human rights discourse, LGBT human rights powerfully illustrate how claims are universalized and relativized in practice.

THE OPACITY OF PROCESSES AND PRACTICES OF HUMAN RIGHTS DEVELOPMENT

While proponents of LGBT human rights stress their universality, detractors emphasize their cultural specificity. Some opponents argue that same-sex sexuality should be discouraged as criminal, unhealthy, or immoral. More nuanced critiques stress that sexual orientation and gender identity are not universally relevant aspects of selfhood, or interrogate the global circulation of LGBT human rights as an imperialist project.[41] What is evident from the hate crimes discussion, however, is that if LGBT human rights are constructed, we must then investigate *who* is doing the constructing, *how,* and *why*—and what remains possible in a framework in flux.

Critics of transnational LGBT advocacy have underscored the ideological and political foundations on which these projects rest.[42] They often highlight the "Western" assumptions that are enmeshed in the ideology and work of LGBT NGOs—typically, those that are individualistic, rights-based, and committed to advancing a particular brand of identity politics. The diffusion of these models is often attributed to NGOs in the North engaging with those in the South.

The distance between ideology and praxis in advocacy is an empirical question, and benefits tremendously from grounded investigation.[43] As Stephen Hopgood observes, however, studies of the internal dynamics of transnational human rights NGOs and the factors that shape their work are rare; as a result, there are few textured depictions of what human rights NGOs actually do and why.[44] The observation certainly applies to LGBT NGOs, which are rarely examined ethnographically.[45] Critical analyses have shown that LGBT NGOs simultaneously unsettle and preserve aspects of the sociopolitical systems in which they operate. Without ethnographic engagement, however, scholars are ill-equipped to show the reverse—how broader sociopolitical systems shape these organizations, their missions, and their tactics, and how individuals animate them with their own beliefs, politics, and goals.

Phrased in the dramaturgical vocabulary of Erving Goffman, most analyses of NGOs survey the *frontstage* of organizational work, particularly the campaigns and publications that are produced for a wider public. What they rarely explore is the *backstage* of organizational work, including the perspectives and skills that staff bring to their advocacy, the projects that never reach fruition, and the dynamics that shape how decisions are made and priorities are determined.[46] As a result, the work of NGOs is discussed in theoretical terms, focusing on the frameworks and discourse they use, the populations they publicly target, and the visible impacts of their interventions. The *practice* of human rights advocacy on behalf of LGBT persons receives little attention.

Ethnography is indispensable in this regard. As Lisa Markowitz suggests,

> Grounding research in the day-to-day work of NGO staff allows identification of the ways quotidian matters and interorganizational relations affect the design, presentation and implementation of projects, and the assumptions embedded within them. Such attention to situated practice also provides an antidote to the generalizations made about NGOs by their advocates and detractors.[47]

Analyses of privilege, hegemony, and imperialism in transnational work are critical, but are most insightful when paired with accounts of the daily motivations, frustrations, and disruptions that shape the work that staff at NGOs actually do.

The processes of constructing, promoting, and institutionalizing human rights can be approached from many levels, from explorations of systemic influences that shape how claims are made to fine-grained analyses of why key actors promote the ideals and goals that they do. In the widest view, the study of social movements, networks, and transnational advocacy has illustrated how NGOs and other organizations "operate in a wider context which both provides them with the aims they pursue and sets limits to the way they may operate."[48] As institutional ethnographers have deftly shown, disciplinary or professional conventions can also profoundly influence what organizations do and how people function within them.[49] In the human rights field, these might include documentation and reporting protocols, the use of technical jargon, or the imperative to assign innocence or blame to identifiable victims and perpetrators.[50] NGOs reproduce these disciplinary conventions in myriad ways—for example, in mission statements, strategic plans, organizational memory, and informal aspects of institutional culture. Actors may resist or subvert conventional ways of recognizing and addressing human rights violations, but these norms inevitably structure how practitioners operate.

Indeed, NGOs are critical sites of inquiry because they can be neither subsumed into the wider society in which they operate nor reduced to the politics of their staff or volunteers at any given time. As Eric Hirsch and David Gellner note:

> Organizations have a view of themselves, both for internal and for external consumption. This means that organizations are not just the sum of their participants' interactions: organizations acquire a life and a momentum independent of the people who make them up. Much organizational time and effort goes into controlling and disciplining those on the inside.[51]

IGLHRC not only projected itself as a singular entity to governments, funders, and partners around the globe. It was also defined as an entity *by* these parties, the media, and the government of the United States, where it was incorporated. Staff were conscious about speaking on behalf of and representing IGLHRC, distinguishing their own views from the organizational line. Although NGOs are not agentive actors, the collective efforts of their staff and supporters do create a kind of fictive agency that acts on the outside world.

Ethnographers are uniquely equipped to explore this human element of organizations—how they are animated by actors whose values, goals, and preoccupations all shape how an NGO functions. This human element is often ignored in studies of social movements and transnational advocacy networks, and risks being obscured when NGOs are treated as monoliths.[52] No organization is completely homogeneous. Each person at IGLHRC had his or her own ideals, priorities, and style, and grounded research is critical in understanding how they worked together to pursue the open-ended goal of advancing LGBT human rights.

A useful framework for this type of inquiry is provided by Norman Long, whose actor-oriented approach has been used to foreground the roles played by those who negotiate, implement, and execute development programs in practice.[53] At its core, the actor-oriented approach focuses on "intermediary actors or brokers operating at the 'interfaces' of different world-views and knowledge systems, and reveals their importance in negotiating roles, relationships, and representations."[54] The emphasis on "brokers" has been prominent in development anthropology, but has not been adopted by anthropologists of sexuality, human rights, or transnational advocacy. In LGBT human rights advocacy, however, brokers play pivotal roles by developing relationships, transmitting information, and negotiating priorities among diverse actors. Indeed, the actor-oriented approach may be especially powerful in ideologically charged fields like human rights, where the routine labor of NGO staff goes unremarked or is poorly understood.

The term "broker" often has a corporate connotation, and calling activists and human rights professionals "brokers" may seem counterintuitive. In development anthropology, however, brokers are those who breathe life into transnational projects, mediating between different constituencies to make those projects possible. As I discuss in chapter 2, brokers at IGLHRC were not homogeneous; the staff included lifelong activists as well as recent graduates who were new to movement work. Some engaged in program work, while others liaised with donors and partners to raise funds, turn out press releases, and keep the organization running smoothly. What the concept of "brokerage" helpfully illustrates is a key theme of this ethnography—that everyone IGLHRC hired actively worked with various constituencies and broader networks to make the organization's work possible.

Focusing on brokers should not divert attention away from the larger systemic and structural conditions that constrain agency and shape behaviors, habits, and motivations.[55] A truly holistic approach to social movements must attempt "to recognize more causal pathways and relevant phenomena than is usually the case in political science; to proceed from a more fragmented understanding of culture than is usually found in history; and to combine ethnography with more attention to political actors than is often the case in anthropology."[56] The core of this approach is anthropological, but the praxis of brokers at LGBT human rights NGOs also implicates history, politics, economics, law, area studies, and postcolonial, feminist, and queer theories. A broad inquiry is especially helpful to contextualize transnational advocacy, which operates across a range of social and political systems to pursue certain goals.

Ultimately, one can recognize that LGBT human rights are historically contingent or socially constructed but still know very little about the background, motivations, and politics of the actors and networks that now promote them. As the hate crimes discussion attests, brokers have complex convictions and motivations for what they do, and these are not always wholly evident to outsiders. To fully understand why and how LGBT human rights are constructed, promoted, and institutionalized, ethnographic engagement with brokers themselves is crucial.

WHY NGOS? IGLHRC AS A SITE OF SOCIOLEGAL PRODUCTION

The project on which this book is based was inspired by my own experiences on the periphery of LGBT human rights NGOs in both the North and South, and was sharpened by the lingering ambivalence I felt about my past anthropological work on LGBT advocacy.

I became interested in LGBT human rights NGOs during the summer of 2006, when I interned at the International Lesbian and Gay Association (ILGA).[57] I arrived in Brussels expecting to campaign, work on policy, and change laws during the summer. In reality, much of my time was spent doing the kind of network maintenance that Annelise Riles has described—for example, translating documents, preparing newsletters, and designing projects that had not yet been funded or fully defined.[58] I was one of four people in the office, only two of whom were full-time staff, and was surprised by how understaffed and underresourced ILGA was relative to the scope of its global mandate.

A similar dissonance between the image and reality of advocacy struck me during my later fieldwork, which examined post-apartheid legal mobilization in South Africa and the ways that activists in the Philippines set agendas and advocated for queer people living in poverty.[59] In my research, I was struck by the extent to which scholarship on the globalization of sexuality pitted fine-grained analyses of sexual politics in the South against a broad caricature of sexual politics in the North. Criticisms of Northern NGOs as individualist, neoliberal, statist, and often aggressively white, Western, and male rang true to an extent, but left little room for the thoughtful transnational work I'd witnessed at ILGA or the distinctive approaches of groups like SRLP, Queers for Economic Justice (QEJ), or Fabulously Independent Educated Radicals for Community Empowerment (FIERCE) in the United States. In the absence of meaningful engagement, critics often conflated the contexts within which activists worked with the values they held and the interventions they made.

With these disjunctures in mind, I made arrangements to conduct doctoral fieldwork at IGLHRC, one of the most prominent transnational LGBT human rights NGOs. As a research fellow, I spent ten months at IGL-HRC's headquarters in New York and three months with the Africa Program in Cape Town. IGLHRC provided a unique vantage point from which to examine the politics and practices of LGBT human rights advocacy. IGLHRC was among the first NGOs in its field, and celebrated its twentieth anniversary during my fieldwork. From its founding, it had been influential in pressuring AI and other NGOs to address the persecution of LGBT persons as a human rights issue. Over two decades, IGLHRC's brokers and partners became prominent actors in the globalization of sexual politics and the development of LGBT human rights, and I had encountered their work in both South Africa and the Philippines.

Fieldwork at IGLHRC spoke to broader questions about the ways in which rights and responsibilities are articulated by activists transnationally. It provided a richer picture of the institution and the brokers who animated it—what influenced their advocacy, what projects they planned and implemented, and what challenges they grappled with as they did so. It also highlighted the relevance of the sociopolitical systems in which they were situated—who populated the terrain on which ideas about humanity and rights were contested, or which kinds of rights proved persuasive in political struggles. Developing this textured understanding of how and why brokers construct, promote, and institutionalize particular rights is fundamental both for critics of human rights advocacy and for those seeking to do that work effectively and responsibly.

The Politics of Method in the Anthropology of Advocacy

Fieldwork with activists is not altogether different from other forms of ethnographic inquiry. It does, however, require careful navigation of perennial anthropological dilemmas regarding access, positionality, and reciprocity. Researchers must determine how they will encounter activists who will shed light on a larger movement, gain facility with terminology and strategy, and, if they are to be present at an NGO full-time, define and perform their affiliation, role, and duties. My prior engagement with transnational LGBT advocacy generated questions before my fieldwork began, but anthropological insights on the field, the method, and the quirks of political ethnography shaped my approach to the project.

My decision to study IGLHRC was heavily informed by scholarship exploring the changing nature of "the field" and the utility of "fieldwork at home" in a globalizing world.[60] Over forty years ago, Laura Nader urged anthropologists to "study up"—to pay attention not only to the most marginalized populations, but to the bureaucracies and institutions that profoundly shape our worlds. As she suggests, a narrow focus on marginalization affects anthropological theory as well as practice: "If one's pivot point is around those who have responsibility by virtue of being delegated power, then the questions change."[61]

My choice of field site was a deliberate attempt to inject a different set of questions into debates about transnational sexual politics. Focusing on an NGO like IGLHRC, which was started and primarily based in the North, does shift the "pivot point" that Nader identifies in a meaningful way. Instead of asking how Southern groups depart from a presumptively Northern baseline of gay and lesbian sexuality or human rights, one might ask whether, why, and how Northern paradigms actually attain solidity and hegemony; where they are and are not perceived to make inroads globally; and whether there is room for creative maneuver that is not apparent in frontstage performances of advocacy.

Addressing these questions requires a range of methodological tools. Even inside NGOs, the work that brokers do on a daily basis is often opaque. Brokers were based in the United States, Argentina, South Africa, and the Philippines, but also traveled to Haiti, the Dominican Republic, Uganda, Kenya, Malawi, Senegal, the Gambia, Morocco, Egypt, Jordan, Indonesia, Austria, Norway, Switzerland, Spain, and elsewhere during my year of fieldwork alone. It was impossible to track what everybody at IGLHRC was doing at any given time, or to be privy to the e-mails, calls, and conversations that constantly shaped their work. Given the limitations of any one researcher, any ethnography of civil society inevitably offers only a "partial truth" of what staff and NGOs do.[62]

To construct a rich composite of an organization, Hugh Gusterson has proposed a method he calls "polymorphous engagement." The method involves "interacting with informants across a number of dispersed sites, not just in local communities, and sometimes in virtual form; and it means collecting data eclectically from a disparate array of sources in many different ways."[63] Although it can include participant observation, it necessarily engages actors and resources beyond any single site.

For this project, I interviewed brokers, but also talked with donors, partners, former staff members, and colleagues at other NGOs. I reviewed archival materials in New York, and former employees shared documents, flyers, and memorabilia from their time with IGLHRC. I monitored press coverage of IGLHRC and disputes over sexual rights as they unfolded in Senegal, Uganda, Rwanda, Malawi, and Kenya. I went to fundraisers to observe how brokers promoted their work, and scrutinized the analytics for IGLHRC's website to see where and how they disseminated their materials. I read IGLHRC's past publications, as well as popular and academic critiques of the organization and the broader field of LGBT human rights NGOs of which it was a part. I also read what brokers wrote, including poetry, plays, and fiction as well as journal articles, book chapters, and essays, to see how they expressed their views outside their work.

What I ended up finding most productive, however, was just doing the work that brokers do. This is what Gavin Brown calls "observant participation," a term he uses to describe his engagement with radical queer groups in London.[64] Brown stresses the value of his own intimate engagement in activist work, noting:

> This level of personal involvement is important to the direction that this work has taken—a less involved observer would be unlikely to appreciate the embodied thrill of participating in cooking in a communal café for a hundred people, building a sadomasochistic play space out of found objects, or facing a line of riot police dressed in pink and silver gender-ambiguous drag. This work is the result of observant participation—rather than the more conventional and detached ethnographic method of participant observation—that engages with the materiality of the practices that constitute these activist networks and spaces.[65]

Brown's shift in emphasis from seeing to doing is central to institutional ethnography.[66] As far back as the Manchester Shop Floor Studies, where ethnographers immersed themselves in industrial work, anthropologists have used hands-on engagement to better understand how people inhabit organizations.[67] Researchers in other disciplines have similarly stressed that participatory research produces very different forms of knowledge and solidarity than the application of extrinsic models.[68]

As a research fellow, I actively participated in IGLHRC's advocacy. Following two departures at the start of my fieldwork, the Communications and Research Department was short-staffed, comprising only a research and policy associate, a web designer, and me. My primary responsibility was to help finish IGLHRC's unreleased publications, including a report on homophobia and transphobia in Senegal, a report on LGBT community centers in sub-Saharan Africa, and an edited volume on blackmail and extortion of LGBT people in sub-Saharan Africa.[69]

Being asked to do substantive work is a common challenge for organizational anthropologists, since "in order to carry out the research he or she may be employed in the organization and therefore have to write reports and carry out tasks like any member of the organization."[70] And indeed, this was a challenge. Critiques of gay imperialism often interrogate the Northern sexual politics that are embedded and exported in the practice of transnational NGOs, and do so by scrutinizing material outputs like reports, training kits, and press releases. I worried that editing or writing portions of those materials for IGLHRC would inevitably introduce my own paradigms and language into them, and would foreclose any critical engagement with that aspect of the organization's work. I contemplated requesting not to do the publications, which would have been an early and jarring break between my roles as an anthropologist and as a research fellow.

After much deliberation, I decided to take the assignment and work on the publications, and they constituted my primary projects throughout my fieldwork. All of them had been conceived and drafted before my arrival at IGLHRC, and my role was that of an editor and author of supplemental content. I found that working on the publications gave me deeper insight into the issues and framings one was expected to present in documentation and writing reports; which language was preferred, which language was avoided, and why; and how legalism and the human rights framework shaped political claims. By running drafts and suggestions past local activists, regional staff, and brokers in New York, I witnessed much of the backstage politics, compromises, and decisions that produced IGLHRC's public, frontstage outputs.[71]

The bulk of my smaller projects were in Communications and Research. I contributed research, writing, and editing to updates on events in India, Indonesia, Tanzania, and Uganda; action alerts regarding episodes in China, Malawi, Turkey, and Uganda; letters to the governments of Malawi, Turkey, and Uganda; and op-eds with IGLHRC's executive director on developments in Senegal and Uganda. In the United States, I helped organize a protest against the Anti-Homosexuality Bill outside of Uganda House in November 2009; assembled panels on LGBT rights in sub-Saharan Africa at the City University of New York (CUNY) and New York University (NYU) in February 2010; and spoke about IGLHRC's work on panels at

Harvard Law School, Rutgers Law School, and the UN NGO Committee on Human Rights. I assisted regional staff with research for the Forty-Fifth Session of the CEDAW Committee; participated in focus groups and research projects; and campaigned with faith-based groups in an effort to discourage Lou Engle, an evangelical pastor, from holding a rally in Kampala while the Anti-Homosexuality Bill was pending. I also helped with development and administrative tasks, and volunteered at benefits in New York, San Francisco, and the Hamptons; monitored press clips; edited funding proposals; and helped revise IGLHRC's employee manual.

Of course, being conscious of my limited time and dual role at IGL-HRC put me in a different position than those who were there as human rights professionals. Nonetheless, by engaging in observant participation I gained a visceral feel for the work that was necessary to understand some of the fears, desires, and pressures that influenced brokers in their advocacy. I grasped why brokers insisted on boundaries between personal and professional life when the executive director called me over Christmas and told me to contact the French Embassy about two dozen men arrested at a party in Senegal. I understood logistical frustrations during a conference call with activists in a country in East Africa that cost hundreds of dollars, but ended when half did not call in and half refused to use landlines for security reasons, and were thus unintelligible. I felt the emotional investment that people had in their work when the report on Senegal, which had been my primary project from October to February, was unexpectedly shelved on the eve of its release. That intimacy with the work shaped how I understood what brokers do, but also forced me to reflect on my own political involvement in the project.

Worrying about my investment in this work was among the biggest challenges of studying activists, especially since a primary attraction of the project was its centrality to my own political and theoretical preoccupations. I identify as queer, and am alarmed by abuses inflicted on sexual subjects by governments and private actors. At the same time, I worry about how claims about LGBT rights are invoked as a measure of "civilization," are co-opted to withhold aid or justify militarism, and erase forms of same-sex eroticism and relationality that cannot be glossed as "LGBT." I believe that sexual justice is critically important, but often doubt that the human rights framework is the best way to promote it.

Nader argues that this investment is not necessarily a liability—to the contrary, "the normative impulse often leads one to ask important questions about a phenomenon that would not be asked otherwise, or to define a problem in a new context."[72] Indeed, the anthropology of advocacy owes a great deal to work that rejects the presumptive neutrality of the ethnographic gaze. A robust defense of politically engaged anthropology has been articulated by Nancy Scheper-Hughes, whose calls for ethical militancy, "barefoot anthropology," and engaged acts of witnessing challenge "two sacred cows that have prevented anthropologists from participating in the struggle: the proud, even haughty distance from political engagement and its accompanying, indeed, its justifying ethic of moral and cultural relativism."[73]

Ethnographies of human rights often implicitly draw on Scheper-Hughes's notion of "witnessing," whereby anthropologists not only observe injustices, but seek to understand, theorize, and ultimately respond to them. As she writes, "Witnessing, the anthropologist as *companheira*, is in the active voice, and it positions the anthropologist inside human events as a responsive, reflexive, and morally committed being, one who will 'take sides' and make judgments, though this flies in the face of the anthropological non-engagement with either ethics or politics."[74]

The witnessing impulse very nearly caused me to restructure my project to focus on the Global South. When I worked on the report on Senegal, for example, I considered leaving IGLHRC early to finish my fieldwork working with activists in that country and examine the politics of human rights reporting.[75] Similarly, as Uganda's Anti-Homosexuality Bill became the highest-profile LGBT human rights issue that brokers could remember, I almost relocated to Kampala to study the impacts that global interventions had on organizing within the country.

In the end, I opted not to relocate the project away from IGLHRC. In part, this was because I grew increasingly convinced that anthropological witnessing need not, and perhaps *should* not, be solely "in the active voice." Anthropologists might also reflect on responses to injustice, think about the ways that claims are made, and challenge those who are committed to justice to think critically about their work. When I arrived at IGLHRC, brokers spent months trying to publicize the draconian provisions of the proposed Anti-Homosexuality Bill in Uganda in the hopes that they could help Ugandan activists stymie its passage. Toward the end of 2009, the story gained momentum as it made international headlines—activists in the North scrambled to say or do something regarding the bill, and world leaders publicly spoke out against the bill and threatened to withdraw development aid. The role of many activists working on the issue transnationally subtly changed as they found themselves trying to tamp down sensationalized coverage, foreground the voices of Ugandans, and direct attention away from misinformation and counterproductive campaigns.

In instances like these, witnessing not only involves documenting injustices against marginalized groups. The problem is often precisely the opposite; fetishizing injustice and responding forcefully are also dangerous, and anthropologists, like activists, walk a fine line between witnessing and fueling sensationalism. Ethnographers invested in witnessing might consider shifting their focus from persecuted groups to those who advocate on their behalf, and to the strategies they use to do responsible work. While engaged anthropology is laudable, something important is lost if its focus is limited to the brutalized, the tortured, or the disappeared and not also to the letter writers, the petition signers, and the placard holders whose attempts at solidarity are also political acts.

What *was* central to my fieldwork was a broader understanding of IGL-HRC's regional programs. The organization had steadily moved toward a regional model, in which the world was divided into four programs—sub-Saharan Africa, LAC, API, and MENA—overseen by brokers who were ideally based in the region in which they worked.[76]

For a number of reasons, my work in the New York office focused predominantly on sub-Saharan Africa. IGLHRC's new executive director had previously been the senior regional specialist for Africa in Johannesburg and then Cape Town, and the research and advocacy being undertaken from New York were heavily influenced by his interests and relationships. As it happened, the incidents that became particularly high profile during my fieldwork—most notably, the Anti-Homosexuality Bill in Uganda, the arrest of Tiwonge Chimbalanga and Steven Monjeza in Malawi, and mob violence against a clinic providing services to men who have sex with men in Kenya—were geographically concentrated in the region. Funding was also more readily available for work in Africa than for work in other regions, giving IGLHRC the structural capacity to expand its staff in the Africa Program.

I took advantage of this de facto focus to more deeply explore the work of regional staff at IGLHRC. After ten months in New York, I spent three months in the office in Cape Town, where I worked with the four brokers who ran the Africa Program. Even though I did not relocate the project away from IGLHRC, working with the Africa Program illuminated a range of challenges and opportunities LGBT human rights activists face as they work transnationally.

I could have navigated this project differently, and a very different ethnography would have been produced as a result. The opportunity to undertake a politically engaged project of witnessing among transnational activists is a rare one, and I opted to get as holistic a view of IGLHRC's work as I possibly could. My hope is that my approach sheds light on processes that are not always visible outside of transnational LGBT human rights work, and that it will be insightful for those taking other approaches to the questions I explore.

Reflexivity in the Anthropology of Advocacy

Even with a sound methodology, anthropologists of advocacy inevitably encounter dilemmas that they must negotiate processually. Positioning oneself among activists and NGOs with discrete objectives invites constant assessment of one's political and philosophical commitments, both from one's own self and from others. For anthropologists who are in some sense colleagues, coworkers, or comrades of their activist informants, questions of reflexivity can decisively shape the interpretation and inscription of data. During my fieldwork, I struggled with three questions about my role at IGLHRC, each of which proved provocative and even generative in its own way.

The first question was whether I could appreciate what is interesting about IGLHRC after being involved in other sexual rights campaigns in the United States and transnationally. Like many anthropologists of advocacy, the movement I explored was not new to me. I entered the project familiar with many of the terms, frameworks, and touchstones of transnational LGBT organizing—as well as the foundations of LGBT politics, human rights, and the particular setting of an NGO in New York. Before starting, I could offhandedly use acronyms like "LGBTIQ," had some grasp of the rights enshrined in the International Covenant on Civil and Political Rights (ICCPR) and International Covenant on Economic, Social, and Cultural Rights (ICESCR), and understood why a consultant had to fill out a 1099 form before she could be paid for her work. My familiarity with the work enriched my understanding, but I also risked taking things for granted that may have surprised or intrigued an outsider.[77]

What makes this dilemma somewhat inevitable in the anthropology of advocacy is that basic familiarity with an organization's work is typically necessary to gain access and be permitted to do fieldwork in the first place. I was only able to spend a year at IGLHRC because I could offer to do research and writing without being a net drain on the staff's time, energy, or resources.[78] Even then, it took a fair amount of persistence to finalize the arrangement. Somebody seeking to simply observe brokers as they worked would almost certainly have been denied the kind of deep, lengthy access I enjoyed.

It is difficult to overstate how much that access mattered to the project. More than I realized, brokers at IGLHRC (and probably most small NGOs) are incredibly busy, and are subject in no small way to the crises that arise unexpectedly in their work. Scheduling interviews or being present for a shorter period of time would have been difficult and misleading, if not impossible.[79] By being present for a year, I witnessed a full cycle of board meetings, donor visits, grant proposals, departmental retreats, fundraisers, and budgeting. I was there as plans were made and executed for annual events like World Human Rights Day, the Transgender Day of Remembrance, the International Day Against Homophobia and Transphobia (IDAHO), and IGLHRC's annual Celebration of Courage fundraisers in New York and San Francisco. I was also present for functions at the UN, including the annual meeting of the Commission on the Status of Women (CSW), submissions to the Universal Periodic Review (UPR) and CEDAW Committee, and meetings of ECOSOC. My familiarity and the duration of the fieldwork it enabled gave me a very different—and hopefully richer—understanding of advocacy than those analyzing it from afar.[80]

What familiarity does require is self-consciousness about the ethnographic encounter and one's own position within it, which is rendered more transparent by tools like self-analysis, a diary, and autobiography.[81] In this project, self-reflection was invaluable. Prior to my arrival at IGLHRC, I made a list of things I would likely take for granted, and revisited it regularly. These included what terminology meant and how it was used, who the organization appealed to in its advocacy and why, and what internal and external pressures brokers felt obligated to comply with.

I was surprised to find that transnational advocacy itself helped considerably in decentering what I took for granted. Working alongside multiple groups with diverse backgrounds and politics regularly threw my assumptions—and theirs—into sharp relief. When American evangelicals were linked to the genesis of the Anti-Homosexuality Bill, African and U.S.-based activists turned a perennial argument on its head and argued that homophobia, not homosexuality, was a Western export. During my fieldwork, IGLHRC printed "Export Hope, Not Homophobia" stickers to echo that refrain. Shortly thereafter, a feminist activist from Lebanon criticized the stickers on a blog, asking, "how about 'don't export anything; fix your own hypocrisy' instead as a lobbying message to the American government?"[82] Some brokers felt the critique missed the point, while others understood the underlying sentiment. These kinds of ruptures routinely stripped away the veneer of any unified, politically homogeneous agenda within transnational LGBT networks—or within transnational LGBT NGOs.

The heterogeneity of LGBT advocacy raised a related question about how my affinities and entanglements with particular activists and NGOs affected my assessments. This aspect of "studying up" is scrutinized by Markowitz, who notes that the ethnography of NGOs often requires "studying over," or carrying out fieldwork among informants one might consider colleagues, fellow activists, or friends:

> I intentionally chose to affiliate with a well-esteemed GSO, doing work I admire, filled with people I like. This choice also came out of the normal ethnographic opportunism based in long-term acquaintance. Some of the staffers in this GSO and other alpaca sector NGOs are fellow social scientists, and some are now friends. Participant observation among them involves chatting in the office, jolting about in pickup trucks, talking politics, and swapping stories in the evening. They also act as key informants in explaining regional NGO turf wars. I find myself, not surprisingly, assuming their point of view: good NGOs are those with whom "my NGOs" collaborate.[83]

Over a year of working together, I inevitably formed opinions of brokers and forged relationships with them. I shared drinks with coworkers, attended dinner parties in their homes, and marked birthdays, engagements, and personal losses with them. I became especially close to certain brokers, and grew familiar with IGLHRC's model rather than those of rival NGOs.

As I wrote this ethnography, I grew less concerned that these relationships might bias my assessments. If anything, I recognized that my rapport with brokers frequently allowed me to interrogate or critique their work without appearing to attack their motivations.[84] Working at IGLHRC gave me a far better understanding of the multiple pressures that shape advocacy beyond any one person's culpability—something that brokers understood quite well, and often complained of themselves. While I have tried not to shy away from critical interrogations of IGLHRC's advocacy, I have also tried to consistently show the reasoning behind it. I was told by the executive director at the outset of my fieldwork that nothing happens at IGLHRC that those who implement it would not be able to explain or defend. Conversations with brokers as I wrote this ethnography helped me adhere as closely as possible to that spirit of open dialogue.

Most of all, though, I have tried to be as transparent as possible with my data so that others can disagree and draw different conclusions from it.[85] Having worked alongside brokers at IGLHRC, I know I am more prone than other critics to sympathetic readings of their advocacy—but then again, my aim is to understand who they are, what they do, and why they do it. I have tried to present my account in such a way that others can ground their analyses in the incidents that I describe, adding nuance and specificity to the scholarship being produced on these critical questions.

The final question I faced is a perennial challenge of anthropology at home—the likelihood that my informants or people who recognize my informants would read what I write.[86] Publicity can have personal, professional, and political consequences for brokers. In the middle of my fieldwork, I remember reading Faye Ginsburg's piece in the *Pleasure and Danger* anthology, which describes the contentious debates over abortion and reproductive rights in a small midwestern town.[87] Although Ginsburg declines to name the town throughout the piece, there is a full page of exposition about it: with its sister city across the river in another state, it has a population of about one hundred thousand, is surrounded by rural farmland, boasts three universities, and is the largest city in the state where Lawrence Welk was born. I immediately recognized the town as Fargo, North Dakota, where I grew up. I was obviously predisposed to see through the anonymization, but technology makes it increasingly easy for anyone to quickly check where Welk was born and know precisely what community, what clinic, and potentially what staff or volunteers Ginsburg was writing about.

I grappled with this at length because very few restrictions were placed on my research at IGLHRC. I suspect brokers had different motivations for this lenience. As activists, many regarded their job at IGLHRC as part of a longer career, and regularly voiced their own well-developed beliefs, critiques, and politics. Most had thought at length about the challenges of LGBT advocacy and recognized why I might be academically interested in the topic.[88] The executive director was the only person who half-jokingly told me in front of a donor that he was putting a lot of trust in me, and that

I had better not let him down. Of course, the fact that I was free labor aided my swift assimilation into the office, but my own self-presentation may have facilitated transparency as well. From the outset, I was a diligent worker, had feminist and queer politics that closely resembled those of others on staff, and was measured in my criticisms of brokers and their advocacy. By contrast, other brokers at IGLHRC were often vocally critical of decisions they disliked, and the wider networks in which they worked were often intensely antagonistic. Frankly, I was probably one of the more agreeable and nonthreatening individuals with whom many brokers interacted.

Although brokers put enormous trust in me, it would be impossible and unproductive to anonymize IGLHRC and still write about the work it does. IGLHRC is unique in the field of transnational LGBT NGOs, and it would be a superficial gesture to hide its identity but still describe its history, mission, and work. If the ethnography itself did not give telling clues to those in the know, a quick search for my name on the Internet would quickly reveal that I was at IGLHRC for a year. I suspect that anonymization would function as an excuse to eschew careful consideration of political repercussions and to write in a more speculative, less rigorous way. For that reason, I opted instead to write openly about IGLHRC and to grapple with questions of transparency and responsibility throughout the process.

Some brokers preferred to use their full names, while others opted for pseudonyms. It is perhaps possible to figure out who worked at IGLHRC at any point in time, but with high turnover and no detailed history of the staff, this is more difficult than it seems. When brokers have been openly critical of the organization's practice, I have sometimes used judgment in anonymizing their comments, giving only as much detail as I feel is relevant in understanding what they are saying and why. Although this saps some texture from the commentary, it strikes a necessary balance between the insights brokers shared and the trust they placed in me as an ethnographer. Like familiarity or affinity, trust is something that anthropologists of advocacy must always negotiate situationally.

A Note on Terminology

One of the most persistent challenges of transnational LGBT human rights work is linguistic and epistemological accuracy. The dizzying diversity of sexual and gendered subjectivities around the globe elude easy categorization. By seeking putatively universal categories and terms, however, human rights frameworks often erase the nuance and specificity that is necessary to describe populations whose behavior, identity, and socially ascribed labels align and diverge in kaleidoscopic ways.

The slippery nature of labels is a theme that recurs throughout this ethnography, but it is still important to give a loose sketch of the terms I use and why. Following the lead of the majority of my informants, I regularly use the acronym "LGBT" or variants like "LGB people," "LBT women," or "Q" for "queer" and "I" for "intersex." The variations tend to reflect regional or organizational preferences for different forms of the LGBT moniker. When a case merits specificity, I narrow the acronym as much as possible and use the terms "gay," "lesbian," "bisexual," and "transgender," "transsexual," or "trans."

When I want to eschew identity-based terminology and describe behavior, I use "men who have sex with men" (MSM), "women who have sex with women" (WSW), or "same-sex practicing." These terms were coined by public health practitioners to avoid assumptions about a person's sexual identity (and the stigma that may be attached to it) in their work. In a similar but slightly different vein, NGOs working in the human rights arena have been careful to avoid uncritically using the terms "gay," "lesbian," or "LGBT." Brokers are aware that these terms do not encompass all genders and sexualities, and are conscious of their politically and socially freighted meanings. To broadly refer to anyone whose gender or sexuality might be nonnormative, some activists use the term "queer," while others speak of "sexual minorities."[89] NGOs in particular have adopted the categorical terminology of "sexual orientation and gender identity" (SOGI). Each of these approaches encompasses a range of sexual subjectivities that are not easily reducible to labels like "gay," "lesbian," or "LGBT."

The terms and translations that activists at IGLHRC opted to use and the various reasons why they did so are explored at length in chapter 3. For my purposes, I tend to use "LGBT" or reference specific subjectivities like *bakla, hijra,* or *meti* when that is the descriptor used by the individual or group in question, use "same-sex practicing" if all that is known is that the individual or group engages in same-sex activity, and use "queer" as an etic term to describe all those who diverge from a normative sex/gender system.[90] Determining how people define themselves vis-à-vis sexual behavior, identity, and communities, along with when and to whom, is difficult, and I do not purport to get it right in every instance. My terminology should be read with some degree of flexibility, recognizing that all of these categories have limitations and there is no language that accurately captures the myriad nuances of sexual and gendered realities.

CHAPTERS AND THEMES

In the chapters that follow, my aim is to provide a clearer view of what actually happens within a transnational NGO headquartered in the North—not to make any definitive pronouncement on LGBT human rights advocacy, but to shed light on the many factors that shape its practice. The resulting ethnography raises larger questions about human rights and the anthropology of advocacy, which I revisit in depth in the conclusion.

In chapter 1, I explore the history of IGLHRC and the growth of a transnational LGBT movement over the two decades since the organization was founded. I reconstruct some of IGLHRC's early campaigns, and trace the shifting mission and priorities of the organization through a variety of transformations up until the present day. IGLHRC's evolution was defined by three decisive shifts—from a grassroots, volunteer organization in San Francisco to a professionalized NGO with a multinational presence; from a primary focus on particular regions to a broad mandate on behalf of LGBT and same-sex practicing people everywhere; and from working directly with at-risk individuals to working primarily with activists and NGOs. The genealogy suggests that IGLHRC's mission, structure, and goals are the products of a very specific history, shaped by both internal and external pressures.

With this history in place, chapter 2 examines brokerage and daily work at IGLHRC. The organization's staff, offices, structure, and funding all shape its advocacy in critical ways, and life history interviews, participant observation, and archival research help illustrate how and why these factors matter. IGLHRC's work takes place within a much wider network of NGOs, funders, journalists, and governments, who also facilitate and constrain the work brokers are able to do.

Chapter 3 focuses on the construction of LGBT human rights, and how brokers understood their mission given the putative constituency and framework with which they operated. I look at who the "LGBT" umbrella included and excluded, at the adjustments that brokers made to the rubric of "human rights," and finally, at the novel possibilities that were created when advocates strategically tacked between LGBT politics and human rights frameworks.

After considering how brokers constructed LGBT human rights, I turn to the ways that brokers promoted these understandings in their work. Chapter 4 unpacks the concept of "partnership," which was the guiding idiom for IGLHRC's relationships with Southern groups. I explore what brokers meant by "partnership," and the qualities that distinguished strong partners from "the only game in town." I then consider the political and ideological differences on which partnerships routinely ran aground, and the ways these were resolved in practice to restore a workable equilibrium.

Chapter 5 examines IGLHRC as a node in networks where information about LGBT human rights is circulated. I observe how brokers produced, verified, and transmitted information about LGBT human rights, and analyze instances where this traffic in information was a decisive part of the political work in which they engaged. Drawing on the concept of power/knowledge, I highlight the forms of mutuality that information politics generated between IGLHRC and its partners, particularly those in the Global South.

The final chapter recognizes that brokers not only promote LGBT human rights, but institutionalize them in law and policy. In chapter 6, I chart efforts to codify LGBT human rights at the UN, in regional mechanisms, and in other arenas in which laws and policies are forged and given the imprimatur of authority. I explore how the politics of daily work at IGLHRC were transformed under the intense pressures of these spaces, and the ways broader values and priorities were revisited in the process. Ultimately, I suggest IGLHRC's work has not been singularly focused on legal and political transformation, but on norm-creation and the normative power of human rights—and that this focus has generated meaningful results.

I conclude by exploring the interplay of universality and specificity in the advancement of controversial human rights. Brokers who invoke universal human rights on behalf of marginalized groups—for example, LGBT persons, indigenous persons, disabled persons, and children—insist on a "right to have rights" with moral as well as legal dimensions.[91] As part of their work, they necessarily construct, promote, and institutionalize particular understandings of rights, and these processes operate in mutually constitutive ways. Whether we critique human rights advocacy or seek to do it more responsibly, being attentive to these dimensions of human rights practice is indispensible if we are to develop a meaningful understanding of what activists do and why.

1 From the Castro to the UN

IGLHRC in Historical Perspective

LGBT rights are often dismissed as new and invented, yet the establishment of the human rights regime and its attentiveness to marginalized populations are also relatively recent phenomena. Contemporary understandings of rights have antecedents stretching back for millennia,[1] but the formation of the UN in 1945 and adoption of the UDHR in 1948 created a formal apparatus to standardize, monitor, and advance human rights as universal principles. As soon as the UN formed, racial minorities in the United States appealed to the nascent body to protect their human rights and hold their government accountable for rampant violations.[2] Over the following decades, countless populations adopted rights-based language and appealed to international institutions to assert political and dignitary claims.[3] The adoption of the Convention on the Elimination of All Forms of Racial Discrimination (CERD) in 1965, Convention on the Elimination of All Forms of Discrimination Against Women (CEDAW) in 1979, and Convention on the Rights of the Child (CRC) in 1989 extended the promise that such efforts might bear fruit.

The founding of an organization that sought to address the human rights of LGBT persons became increasingly plausible with time. In the 1950s and 1960s, gay and lesbian activists in the United States embraced identity-based understandings of sexuality, analogizing sexual minorities to racial minorities to demand civil rights.[4] As the concept of human rights grew in popularity, gay and lesbian activists took advantage of the framework to make their claims more palatable. When it was founded in 1980, the Human Rights Campaign—which remains the largest LGBT organization in the United States—adopted an asexual, euphemistic name that would maximize its appeal, even though it was a domestic operation that did not engage human rights bodies or instruments in any meaningful sense.

IGLHRC, founded in 1990 by an American activist in her mid-twenties, was among the first organizations devoted to transnational human rights work on behalf of gay and lesbian persons. By 2010, IGLHRC had grown considerably, with eighteen full-time staff in New York, Buenos Aires, Cape Town, and Manila, a budget of over $2 million, and influence extending from grassroots NGOs to the UN. Today, LGBT and same-sex practicing persons assert a visible presence in international agencies and the halls of the UN; regional mechanisms like the European Court of Human Rights, the Inter-American Court of Human Rights, and the African Commission on Human and Peoples' Rights (ACHPR); and domestic human rights mechanisms and judiciaries on every continent.

In retrospect, the formation of a group that promotes LGBT human rights seems almost inevitable. NGOs have formed to advocate for virtually any group one can think of, and a substantial portion do so using the human rights framework. Yet human rights advocacy is a heterogeneous field, and the demands NGOs make, and how they make them, vary widely. IGLHRC's history evinces a resolutely specific narrative driven not only by geopolitical trends, but by the politics, skills, and circumstances of activists who have animated the organization.

Since its founding, IGLHRC's mission, priorities, and tactics have shifted under pressures that were both internal and external to the organization. The processes by which these shifts occurred are crucial to any understanding of IGLHRC as a site for the construction, promotion, and institutionalization of rights. They provide a helpful corrective to acontextual narratives of LGBT human rights advocacy as either progressive enlightenment or Western imperialism. As IGLHRC's history suggests, any accurate description of LGBT advocacy must recognize the contingency of aims and rhetoric, as well as the promise of political alternatives that such contingency enables.

IGLHRC's Founding and Early Advocacy: 1990–1999

IGLHRC was the brainchild of Julie Dorf, who founded the organization when she was twenty-five. Dorf was raised in Madison, Wisconsin, in a business-minded, Republican-leaning Jewish family. Her interest in human rights deepened as a Soviet studies major at Wesleyan University,[5] where she was involved in the Latin American solidarity and anti-apartheid movements.

When she visited the Soviet Union in 1984, Dorf, who identified as bisexual, was introduced to a number of gay and lesbian individuals who faced arrest or harassment at the hands of the state. Article 121 of the Criminal Code, which Josef Stalin promulgated in 1933 to prohibit same-sex activity between men, was still selectively used to prosecute gay men and suspected dissidents. Through her encounters, Dorf became close to a number of gay and lesbian Soviets, and developed a global consciousness about the ways in which anti-LGBT sentiment transcended political contexts. In an interview, she recalled being at a dinner party where a man arrived, still in his prison uniform, after being jailed for over two years on charges of homosexuality:

> Just as I believed the opposite of the propaganda I was told, they believed the opposite of the propaganda they were told. They thought the United States was this completely wonderful place for gay people. Ronald Reagan was the president at the time. And the guy proceeds to take the writer's typewriter, and write letters to the U.S. Congress, and to President Reagan, pleading for their help to undo the sodomy law in the Soviet Union. He writes this personal plea, and begs me to take it back to the United States to help get the sodomy law changed in the Soviet Union. Because, you know, we had the power to do that, apparently [*laughs*]. Interestingly, he wouldn't believe that we had sodomy laws—which was classic. But for me, it was one of the catalyzing moments, of, okay, we've got this worldwide problem.

Dorf's belief that solidarity could benefit gay and lesbian Soviets was not only a product of these interpersonal encounters, but resonated with the global social movements of the 1980s. After the Bhopal disaster in 1984, Dorf and other students protested at Union Carbide's headquarters, which was a short distance from Wesleyan. The protest immediately drew attention; they found themselves being interviewed by the Associated Press and addressed by company spokespeople. Over twenty-five years later, Dorf remembered the episode as a galvanizing moment of transnational solidarity:

> The Yiddish word would be *chutzpadik,* you know, to have enough balls to just talk about something we knew *nothing* about. I get quoted saying, "We demand that Union Carbide takes account for these horrible actions for the people of India," or something like that, right? All of a sudden, about a month later, I start getting all these letters in my postbox: "Julie Dorf, Wesleyan University, Connecticut, United States." Like, that's all the information they had from these reports. I started getting letters from people in India, saying thank you for caring.

For me, the particular juxtaposition of that action and the solidarity, anti-apartheid stuff really made me feel like I personally needed to devote my activism with real people, who I knew were going to benefit from the activism we did in the United States, and where that link was strong enough that I could not just reap the rewards of their appreciation [laughs], but know that this was the right thing to do. . . . Where did I have it? I had it in the Soviet Union, that's where I knew people.

Dorf's political consciousness—and IGLHRC's genesis—were born of this "cycle of protest," a series of social movements that provided discursive and tactical models for the activists and movements that followed.[6] The solidarity campaigns of the late 1980s not only emphasized the global interconnections that facilitated political repression, but took advantage of the growing power of human rights discourse to link various struggles around the world.

The late 1980s were also a heady time for queer politics in the United States, especially San Francisco, where Dorf moved after finishing her degree at Wesleyan. The radicalization of gay and lesbian and HIV movements, embodied by direct-action groups like the AIDS Coalition To Unleash Power (ACT-UP), shaped the tactical repertoire that Dorf and her colleagues drew on in their early advocacy. In IGLHRC's twentieth anniversary video, Dorf traced IGLHRC's genesis to "a bunch of ragtag street activists and immigrants who really came out of that era in the late '80s and early '90s of ACT-UP and Queer Nation to fight for LGBT rights, in the United States and out." At the height of the AIDS epidemic, queer advocacy took on an urgency and importance that activists felt viscerally; with street protests, direct action, and letter-writing campaigns, Dorf and her fellow activists took cues from the radical queer movements in which they participated. They also had to fight to make their issues visible and be taken seriously; with the profound crises facing queer activists domestically, it was difficult to focus attention on international issues. As Dorf recalled, the name International Gay and Lesbian Human Rights Commission was used to give the group an air of credibility when it was little more than an activist collective.

When Dorf officially founded IGLHRC in 1990, it was not out of any deep commitment to bureaucracy or professionalization. Instead, she incorporated IGLHRC as an NGO largely out of necessity. Her early activism rang up thousands of dollars in international telephone bills, and forming an organization made this advocacy financially sustainable. In 1991, IGLHRC

moved into a one-room office on San Francisco's Castro Street and registered as a charitable organization under Section 501(c)(3) of the Internal
Revenue Code, which allowed Dorf to fundraise more aggressively. Russ
Gage became IGLHRC's first program director, and the only paid staff
besides Dorf in IGLHRC's earliest years.

IGLHRC's first projects, coordinated by volunteers working from kitch-
ens and living rooms, were a gay and lesbian conference and film festival in
Moscow, a campaign to pressure AI to include gay and lesbian people in its
mandate, and protests against restrictions on the freedom of expression in
Mexico and Argentina. As Dorf recalled:

> Those initial campaigns were the things that helped define us and forced us
> to learn to couch the issues in human rights terms, for our own identity as a
> human rights organization.... Every human rights organization I know was
> started by human rights lawyers. We were started by folks who knew how to
> do posters and chants in front of embassies. But that constellation of stuff is
> how we ended up deciding who we were and what we wanted to accomplish.

From these self-defining campaigns, IGLHRC began to take shape as an
institution. In its early days, activists primarily responded to incidents in
Eastern Europe or Latin America—where they had personal ties—that were
brought to their attention. In 1992, activists from IGLHRC and U.S. Representative Barney Frank traveled to Russia to lobby for the repeal of Article 121. When Russia repealed the law in 1993, Masha Gessen, a volunteer,
conducted documentation there to ensure that prisoners detained under
the law were freed. The project produced IGLHRC's first book-length
human rights report, *The Rights of Lesbians and Gay Men in the Russian
Federation*. In Latin America, IGLHRC helped Communidad Homosexual de Argentina become a registered nonprofit in 1992; worked with
activists in Mexico, Brazil, and Ecuador; and collaborated with Juan Pablo
Ordoñez on the report *No Human Being Is Disposable: Social Cleansing,
Human Rights, and Sexual Orientation in Colombia*.

In the pre-Internet era, transnational relationships were especially critical for compiling information on conditions facing gay and lesbian persons abroad, which IGLHRC's activists began using in asylum proceedings.
In 1992, brokers at IGLHRC provided documentation for a gay man from
Argentina seeking asylum in Canada, who became the first person known
to be granted asylum on the basis of sexual orientation. Their first major

victory in the United States occurred in 1993, when a judge in San Francisco granted asylum to Marcelo Tenorio, a Brazilian, ruling that sexual orientation could constitute membership in a persecuted "social group" under U.S. immigration law. That year, IGLHRC formally launched its Asylum Program, which was run by Sydney Levy and became one of the hallmarks of its advocacy throughout the 1990s and early 2000s.

At its peak, the Asylum Program processed nearly one thousand cases per year, and kept voluminous country files for asylum seekers and lawyers seeking scarce information about conditions for gay and lesbian people outside the United States. In the 1990s, with a paucity of available information and limited technical capacity, this required extensive work and record-keeping. As Dorf recalled:

> We were attempting from the get-go to have files on every country in the world, documenting the situation for gay people. We had this group of clippers, these volunteers who, for years, would come in once a week in the evening for like three hours and go through newspapers and clip stuff and put them into the files. It was way predigital anything. We attempted to be as comprehensive as we could in documenting gay life around the world, both positive and negative. And the biggest consumer of that information was asylum seekers—and not just in the U.S., all over.

In those very early days when information on LGBT lives was scarce, Dorf remembered, "we were positioning ourselves as experts for the whole world, even though most of the world we knew zero about." With time, this changed. As the Asylum Project researched country conditions and IGLHRC began to become more visible internationally, activists at IGLHRC not only utilized their existing personal ties, but began to form relationships with activists and groups around the globe. According to Dorf:

> Usually, by the time we connected with them, there was something organized, even if it was underground and not legal, or at least some leader with a group of people who they could lead. Sometimes, it was around expats, but not usually. I mean, the truth is, mostly people got in touch with us, as opposed to our finding them, most of those ten years. By the time we got big enough that we actually had regional program people, obviously they would do what they could to uncover groups that were new to us, but for the most part people would contact us, because they needed something, usually.

The recognition that LGBT individuals and groups around the world faced similar challenges encouraged staff at IGLHRC to think globally about their work. During IGLHRC's early years, the UN and regional mechanisms provided little space for advocacy on behalf of gay and lesbian persons. Before 1993, the only direct references to anything "sexual" in intergovernmental documents were Articles 19 and 34 of the CRC, which specifically pertained to sexual abuse and exploitation.[7] IGLHRC seized opportunities when they arose, and actively strategized around advances like the UN Human Rights Committee's opinion in *Toonen v. Australia,* which found that Tasmania's sodomy law violated the ICCPR.[8] IGLHRC's engagement with formal human rights mechanisms increased markedly in 1994, when brokers prepared for the UN's Fourth World Conference on Women, held in Beijing. Preparations for the summit were spearheaded by Rachel Rosenbloom, a graduate student from the University of California at Berkeley. When Rosenbloom was hired to work for IGLHRC full time, she compiled *Unspoken Rules: Sexual Orientation and Women's Human Rights,* a collection of written reports on thirty different countries by lesbian, bisexual, and allied attorneys and activists from those countries.[9]

Even in their early efforts at the UN, however, brokers at IGLHRC primarily agitated from outside the halls of power. In Beijing, they crafted a petition with six thousand signatures to "put sexuality on the agenda," coordinated the Lesbian Tent at the NGO Forum, and fought for the inclusion of language regarding sexual rights and sexual orientation in the Platform for Action.[10] Activists were ejected from a plenary session for unfurling a banner that said "Lesbian Rights are Human Rights," and had to be sprung from security by U.S. Representative Bella Abzug.[11] Although IGLHRC pressured governments, its primary role was that of an agitator seeking entry into the system. The sheer volume of work that went into securing language on sexual rights and sexual orientation—and its perceived importance as precedent—was suggestive of a movement seeking a seat at the human rights table.

In Beijing and beyond, IGLHRC's early forays into UN advocacy owed a great deal to the women's rights movement. Brokers explicitly situated their work within the broader sexual rights movement,[12] worked closely with activists like Charlotte Bunch of the Center for Women's Global Leadership, and borrowed frames and tactics for their own advocacy from women's rights advocates. One example was the Beijing Tribunal on Accountability for Women's Human Rights, a quasi-judicial hearing organized by NGOs to give voice to women who were subject to human rights violations. IGL-HRC arranged for Daphne Scholinski of Des Plaines, Illinois, who was diagnosed with gender identity disorder and institutionalized as a teenager, to testify.[13] IGLHRC later replicated this tactic with the International Tribunal on Human Rights Violations Against Sexual Minorities, held in New York for the fiftieth anniversary of the founding of the UN. There, Scholinski testified alongside individuals from Zimbabwe, Romania, the Philippines, El Salvador, India, Turkey, and Argentina about violations they experienced based on SOGI. IGLHRC's work around Beijing had lasting effects on its own advocacy; the research for *Unspoken Rules* significantly expanded IGLHRC's documentation on lesbian and bisexual women and trans men, which became a resource for the Asylum Project as well.

IGLHRC deepened its regional programming in the years after Beijing, with new hires playing a decisive role in defining regions and carrying out projects. Jorge Cortiñas succeeded Gage as program director, and his connections reinforced IGLHRC's heavy focus on Latin America in the mid-1990s. Levy moved to a role that focused on IGLHRC's communications, and Dusty Araujo was hired to take over the Asylum Program. The first regional staff position was created when Kagendo Murungi, a Kenyan immigrant to the United States, became regional specialist for Africa, the Caribbean, and the Middle East.[14] Shortly thereafter, Daniel Lee was hired as regional specialist for Asia and the Pacific, Scott Long was hired as advocacy coordinator and regional specialist for Europe, and Mirka Negroni was hired as regional specialist for Latin America, Canada, and the United States. These regions were repeatedly realigned in kaleidoscopic ways, primarily reflecting the competencies of new staff. With Murungi's departure, Kamal Fizazi became the regional program coordinator for Africa and Southwest Asia, and the programs were reorganized again when Long became policy director and Negroni left IGLHRC.[15] By the end of the decade, IGLHRC hired Alejandra Sardá to operate remotely from Buenos Aires as the program officer for LAC, a move that eventually would be replicated elsewhere as regional offices were established in the 2000s.[16]

During IGLHRC's first ten years, the board of directors took an active role in operational and programmatic work. Members like Alexandra Chasin, Gara LaMarche, Tinku Ali Ishtiaq, Stephanie Roth, and Judith Butler—who reflects on her time as IGLHRC's board chair in the preface to the tenth anniversary edition of *Gender Trouble*[17]—weighed in on strategic decisions that meaningfully defined IGLHRC's trajectory. When IGLHRC opened a satellite office housed at HRW in New York, for example, Dorf raised the possibility of merging the organization into HRW. The board pushed back against the idea, stressing that IGLHRC had something unique to add as an LGBT-identified human rights organization, and the organization remained an independent entity.[18] When Ise Bosch turned to IGL-HRC for assistance identifying LGBT groups as grant recipients, Dorf approached the board about incorporating grantmaking into IGLHRC's work in a more systematic way. The board expressed concern that becoming a funder would change IGLHRC's relationship to activists around the globe, and suggested the money belonged at the Astraea Foundation instead. When ILGA came under scrutiny for its affiliation with the North American Man/Boy Love Association (NAMBLA)—an incident I explore in chapter 6—members of the International Advisory Board (IAB) weighed in as well. Harry Hay, a cofounder of the Radical Faeries, resigned when IGLHRC would not back NAMBLA, while Representative Frank resigned because he felt IGLHRC was not distancing itself from NAMBLA enough. Butler and Dorf spent months after the incident hammering out a nuanced position on children's rights, which was shaped by these debates as well as their own politics. In each of these episodes, the board's active engagement shaped how IGLHRC evolved.

IGLHRC's early history also reflects the changing politics of LGBT activism in the United States. From its founding, IGLHRC's title identified its constituency as "gay and lesbian," although as former staff point out, much of IGLHRC's early work was with individuals who represented a far broader spectrum of genders and sexualities.[19] During the 1990s, brokers also explicitly focused on HIV/AIDS, which was then central to LGBT activism in the United States. Descriptions of their advocacy reflected an evolving recognition and definition of this constituency. IGLHRC's 1993 Annual Report referred to the organization's work on behalf of "lesbians, gay men, and people with AIDS and HIV." Characterizations of IGLHRC's constituency expanded by 1995, when its publications stated: "IGLHRC advocates for a world in which the fundamental human rights of gay men, lesbians, bisexuals, transgendered people, and people with HIV/AIDS are respected and accorded the protection of international human rights law." The acronym "l/g/b/t" first appeared in the 1996/1997 Annual Report, although "gay and lesbian" or "sexual minorities" were more commonly used to describe IGLHRC's constituency. By the 1998/1999 Annual Report, however, IGLHRC used "LGBT" as a standardized acronym in its outputs.

The way IGLHRC described its mandate also underwent subtle changes in the 1990s. In 1997, publications stated that "IGLHRC responds to human rights violations on the basis of sexual orientation, gender identity, and HIV serostatus through monitoring, documentation, and advocacy." By 1998, IGLHRC's mission was "to protect and advance the human rights of all people and communities subject to discrimination or abuse on the basis of sexual orientation, gender identity or HIV status." In its early mission, IGLHRC *responded* to violations, typically by mobilizing its Emergency Response Network (ERN) to write letters and stage public demonstrations. In its later mission, IGLHRC sought to *protect and advance* human rights, signaling a more proactive understanding of its role in developing policy and programming for LGBT persons.

This shift was evident in the tactics that brokers used and emphasized as the organization grew. Near the end of the decade, IGLHRC's publications included a more holistic description of its constituency and tactics appended to its mission, which read:

> IGLHRC's mission is to protect and advance the human rights of all people and communities subject to discrimination or abuse on the basis of sexual orientation, gender identity, or HIV status. Our constituency, therefore, includes people who are lesbian, gay, bisexual, transgendered, and anyone living with HIV or AIDS. Established in 1990 as a US-based non-profit, non-governmental organization, IGLHRC responds to such human rights violations around the world through documentation, advocacy, coalition building, public education, and technical assistance.

From its founding, IGLHRC's tactics were never strictly limited, and brokers always used a variety of methods both inside and outside of the human rights arena to press their claims. The list of approaches included at the end of the statement above specifically identifies a number of these, however, and illustrates the hybrid space that IGLHRC came to occupy. The standard human rights tactics of "monitoring, documentation, and advocacy" emphasized in IGLHRC's early work were supplemented by "coalition building, public education, and technical assistance," marking a fusion of traditional human rights models with more aggressive forms of social movement mobilization.

The ability to undertake this broader spectrum of transnational work was greatly enhanced by IGLHRC's robust fundraising throughout the 1990s.

Just ten years after it began as a volunteer operation, IGLHRC had an annual income of $864,367. Its sources of funding also shifted markedly throughout this period; in 1993, IGLHRC received 60 percent of its revenue from individual donations, and just 15 percent from foundation and corporate grants. By 1999, individual donations constituted only about 40 percent of its revenue, while 57 percent was secured through grants. This shift enabled IGLHRC to plan longer-term projects, but also made brokers accountable to a different set of actors in the human rights field.

As its tenth anniversary approached, IGLHRC had long ceased to be a ragtag band of volunteers organizing phone trees in a kitchen. With a growing staff in the United States and Argentina, newfound access to policy-makers and the UN, and its first large grant from a major funder, the Ford Foundation, IGLHRC was on the cusp of major changes to its staff, structure, and advocacy. The ways brokers navigated these rapid changes decisively shaped IGLHRC's work and public profile for the decade to come.

Entrenchment, Expansion, and Navigating Possibilities: 1999–2009

In 1999, Dorf announced her resignation as executive director to spend more time with her family. Dorf was a new parent and committed breast-feeder, which made the demands of a seventy-hour workweek and global travel difficult. Looking back on her reasons for leaving IGLHRC, she wryly recalled, "I kind of naively thought that I could be a parent and run an international organization."

Just before leaving, Dorf participated in an IGLHRC-sponsored training of African activists gathered in South Africa in 1999. After spending ten years utilizing virtually every tool in the human rights toolkit, she felt the experience affirmed that IGLHRC's future might best be spent focusing on the capacity building of activists around the world. As she recalled:

> I felt like, okay, we did a good training, but *we* weren't the right ones to have done that training, actually, and what would have made more sense is to train a South African group to be a trainer for Africa, or a Zimbabwean group, or whatever. And it wasn't whether we were African or white American, it wasn't so much that. It was purely our location in the U.S. It didn't make sense. . . .
> I felt like, had I stayed, I think what I would have done with IGLHRC—which is very different than what happened—was actually have IGLHRC incubate regional hubs, and help get them money to get them started, and

then left, basically, and stayed a U.S. organization that focused on a domestic U.S. constituency, but helped to incubate better, more regionally specific technical assistance hubs for groups that needed more than amplification of their campaigns.

When Dorf departed, however, conventional wisdom in nonprofit circles was that it was healthiest to make a clean break between the founding executive director and successive leadership. As a result, the strategic planning process was left to Dorf's successor to guide the organization going forward.

After a brief period with an interim executive director, Surina Khan was selected to fill the role. Khan had first worked at a gay and lesbian newspaper in Connecticut, *Metroline,* and then at Political Research Associates (PRA) in Massachusetts, where she researched right-wing movements in the United States. When she took the helm at IGLHRC in April 2000, Khan was thirty-two years old, and her background was primarily in domestic LGBT and progressive activism rather than human rights advocacy. As she noted in a letter to supporters in the 1999/2000 Annual Report, "While some of the specifics of the human rights framework have been new to me, its underlying principles of justice and respect for the dignity of all people remain familiar and compelling." In outlining new directions for the organization, Khan stressed, "I believe that IGLHRC has much to gain from developing our connections with progressive organizations that challenge the right wing in the US." In a variety of ways, these investments shaped IGLHRC's work during Khan's tenure.[20]

As the first executive director after IGLHRC's founder, Khan faced a number of challenges that were institutional as well as programmatic. As she recalled in an interview:

> There were challenges that were internal to the organization, in terms of the challenges that come with following a founding director. The staff were somewhat traumatized, I would say, when I got there, and so there was a lot of work to do to strengthen the organization from an internal perspective. And then I think externally, the challenges were some of the dilemmas we were facing around what was going to be our major identity, in terms of a human rights organization or an organization that was doing movement-building work. So there were some big conversations there that were happening.

The tension that Khan observes between formal human rights work and a commitment to build movements globally has in fact persisted throughout

IGLHRC's institutional history. As sustained activism at the UN became a distinct possibility and other human rights groups began to focus on LGBT rights, IGLHRC's role in the movement was a topic of ongoing debate. During Khan's tenure, a decision was made to amplify IGLHRC's work at the UN and other human rights mechanisms. As she recalled:

> Ultimately, when I got there, we started to do a strategic plan, and decided to really remain focused on the human rights aspect of the work, because that's where we had our expertise and history. In hindsight, I do think it would have been good to really further explore the movement building role of IGLHRC because of the limitations of the human rights framework.

The most high-profile instance of IGLHRC's increasing assertiveness in the human rights arena was in 2001, when Karyn Kaplan, the HIV Program officer, was invited to speak at a roundtable at the UNGA Special Session on HIV/AIDS. Kaplan had been invited to participate in the discussion by UNGA president Harri Holkeri of Finland, but was barred from doing so when the Egyptian, Iranian, Libyan, Malaysian, Moroccan, Pakistani, Saudi Arabian, Sudanese, and Syrian delegations objected, threatening to walk out of the session in protest. In response, Argentina, Canada, and Norway filed a motion objecting to Kaplan's exclusion, triggering the first debate about a gay or lesbian issue in the UNGA.[21] Overnight, IGLHRC was able to mobilize supporters, and to force a discussion of MSM as an at-risk population in the pandemic. Following an action alert and lobbying by IGLHRC, Kaplan was reinstated by a vote of 62–30–0 and addressed the Special Session.

During Khan's tenure, IGLHRC's entry into the human rights arena also accelerated in more subtle ways. Brokers engaged with Special Procedures, sending a letter to UN Special Rapporteur on Violence Against Women Radhika Coomaraswamy on family and state oppression of lesbians and gender-nonconforming women. They facilitated a meeting between Argentinian transgender activist Lohana Berkins and UN officials in Geneva in April 2001; the Special Rapporteur on Freedom of Opinion and Expression, Abid Hussain, followed up on this overture by meeting with three transgender groups in Argentina in June 2001. By 2002, when Khan announced her departure, the Working Group on Arbitrary Detention had issued an opinion condemning detention based on sexual orientation, the first of its kind from the UN.[22] The Human Rights Committee had begun including questions about sexual orientation on its list of issues to address when reviewing states. IGLHRC had been a co-petitioner in the first case before the Inter-American Commission on Human Rights (IACHR) directly addressing homosexuality, in which an incarcerated Colombian lesbian sued for her right to receive conjugal visits. These formal interventions were central to IGLHRC's mission at the time, even as the idea of movement building gained internal momentum.

This did not preclude brokers from working with local movements during Khan's three years at IGLHRC. They did, and Khan also remembers that as a legacy of her tenure. Brokers focused heavily on Asia and Africa, on gender and the needs of those who were less visible than gay or same-sex practicing men, and on power and questions of representation within LGBT movements. In what they then called Southwest Asia, brokers met with Lebanese, Tunisian, and Moroccan groups, attended international conferences for Arab women and gay Muslims, and helped mobilize a response to the threatened closure of a gay-themed Internet portal in Lebanon. In Asia and the Pacific, brokers supported groups that were trying to maintain protections for LGBT persons in Fiji and attempting to secure antidiscrimination legislation in Hong Kong and the Philippines. They also worked closely with the Japan Association for the Lesbian and Gay Movement (OCCUR) on its successful campaign to reintroduce sexual orientation into Tokyo's human rights guidelines. The senior program officer for Asia and the Pacific, Daniel Lee, met with more than seventy-five activists in India to determine how IGLHRC might best support a legal challenge to Section 377, the law prohibiting same-sex activity between men. In Africa, brokers mobilized a public outcry (and the U.S. State Department) to secure the release of a gay man arrested in Uganda after the president called for a "crackdown" on homosexuals. During this period, IGLHRC worked with HRW on *More Than a Name: State-Sponsored Homophobia and Its Consequences in Southern Africa*, a report that the groups jointly published in 2003. In the LAC region, brokers advocated for legal reforms in Jamaica and Trinidad and Tobago, and helped the first LGBT organization in Panama fight for official recognition. They also publicized murders and death threats in Brazil and Argentina and petitioned the Salvadoran police to provide much-needed protection to activist William Hernandez. In this work, brokers continued to look beyond exclusively gay and lesbian issues, protesting the abuse of transgender individuals in Venezuela, Argentina, and Guatemala and a mayoral proposal to expel sex workers from downtown Veracruz, Mexico.

Although IGLHRC campaigned on a wide variety of issues, brokers made a conscious effort to pay attention to power dynamics and the needs of local activists. As Khan recalled:

> I'm not sure of this, but my perception is that when I was at IGLHRC, we really—I really—tried to take very seriously the values that we articulated in the strategic plan, [that] those that are most impacted by problems in their communities are the ones that are coming up with the solutions on a daily level and should be the ones to really lead in those efforts. And I'm not sure that that was a value that was recognized by IGLHRC or one that was there before.

This emphasis on local leadership supported from the North was a central part of IGLHRC's philosophy, but also drew attention to marginalization that was not primarily juridical. Brokers began to publish a short-lived newsletter, *Asia/Pacific Bridges,* to build networks in the Asia–Pacific region. With "Representing a New South Africa," they raised funds to commission artwork with gay and lesbian themes for the repurposed Constitutional Court building in South Africa. To counter right-wing appropriation of "the family," IGLHRC released *Conceiving Parenthood,* a report on LGBT parents, their children, and their rights.

Indeed, many of the stances that IGLHRC became most famous for during this period were not expressly aimed at supranational human rights bodies. As Khan promised at the beginning of her tenure, brokers made common cause with self-identified progressive groups and embraced wider understandings of social justice and human rights. In 2000, brokers spoke on a National Gay and Lesbian Task Force panel exploring why the death penalty is a queer issue, and after the September 11, 2001, attacks on the World Trade Center and Pentagon, IGLHRC was one of the first U.S.-based LGBT organizations to publicly oppose the bombing of Afghanistan. The latter position attracted a considerable amount of publicity, much of it negative, after Khan expressed it in an interview with the LGBT newspaper *Bay Windows,* but IGLHRC's staff and board stood by it.

Throughout this period, IGLHRC also maintained a distinctive focus on HIV/AIDS. Kaplan's hiring as the HIV Program officer created an institutional point person for this work, and legitimated HIV advocacy that was not primarily about sex or LGBT people. Among other projects, for example, Kaplan spent five weeks interviewing injection drug users (IDUs) in three provinces of Thailand for a joint harm-reduction project with Thai HIV/AIDS activists. IGLHRC produced two action kits to help activists lobby around trade barriers, intellectual property law, and HIV, and organized at the Thirteenth International AIDS Conference in Durban and the World Trade Organization meeting in Seattle. All of these initiatives took IGLHRC beyond any narrow understanding of LGBT human rights advocacy and toward more expansive understandings of the conditions that denied justice to marginalized populations.

What was scaled back near the end of Khan's tenure, however, was the Asylum Program, which was renamed the Asylum Documentation Program (ADP). The 2002 Annual Report explained that the move was designed to return the program to its original focus—providing documentation and advocacy but "forward[ing] all calls for direct assistance to immigration attorneys and advocates." Although the ADP's programmatic focus was narrowed, Araujo, the longtime head of the Asylum Program, continued to compile and disseminate packets of information about the treatment of LGBT people in different countries.

The broad range of possibilities that IGLHRC navigated during the early 2000s widened further after Khan's tenure ended. Khan left the organization in December 2002 to move with her partner, an academic who had just taken a job at the University of California, Irvine. Given IGLHRC's increasingly active work within formal human rights mechanisms, the possibility was raised that IGLHRC would move to New York. Khan had opposed the move, believing it would sap IGLHRC's institutional memory and expend valuable resources that could be better spent on programmatic work. With a new executive director, however, the move became a real possibility.

To replace Khan, the board hired Paula Ettelbrick, a well-known feminist civil rights lawyer, academic, and activist in New York who had been instrumental in the development of legal strategies around family law for LGBT people. As when Khan started, there were both institutional and programmatic challenges facing IGLHRC. As Ettelbrick recalled:

> I didn't have a deep human rights background, but I had a longstanding international background in terms of doing some of the work. So when I came to IGLHRC, I was sort of recruited there mostly because the organization was in a tremendous transition and needed somebody who just, structurally, knew the donors, knew how to run organizations. You know, on some level, my

job was to hire the human rights experts, but to make sure there was an organization to hire them to, at that point.

Like Khan, Ettelbrick's tenure was marked by key shifts at IGLHRC, which
were tied to her background and priorities as much as any overarching ideology. Ettelbrick was not only open to moving IGLHRC to New York—
and did so in 2004—but embraced the programmatic priorities that
justified such a move. As she remarked:

> That was just a necessary move. The only reason IGLHRC existed in San
> Francisco was because that's where Julie lived, and she was the founder. She
> was the first to say that. That's why they were there, but they should always
> have been in New York. You just can't do this work in the U.S. and not have
> a very strong base, if not your base, in New York. Because that's where every-
> one comes in and out of, it's the UN, it's the missions, it's the U.S. It's every-
> thing. You're down to D.C. easily. It just made no sense not to be.

The staff largely turned over with the move to New York, and former staff
lamented that much of IGLHRC's institutional memory from its earliest
days was lost or left behind in the transition. Yet IGLHRC grew in new
directions as well. Ettelbrick placed a high premium on regional expansion, and on the placement of brokers in the regions in which they worked.
IGLHRC's model shifted from the fluid portfolios created to reflect the
competencies of staff in San Francisco or New York to a more permanent
division of the globe into discrete regions with brokers operating within
them. As Ettelbrick recalled, her own experience doing domestic LGBT
legal work from New York informed this transition:

> The thing I wanted to do, which I did, was to move us from being a U.S.-
> based organization with U.S.-based staff, to an international organization
> with international staff of and from the regions. I mean, as a microcosm in
> the U.S., if you really want a national group, you've got to also deal with
> people in the states and cities across the country. You can't have New York-
> ers speaking for people in Alabama, obviously. I really wanted a chance to
> do that, and that was my vision that I brought to the organization, that we
> really needed to expand, we really needed staff from the regions.

Under Ettelbrick's leadership, the first regional office opened in Buenos Aires
in 2004. In 2007, IGLHRC opened another office in South Africa headed

by Cary Alan Johnson, who had fundraised, supported, and served as a board member for IGLHRC while working with NGOs across Africa. The same year, IGLHRC relaunched its API program with brokers in the United States and the Philippines.

Despite these shifts, much of the programming continued during Ettelbrick's tenure. In keeping with the decision to move to New York, IGLHRC's advocacy at the UN and with foreign embassies and missions accelerated. This work saw a milestone in 2003, after diplomats from Brazil introduced a nonbinding resolution to recognize that SOGI renders people vulnerable and to call on states to promote and protect human rights for all persons. IGLHRC claimed a leading role in pushing for the passage of the Brazil Resolution; it brought the largest delegation of LGBT activists—nearly fifty—to lobby the CHR, assembled an advocacy kit, held strategy sessions, and worked in coalition with other groups seeking passage of the resolution. While the effort was ultimately unsuccessful, the coalition continued to cooperate on other UN initiatives, including the development of nonbinding statements of support at the UNGA.

Brokers continued to engage the UN at multiple levels. They assisted Helem, a Lebanese NGO, with the production of a shadow report for the CEDAW Committee, and flew an activist to New York to present recommendations that called for the decriminalization of abortion and same-sex activity, comprehensive sex education, and antidiscrimination legislation in Lebanon. In the LAC region, brokers assisted with Chilean and Brazilian submissions to the Special Rapporteur on Education and with an appeal to the Human Rights Committee on Nicaragua's sodomy law. After the rape and murder of FannyAnn Eddy of the Sierra Leone Lesbian and Gay Association in 2004, brokers themselves submitted a briefing to the UN Special Representative on Human Rights Defenders, highlighting the vulnerability of those who vocally stood for LGBT rights.

Brokers also increasingly engaged with regional mechanisms. In Latin America, they secured attorneys to support Karen Atala as she brought her custody dispute before the IACHR, and provided documentation to Honduran groups who filed a complaint with the IACHR and were subsequently registered by their government. They sought to develop regional jurisprudence as well, and helped secure a landmark declaration from the Common Market of the South (Mercosur) human rights body recognizing and seeking to end discrimination on the basis of SOGI. IGLHRC also participated in the campaign for an Inter-American Convention on Sexual and

Reproductive Rights, which was active throughout the 2000s. In Africa, staff brought LGBT groups from the region together to develop a strategy for engaging with the African Commission.[23] As a result of that meeting, IGLHRC began submitting shadow reports and briefing papers to ACHPR commissioners, and brought the first openly lesbian individual, Sybille Nyeck of Cameroon, to address the body.

Within the United States, the ADP continued to play a role in developing jurisprudence on immigration, asylum, and refugee claims. One prominent example of the productiveness of this engagement was *Hernandez-Montiel v. INS*. In that case, attorneys using documentation provided by the ADP challenged the denial of asylum to a transgender person being threatened with deportation to El Salvador. In a landmark ruling, the U.S. Court of Appeals for the Ninth Circuit found that harassment by a government agent is not a prerequisite for a successful asylum claim, which may instead be based on the state's encouragement of, or indifference to, victimization on the basis of sexual identity. Like feminist jurisprudence seeking to hold states accountable for so-called private violence,[24] these precedents were impactful for clients but also reshaped the ways that laws and obligations were understood by governments.

Alongside these institutional appeals, brokers trained activists in various regions to take advantage of the human rights apparatus themselves. In 2004 alone, IGLHRC organized trainings in India, Uganda, Hungary, Thailand, Canada, Paraguay, Brazil, Mexico, Macedonia, the Netherlands, and Peru. In 2005, staff held a first-of-its-kind Activist Institute with transgender and intersex activists in the LAC region; co-hosted trainings and strategy sessions with HRW in Porto Alegre, Brazil, and Colombo, Sri Lanka; and hosted trainings or workshops for activists in the Balkans and China. In 2006, IGLHRC organized trainings on human rights documentation and a discussion on Pride in Eastern Europe with ILGA-Europe. In 2007, it held its second Activist Institute on lesbian and bisexual women's issues in the LAC region.

During this period, IGLHRC's work on emergency response and movement building also continued in a variety of forms. In one instance, IGLHRC galvanized its six-thousand-person-strong ERN to pressure the government of Nepal to release thirty-nine *metis* who had been arrested in Kathmandu; wired money to supply food and water to the detainees; and provided documentation and advice to support a local group, the Blue Diamond Society, as it sought registration with the government. In under two weeks, the detainees were released. Another high-profile campaign was conducted in Cameroon, where seventeen individuals were detained at a nightclub purportedly frequented by gays and lesbians. Eleven of the detainees were kept in custody under Section 347 of the Penal Code, which criminalizes same-sex activity with up to five years in prison. In the absence of known LGBT organizations in Cameroon, IGLHRC worked with LGBT individuals and allies in Cameroon to find a lawyer for the detainees, supported their defense, and worked with the Human Rights Clinic and Education Center (HURCLED), African Human Rights Organization (AFHRO), and Trauma Rehabilitation Center in Cameroon on the case.

A broader feminist and social justice perspective was explicitly incorporated into much of this work, particularly after the hiring of Susana Fried and Sangeeta Budhiraja in October 2003.[25] During these years, Sardá also worked with groups in Bolivia, Brazil, Colombia, Honduras, and Mexico to draw attention to the ways that discrimination negatively affects the economic situation of lesbian and bisexual women. The research was compiled and released in the report *"Unnatural," "Unsuitable," Unemployed! Lesbians and Workplace Discrimination in Bolivia, Brazil, Colombia, Honduras, and Mexico.*[26]

In keeping with its expanding workload and geographic reach, IGLHRC's mission also subtly changed throughout the mid-2000s. From 2004 to 2008, IGLHRC's annual reports transcended a prior commitment to "protect and advance" human rights and stated:

> The mission of the International Gay and Lesbian Human Rights Commission is to secure the full enjoyment of the human rights of all people and communities subject to discrimination or abuse on the basis of sexual orientation or expression, gender identity or expression, and/or HIV status.

Just shy of Ettelbrick's departure, the Strategic Plan of February 7, 2009, described IGLHRC's mission as

> advancing human rights for everyone, everywhere to end discrimination based on sexual orientation, gender identity, or gender expression.

By that point, IGLHRC fully embraced universality in its stated goal of "advancing human rights for everyone, everywhere." At the same time, IGLHRC tactically dropped its explicit commitment to addressing discrimination on the basis of HIV status, which had animated many of its campaigns in the 1990s and justified its work on IDUs and trade barriers in the early 2000s. This was reflective of larger changes at IGLHRC; the HIV Program officer position did not follow the organization when it moved to New York, and its work had begun to focus almost exclusively on issues related to SOGI.[27] A period of heightened intersex advocacy also abated after the period when Mauro Cabral and others worked on IGLHRC's trans- and intersex convening in the LAC region.[28]

IGLHRC's tactics, too, remained in flux. Rather than framing formal legal advocacy and movement building as strategic alternatives, brokers began to more earnestly describe them as complementary components of their work. IGLHRC's campaigns reflect this emphasis on blending human rights advocacy with movement building. After setting out IGLHRC's mission, the Annual Report for 2007/2008 explicitly stated: "We believe that realizing this vision requires the development of strong human rights movements globally; building partnerships is at the heart of what we do." The report laid out three ways this was done, explaining that "as partners, we work hand-in-hand with local activists to: respond to emergencies ... expose human rights violations ... [and] strengthen capacity."[29]

Programs that were not compatible with that approach were cut, including the ADP, which was dropped after over a decade of work to focus more intensively on advocacy and movement building.[30] As Araujo recalled in an interview, IGLHRC's emphasis on movement building in countries around the world sat uneasily with its commitment to help LGBT people, including activists, leave those countries and seek asylum abroad.[31] Even so, this did little to focus IGLHRC's energies. One survey of international groups from 2008 linked IGLHRC to seven of the ten forms of advocacy listed, namely, international/UN advocacy, regional advocacy, national advocacy, local advocacy, documenting human rights abuses, responding to human rights abuses, and legal representation and referrals. IGLHRC did not report work in health/service provision/referrals, media work, or general public education.[32] The wisdom of working in all of these areas was regularly revisited, including during my fieldwork.

After six years, Ettelbrick left IGLHRC on March 1, 2009, and Johnson moved from the office in Cape Town to the headquarters in New York to assume the position of executive director. Under his leadership, much of IGLHRC's work focused on Africa, a shift in focus that powerfully illustrates how personal, political, and structural dynamics converge to shape agendas and advocacy.

Prior to IGLHRC, Johnson worked for a number of NGOs in Africa, including the Margaret Sanger Center International, Africare, and the UN High Commissioner for Refugees. He also held an MA in international affairs and a certificate in African studies from Columbia University. As the former head of IGLHRC's Africa Program, Johnson was well connected in the region, and had on-the-ground experience that Dorf, Khan, and Ettelbrick did not have when they became executive directors. As a result, he was able to turn to his existing networks to get advice, forge partnerships, carry on unfinished projects, and assist grassroots work.

Johnson brought a number of projects from the Cape Town office to New York, most notably reports on blackmail and extortion, community centers, issues facing transgender Africans, and violations of human rights on the basis of SOGI in Senegal and Cameroon. Politically, these gained new salience in light of a series of developments in late 2009 and early 2010, including the tabling of the Anti-Homosexuality Bill in Uganda, reports that Rwanda was considering criminalizing same-sex activity between men, the arrest of Steven Monjeza and Tiwonge Chimbalanga in Malawi, and mob violence against MSM in Kenya. IGLHRC's prolonged focus on these episodes was due not only to their scope and severity, but to the attention paid to them by governments and a media narrative that made each instantly prominent.

These situational factors coincided with systemic conditions that encouraged NGOs to focus on human rights violations in Africa. Throughout my fieldwork, available funding for human rights and public health work was disproportionately targeted at sub-Saharan Africa. Groups working with MSM in particular were able to take advantage of considerable amounts of money devoted to combating HIV/AIDS. IGLHRC's work in Africa benefited from this increased funding, which allowed Johnson to hire a staff member in the Cape Town office and to allocate additional resources to the Africa Program. It also allowed IGLHRC to focus its own general operating funds on regions that were of less interest to global donors, ensuring that they would not be overlooked.

Of course, this collision of factors opened some avenues of work and implicitly foreclosed others. Johnson's background was primarily with activists and grassroots groups in Africa. He was not a lawyer—in fact, when he became executive director, none of IGLHRC's top management positions were occupied by lawyers—and human rights law and navigating the UN and regional mechanisms were not his primary areas of expertise.

Under Johnson, brokers again revisited whether they would focus on human rights advocacy per se or on building LGBT movements globally. During my fieldwork, most identified movement building as their primary function. Of course, in each of the regions, the human rights framework typically structured the movement building that brokers undertook. It was notable, however, that IGLHRC was no longer a lone voice in the wilderness on LGBT human rights, and brokers, funders, and the board recognized that the landscape of the movement was changing. Johnson questioned whether IGLHRC had a unique role to play in documenting human rights abuses; grassroots activists had greater proximity to events as they unfolded, and large NGOs like AI and HRW had more resources to do thorough, substantive documentation. Beyond the world of advocacy, donors, journalists, and foreign missions were increasingly documenting human rights abuses for their own purposes, and doing so on site as situations unfolded. After the demise of its report on Senegal, which I discuss in chapter 4, brokers weighed whether IGLHRC's role was not to do documentation, but to primarily assist and train activists on the ground to do documentation, and to build local movements' capacity to do this work themselves.

A number of other considerations made movement building an ascendant priority. Some brokers in New York voiced concern that IGLHRC lacked focus; that staff were overworked; and that work at the UN was too costly, too slow, and too technical to be an organizational priority.[33] With ARC International coordinating shadow reports to the UPR and leading a coalition for initiatives at the UN, IGLHRC's role was not clear-cut. Brokers who were committed to advocacy at the UN insisted that IGLHRC still played a valuable role by acting as a conduit for groups around the world. Since ARC International was based in Canada and Switzerland, IGLHRC was uniquely poised to access the UN, monitor proceedings, and meet with foreign missions in New York. The research and policy associate— who had a law degree and was personally committed to this aspect of IGLHRC's work—the program director, and the regional coordinators for API and LAC played important roles by assisting groups with shadow reports to CEDAW, securing consultative status for IGLHRC at ECOSOC, and rallying support to restore the phrase "sexual orientation" to a standing resolution on extrajudicial executions. Thanks in large part to their insistence and initiative, IGLHRC's work at the UN continued, albeit amid a broader shift toward movement building as IGLHRC's primary focus.

Context Matters: IGLHRC in the Broader Environment for LGBT Human Rights

In the midst of these changes, IGLHRC's core commitments to an LGBT constituency and to the human rights framework were consistently central to its work. Structurally, too, IGLHRC remained a U.S.-based organization, operating mainly in English, and using particular tactics and technologies to pursue its goals.

Yet notably, the contexts in which IGLHRC operates have changed dramatically. A number of these transformations shaped global civil society in the 1990s and 2000s: the growing number of NGOs engaged in advocacy and lobbying, uncertainty about the role of Northern NGOs as donors began bypassing intermediaries and directly funding Southern groups, and the general shift from Northern campaigns and service provision to capacity building with Southern partners.[34] IGLHRC could be productively analyzed as a case study in relation to any of these trends. As I describe below, brokers at IGLHRC have largely surrendered campaigning to Southern partners, and have focused instead on building movements. Other interrelated pressures have impacted their work: to secure funding; to professionalize; and to be accountable to activists, funders, and journalists as technological developments make transnational advocacy increasingly transparent.

One of the most influential changes since 1990 has been the rise of a robust network of actors engaged with LGBT issues transnationally. When IGLHRC was founded, transnational human rights NGOs did not proactively advocate on behalf of LGBT persons. Since then, AI and HRW have both embraced LGBT rights in their programming, and countless smaller actors promoting LGBT rights have emerged worldwide. Notably, this was partially a product of IGLHRC's own advocacy. Under Dorf, IGLHRC publicly pressured AI, HRW, the Lawyers Committee for Human Rights,[35] and other NGOs to adopt LGBT issues into their mandates, bolstering the demands of Amnesty International Members for Lesbian and Gay Concerns (AIMLGC) and making it difficult for generalist human rights NGOs to ignore violations against LGBT people. After Long, IGLHRC's program director, began working for HRW in 2002, he became the founding director of HRW's LGBT Rights Program in 2004, continuing a collaborative relationship between the two NGOs that generated multiple projects and publications.

While large human rights organizations are among the most prominent players in these networks, smaller organizations have also promoted LGBT human rights in critical ways. ILGA and its regional branches (ILGA-Europe, Pan-African ILGA, ILGA-LAC, ILGA-Asia, and ILGA-Oceania) have federated LGBT groups around the globe whose work is not necessarily or exclusively grounded in a human rights framework. ARC International has been particularly proactive with UN advocacy, and a working group of LGBT human rights organizations has shared information and coordinated efforts at the UN. A number of these NGOs were involved with the development and promotion of the Yogyakarta Principles, a set of guidelines launched in 2007 to affirm binding state obligations to safeguard the human rights of all persons, regardless of SOGI.

Other groups periodically engaged with IGLHRC on projects and proposals, including Human Rights First (HRF), Heartland Alliance, Global Rights, and the Unitarian Universalists' United Nations Office (UU-UNO), which sponsored a number of convenings to respond to the exportation of religious homophobia from the United States. Organizations continue to emerge. In late 2010, a group of young activists launched an online platform, All Out, which sought to build a grassroots movement that would be more broadly galvanizing than the advocacy of existing organizations.

In recent years, regional networks have also formed to coordinate initiatives in particular areas of the globe. ILGA-Europe, a largely autonomous branch of ILGA funded by the European Commission, has perhaps been the best-resourced of these. In the Global South, Asia-Pacific Rainbow, the Coalition of African Lesbians (CAL), and African Men for Sexual Health and Rights (AMSHeR) have formed as well.[36] As I discuss in chapter 4, these networks at times posed challenges to the regional offices and bilateral partnerships that IGLHRC adopted as models throughout the 2000s.

The growth of LGBT human rights networks has been recent and rapid. Almost 90 percent of international LGBT organizations and programs formed after 1990.[37] A major catalyst for these networks has been increasing material support for their work. In 2008, the largest and best-resourced LGBT programs were IGLHRC, with a projected budget of $1,785,000, followed by ILGA with $749,000, Heartland Alliance with $600,000, the HRW LGBT Rights Program with $582,000, INTERIGHTS with $480,000, ARC International with $400,000, and Global Rights with $347,000.[38] IGLHRC's prominence in transnational LGBT NGO advocacy has been due in part to its large budget relative to other NGOs in this field.[39]

IGLHRC's own funding shaped the organization's work in a number of ways. Unlike in 1993, when the bulk of IGLHRC's funding was from individual donors, 77 percent of IGLHRC's revenue during my fieldwork was derived from foundations, and less than 10 percent came from individual donors. Established relationships with foundations generated multiyear commitments that enabled brokers to predict the funding they could expect each year with some accuracy. In 2011, this included $500,000 from a regular anonymous donor, $300,000 from the Swedish International Development Cooperation Agency (SIDA), $275,000 from various parts of the Open Society Institute (OSI), $200,000 from the Arcus Gay and Lesbian Fund, $150,000 from the Ford Foundation, $125,000 from the Sigrid Rausing Trust, $50,000 from the Arcus API Institute, $50,000 from Atlantic Philanthropies, $35,000 from Hivos, and $25,000 from the Levi Strauss Foundation. (The executive director of the Levi Strauss Foundation was Daniel Lee, IGLHRC's former Asia-Pacific coordinator.) Other foundations gave $90,000, making up $1,800,000 of IGLHRC's $2,345,550 in revenue for the year.

Unlike ILGA-Europe, IGLHRC had a longstanding policy to refuse money from governments to avoid any influence over its advocacy and programming. During my fieldwork, this was revisited. IGLHRC's board agreed to accept funding from governments so long as this made up less than 50 percent of IGLHRC's budget and brokers felt free to respond to abuses by donor states. Throughout my fieldwork, however, IGLHRC received a relatively small portion of its funding through governmental sources. The exceptions were grants from SIDA and the Norwegian Ministry of Foreign Affairs, which each supported IGLHRC's work.

The structure of IGLHRC's funding streams shaped where money was spent and why. The size and capacity of IGLHRC's regional programs were not solely the result of ideological priorities, but were decisively shaped by the funding available for work in different regions. Ettelbrick recalled that, during her tenure, "European foundations couldn't care less about Latin America. They were all into Africa during that particular timeframe. A little bit into Asia, but not even so much there."[40] Although strategic choices made some difference, these geopolitical realities had material effects on IGLHRC's work.

Of course, brokers' individual competencies also influenced fundraising and IGLHRC's allocation of resources. As Ettelbrick noted, "That was one of the reasons the programs grew differently, because of who was in charge of them." Brokers have diverse skill sets, and for myriad reasons, some had better luck raising funds than others. Having a diverse staff made this somewhat inevitable; those with experience in the idiosyncratic world of American philanthropy might approach fundraising differently than those who had primarily organized in contexts with state funding for advocacy and outreach.[41] This remained true during my fieldwork. As the deputy director of development remarked about the considerable funding that was earmarked for Africa, "a large part has to do with, certainly, the region, but I think a large part actually is Cary, and his conceptualization of projects in the region, and his willingness and his experience working and cultivating foundations."

Funding considerations made some proposals more feasible than others. Some were deemed too costly or difficult for funders to support, which frustrated brokers who wanted to assist groups in the API and MENA regions with long-term needs that were neither inexpensive nor immediately impactful. The demand by foundations for demonstrable outcomes and outputs meant that cultural work, dialogues with religious hardliners, and individual cases were difficult to fund, whereas line items that fit in a more traditional human rights framework—for example, documentation and publishing reports—were often much easier.

Pursuing funding thus entailed renegotiating priorities. When money came with strings attached, brokers both expanded their advocacy and continued existing advocacy within the grant's guidelines. The SIDA funding, for example, not only allowed IGLHRC to hire a staff person to expand work on health and human rights in Africa. It also meant that a component on the intersection of health and human rights was more explicitly incorporated into projects in the Africa Program.

Since the bulk of IGLHRC's funding was multiyear, unrestricted, and somewhat predictable, however, the biggest pressure from funders was to define and concretize IGLHRC's mission. As one broker observed:

> [Our funders] really drill us, but they drill us for a reason. They don't just drill us and leave us hanging. . . . [A donor] really wants us to narrow our focus, and that's what he's pushing us to do. Not to just pick one of our four strategies, but to really strategically think about those four, or any other strategy. . . . We're only a staff of twenty, and we need to be able to make an impact.

In part, this was because the same few funders supported many international, regional, national, and local LGBT organizations, and wanted IGLHRC to define its added value to the movement. Unlike the 1990s, it no longer sufficed for IGLHRC to simply support its partners. A broker estimated that IGLHRC supplied $15,000 to fight the Anti-Homosexuality Bill in the year after it was tabled. In another interview, a major funder estimated that the donor community had spent over $220,000 for the same purpose.

By 2010, brokers generally did not award grants to local groups for their routine expenses, especially since IGLHRC's funders increasingly supported partner organizations directly. Instead, it provided monetary support for certain projects: holding convenings and trainings; producing reports; hosting conference calls to collectively strategize; traveling to venues like the UN; and helping LGBT people secure passports, travel, and stay in safe houses during crises. Yet as ethnographers of transnational advocacy networks have cautioned, "An overly narrow view of resources as merely financial may also distort the picture of how transnational organizing works. Resources certainly include money but may also include access, reputation, influence, and other intangible benefits."[42] Although it was not a funder, IGLHRC provided nonmonetary capital to partners by helping activists access international forums; publicize their research and advocacy; and stay visible to NGOs, funders, and governments in transnational LGBT networks.

IGLHRC's professionalization and compliance with U.S. financial regulations also made some expenditures untenable. Brokers could disburse money to third parties to support activist work, but receipts were required to account for all money wired abroad. This made it difficult to send money to activists who did not have bank accounts, or to fund urgent needs that could not be documented—for example, informally paying an official to help an activist recover a confiscated passport. MoneyGrams required that recipients present state-issued identification, which was particularly problematic for transgender brokers who lacked access to accurate, gender-affirming documentation or activists trying not to draw attention to their ties with Northern LGBT groups.

The growing support of governments also reshaped the landscape in which brokers operated. Groups like ARC International, ILGA-Europe, and the Council for Global Equality (CGE) have persistently engaged international, regional, and domestic actors to promote the recognition of LGBT rights as human rights. Brokers operating within the UN system have worked closely with foreign missions from a number of different countries, and some of these, including Argentina, Belgium, Brazil, Croatia, France, Gabon, the

Netherlands, New Zealand, Norway, Romania, Sweden, the United States, and the European Union, have been visibly supportive of LGBT NGOs. The European Union has incorporated LGBT rights into its understanding of human rights and its criteria for accession, and the U.S. State Department now routinely includes violations on the basis of SOGI in its annual human rights reports.[43] Supportive governments have created openings for advocacy, but they have also generated complex entanglements. It can be challenging for brokers to distance themselves from state interventions they consider regressive or counterproductive, and governments often qualify their support of NGOs that endorse a broader range of sexual and reproductive rights than they themselves recognize.

Since 1990, these varied actors have subtly shaped IGLHRC's mission and programs in numerous ways. The expanding universe of LGBT human rights NGOs, particularly the growing transnational leadership in the South,[44] has led brokers to seek new ways of adding value to the movement. Foundations, which provide the bulk of IGLHRC's funding, have identified priorities that influence how brokers spend time and resources. Governments seek out trusted, credible intermediaries for their own foreign policy interventions. Now, brokers not only struggle to make their voices heard, but navigate new opportunities and relationships in a world where NGOs, foundations, and governments support LGBT human rights for their own particular ends.

CONTINGENCY, DYNAMISM, AND THE ELUSIVE LGBT HUMAN RIGHTS AGENDA

IGLHRC's history demonstrates that LGBT human rights advocacy is not a purely ideological project, but emerges from the messy interplay of personal, organizational, and systemic factors. IGLHRC's advocacy would look different if individual staff members had not arrived or left, if it had not incorporated as a 501(c)(3) or moved to New York, or if support for LGBT human rights advocacy had not grown dramatically. Questions about what IGLHRC is, for whom, and how it should operate persist amid perennial discussions of the merits of documenting and reporting, working within the formal human rights arena, and building grassroots movements. Yet three broad trends have been particularly pronounced, and these decisively structured how IGLHRC operated at the time of my fieldwork.

First, IGLHRC professionalized dramatically over twenty years, transforming from a volunteer operation to a transnational NGO with an annual budget of approximately $2 million. While early members reminisced about brainstorming in people's homes, calling each other on phone trees, and taking to the streets to protest to anyone who would listen, brokers now attend global convenings and strategy sessions, use new technologies to monitor and navigate crises as they unfold, and work with journalists, governments, and UN agencies to promote LGBT human rights.

Professionalization facilitated advocacy in countless ways. It helped brokers secure funding for large-scale projects and place regional staff in Argentina, South Africa, and the Philippines. As it grew, IGLHRC was increasingly recognized as a legitimate stakeholder by journalists, diplomats, and politicians. Brokers were not only able to agitate as outsiders, but could increasingly supply information, research, and expertise to influence policy, both publicly and privately.

Yet professionalization also complicated IGLHRC's mission. Management expected brokers to produce polished, high-quality work, and Johnson often reminded staff to "be rigorous," "step it up," or "take it to the next level." Brokers agreed that work should be professional, but in an activist setting where flexibility and inventiveness were valued, brokers could reasonably disagree about what professionalism entailed. Brokers sometimes felt rules and hierarchy were arbitrary, and at other times felt it was important to maintain more rigid standards.

In part, this was because brokers considered themselves activists, but many also regarded their job at IGLHRC as just that—a job. One broker highlighted some of the economic and professional considerations that made professional advocacy with an NGO attractive:

> I just got tired of being poor [*laughs*].... I'm like, man, I can't deal with this anymore. I need health insurance, I need to get a paycheck, I need to move to a bigger apartment. And just as I was just burning out . . . somebody mentioned this job at IGLHRC.

Of course, this did not mean that brokers took their work less seriously; working at an NGO offered some degree of stability and made it possible to embark on projects it was difficult to conduct as an unaffiliated activist. All the brokers employed during my fieldwork had activist backgrounds and were dedicated to their work, but many of them also came to IGLHRC with the expectation that it would be a stable, professional job. They often stressed the importance of boundaries separating their personal and professional lives. While they frequently put in extra time on projects they were invested in, some were frustrated by requests to do work they considered outside their job description or to work on nights and weekends. As IGLHRC professionalized, it expanded the scope of the work that brokers undertook, but also introduced the tensions of a professional workplace.

Second, IGLHRC placed a growing emphasis on universality. Brokers expanded their constituency from gay and lesbian persons to LGBT persons to anyone facing violations on the basis of "actual or perceived sexual orientation, gender identity or expression." IGLHRC's constituency contracted in some respects, including when brokers stopped overtly focusing on people living with HIV/AIDS. Still, brokers moved far beyond their original lesbian and gay constituency. The tagline IGLHRC adopted, "Human Rights for Everyone, Everywhere," is testament to a far more ambitious political project.

Brokers also widened their geographic scope, although the depth of their engagement varied over time. IGLHRC's work initially focused on countries where brokers had personal relationships with LGBT individuals, particularly in Eastern Europe and Latin America. Over time, brokers built a knowledge base about the conditions LGBT people experienced elsewhere by compiling country files, which helped them to form new relationships and speak about other contexts with some credibility.

With the elimination of the ADP, IGLHRC moved its country files to Araujo's new position at the Heartland Alliance. IGLHRC's restructured website, however, acted as a public repository for country information. Each country had a separate page with articles, news from local partners, reports, press releases, action alerts, and information on LGBT rights. For countries like Argentina, the Philippines, or Uganda, these pages of links were updated regularly. For the vast majority of countries, however, they were updated infrequently. Countries like Mali, Macedonia, and the Seychelles had no information, and many others had not been updated in years. Although IGLHRC did not have close partners in every country, it shifted from a corpus of comprehensive country files to a system where primary information about local conditions was fielded from regional programs and partner organizations.

In recognition of their limited capacity, brokers tried to narrow their focus. During my fieldwork, priority countries were nominally identified in IGLHRC's strategic planning, but when I asked, brokers were frequently unable to remember which countries those were. As IGLHRC began to develop a new strategic plan, brokers were in the process of more rigorously identifying these countries, but still recalibrated their advocacy to respond to events in other countries as they unfolded. The countries in which brokers worked on a daily basis were not necessarily those identified in the strategic plan, but were those where conditions were worst, where emergencies arose, or where brokers felt they had an opportunity to make a meaningful difference.

Third, IGLHRC gradually foregrounded its work with individuals who were activists or advocates for LGBT communities. In its early days, IGLHRC was heavily involved in refugee and asylum work, and this remained a centerpiece of its advocacy into the 2000s. With the decision to move to New York and focus on institutional advocacy and regional outreach, the ADP was deemed peripheral to IGLHRC's mission and was shifted to an immigrant service provider. Although IGLHRC continued to advocate for at-risk individuals and respond to emergencies, its work with human rights defenders became increasingly central to its mission.

This shift from direct, one-on-one engagement with at-risk individuals toward engagement with movements and human rights defenders was evident in IGLHRC's formalized goals. The Strategic Plan for 2009–2014, which was already being rewritten during my time with the organization, outlined four strategic goals for IGLHRC: "Advocate for the elimination of discriminatory laws, policies, and practices; support the enactment and implementation of anti-discrimination laws, policies, and practices; reduce family, community, and state-sponsored violence; and promote economic, social, and cultural rights."

In practice, these goals were pursued by doing what brokers called "defending the defenders." Instead of intervening directly, brokers tried first and foremost to ensure that those in regional, national, and local LGBT movements were safe and able to defend those at risk in their area. As groups emerged locally, regionally, and transnationally that were able to deal with incidents in a nuanced, attentive way, IGLHRC reevaluated its mandate and refocused on the concept of movement building. As I suggest in later chapters, this generated a whole series of challenges and possibilities of its own.

Conclusion: Excavating Activist Histories

IGLHRC's name suggests a static emphasis on work that is international, focused on gay and lesbian persons, and uses a human rights lens, but what that involves has evolved considerably. IGLHRC changed from a grassroots group of volunteers in San Francisco to a professionalized NGO with full-time staff in New York, Buenos Aires, Cape Town, and Manila. It expanded from its early focus on a small number of countries to a putatively universal focus on LGBT and same-sex practicing people everywhere. And finally, it largely ceased to work directly with individuals at risk, working instead to support human rights defenders who mediate their claims and advocate on their behalf. These shifts have not been linear; within a single LGBT human rights organization, brokers have expressly included and implicitly excluded different constituencies, chased after radically different practical and symbolic goals, and variously located the heart of their enterprise in activities as diverse as movement building, lobbying at the UN, targeting governments, information sharing and training, and service provision.

With the staff turnover of a small NGO, the most gradual trends sometimes escape notice. Yet history does shape how brokers understand the models they inherit and the work they do. The ways that IGLHRC's history is narrated by brokers and subsumed into its mission was perhaps most evident at the twentieth anniversary Celebration of Courage fundraiser. In a commemorative video, Dorf, Frank, Ettelbrick, Johnson, and IGLHRC's brokers and partners emphasized the importance of IGLHRC's work and the groundbreaking victories it has won for LGBT people worldwide. The video understandably omits any mention of internal tensions, staff who resigned or were fired, and disagreements about the organization's mission that have made it dynamic over the past two decades. Instead, it celebrates a determined, feisty organization that has consistently insisted on human rights for everyone, everywhere.

The ways in which brokers at IGLHRC make the strategic choices before them are elaborated in the chapters that follow, but IGLHRC's history offers at least one preliminary lesson to defenders and critics of LGBT human rights transnationally. Both universal human rights and Western gay politics are often treated as monolithic ideologies, and scholars have convincingly objected that these are much richer, more internally heterogeneous bodies of knowledge than these treatments suggest. IGLHRC's history adds another crucial complication to this vein of scholarship—beyond ideological heterogeneity, the goals and tactics that human rights organizations adopt are dynamic, sometimes conflicting or contradictory, and always shaped by the human actors who bring their whole selves to their work. Ultimately, the way that LGBT human rights advocacy takes place in practice is profoundly influenced by the brokers who animate IGLHRC as an entity and the internal and external pressures that shape their work.

2 Bodies of Law

Activists and Brokerage in Practice

LGBT human rights advocacy is often described in monolithic terms. In politics and popular media, references to a "gay agenda" or a "gay rights movement" are ubiquitous. Often, this oversimplification is reproduced in otherwise exemplary scholarly work. Joseph Massad, for instance, glosses ILGA, IGLHRC, and other advocates of LGBT human rights as "the Gay International," a vast array of "missionary tasks, the discourse that produces them, and the organizations that represent them."[1] Such broad generalizations assume that LGBT human rights NGOs share certain frameworks, motivations, and goals. Yet as chapter 1 illustrates, there are reasons to doubt this homogeneity. IGLHRC's mandate, like others, is a contingent outcome of ongoing and highly particular choices about constituencies, priorities, and tactics, which are often shaped by individual activists.

As anthropologists have noted, NGOs, like cultures, are not bounded, static, or whole.[2] The use of participant observation and firsthand accounts of organizational practice demonstrate *how* this is true, foregrounding the daily dynamism of brokerage in transnational advocacy. As David Lewis argues, ethnographic work informs assessments of civil society by "*revealing* (exposing areas of the third sector that presently receive little attention); *widening* (opening up important nonwestern perspectives on third-sector organizations); and *deepening* (a distinctive critical perspective on third-sector organizations and their contexts)."[3] Studies of the World Bank and other large institutions show how individual, organizational, and structural factors intertwine to produce particular frameworks and approaches.[4] Ethnography enriches our understandings of *what* brokers do on a daily basis, but it also explores *why* they do it.

Brokers at IGLHRC deliberately hired activists, who brought distinctive politics and styles to their work. Brokers disagreed passionately, found common ground, and stretched the organization's agenda based on their own expertise, ongoing relationships with different communities, and normative commitments. Ultimately, their interactions were shaped not only by understandings of justice and equality but also by mundane considerations like the layout of an office or the ambiguity of a job description. The fact that IGLHRC's institutional positions were often flexible or implicit allowed brokers to negotiate how they would carry out their advocacy. Understanding how brokers' backgrounds and interactions shaped political interventions cautions against any monolithic assessment of LGBT human rights advocacy, but also sheds light on some of the ways in which tensions arise and particular agendas prevail.

IGLHRC's Brokers and Brokerage

None of IGLHRC's advocacy took place without human agency and deliberation. Each partnership, publication, and campaign was undertaken by brokers who animated the organization. Brokers not only brought distinctive politics and ideologies to the table but also drew on their own management styles, relationships, and personality traits.

IGLHRC's executive director during my fieldwork was Cary Alan Johnson, who had been involved with IGLHRC since its founding. He had pressed AI to take up LGBT rights as part of AIMLGC, fundraised for IGLHRC when it was still a relatively unknown organization, and served on IGLHRC's board and IAB before being formally hired to head its Africa Program. His background was not exclusively in human rights, but instead spanned a much wider range of development and public health initiatives. This was reflected in Johnson's work in the Africa Program, where he spearheaded efforts to bring LGBT and MSM activists to the International Conference on AIDS and STIs in Africa (ICASA) in Dakar, Senegal, in 2008, and authored *Off the Map: How HIV/AIDS Programming Is Failing Same-Sex Practicing People in Africa.*

Johnson answered to IGLHRC's board. The board, comprising roughly a dozen people, ensured that IGLHRC remained functional and fiscally solvent. It was almost exclusively American; a former executive director explained this was because its roles were to fundraise and manage the organizational needs of a U.S.-based NGO. Its members were not typically involved in the day-to-day work of brokers, who rarely interacted with them.

Johnson did ask board members with expertise in specific movements or institutions to comment on draft publications and strategies, although this feedback was advisory rather than binding. For guidance that was more representative of IGLHRC's global constituency, the board coexisted with the IAB, made up of prominent activists around the world who were occasionally consulted by brokers.

During my fieldwork, IGLHRC was in a state of transition. I had arranged my research with the program director, Adrian Coman, who left to work at the European Parliament shortly before I arrived. A consultant, Debra Schultz, was hired as interim program director until a permanent replacement could be found. Schultz had co-founded the Soros Foundation's International Women's Program, but had also taught history and women's studies at the New School and Rutgers University. (Schultz, like Johnson, grew up in Brooklyn, and the two had attended high school together.) During her brief tenure, Schultz was well liked as a warm and sympathetic manager, particularly by the regional staff.

Of the regional programs she oversaw, the LAC Program was the most established. The program coordinator for LAC, Marcelo Ferreyra, began volunteering as a translator for IGLHRC in 2000, then was hired as an assistant for Sardá in 2002 and took over her position when she left in 2006. Ferreyra had been a founder of Biblioteca Gay Lésbica Travesti Transexual y Bisexual and Gays y Lesbianas por los Derechos Civiles, and helped secure language protecting sexual orientation in the Buenos Aires City Constitution. The program associate for LAC, Fernando D'Elio, had trained as an accountant, but advised a number of Argentinean NGOs working on LGBT issues, women's rights, and HIV/AIDS. He was hired when Ferreyra was promoted.

The Africa Program was newer and already larger than the LAC Program, and its headquarters in Cape Town was the regional office with which I became best acquainted. The Africa Program coordinator, Esther Kilonzo, joined IGLHRC in June 2009. Kilonzo, who was Kenyan, held degrees in law from the University of Nairobi and University of Pretoria. She had previously worked in the Kenyan Section of the International Commission of Jurists (ICJ), and had litigated cases and written on women's rights, reproductive rights, and minority groups in Africa. Kilonzo was particularly well connected to the Gay and Lesbian Coalition of Kenya (GALCK). She maintained close contacts with human rights professionals across Africa, including many outside of LGBT movements.

Other staff had been hired by Johnson, but remained through the subsequent transition in leadership. Victor Mukasa, the program associate for the Horn, East, and Central Africa, was a Ugandan activist who had helped found a number of influential groups, including Sexual Minorities Uganda (SMUG), Freedom and Roam Uganda (FARUG), and the East and Horn of Africa Human Rights Defenders Project. Mukasa was the only publicly identified trans broker at IGLHRC; he identified as a trans lesbian. The last addition to the office was Chivuli Ukwimi, the Health and Human Rights Program officer, who was hired during my fieldwork in January 2010. Ukwimi, whose background was in biological science, had previously worked at Population Services International (PSI) in Zambia on HIV and human rights, particularly concentrating on male circumcision and expanding outreach and service provision for MSM. Ukwimi, who was Zambian, was also active in a domestic LGBT group, Friends of Rainka, and served on the executive committee of AMSHeR.

The API Program had only two staff, and no physical office. Grace Poore, the regional coordinator for API, was a Malaysian activist and filmmaker who had focused primarily on issues of sexual abuse and child abuse. Ging Cristobal, the project coordinator for API, had cofounded Lesbian Advocates Philippines (LeAP) and was a member of Ang Ladlad and Asia-Pacific Rainbow. I had originally met Cristobal during an earlier period of fieldwork with LGBT activists in the Philippines, and she remained closely linked to LGBT movements in the region.

The fledgling MENA Program was run by Hossein Alizadeh, the MENA Program coordinator, who began working for IGLHRC in 2006 after the ADP assisted him with his asylum claim. Alizadeh, who was Iranian, closely followed movements in Iran and Iraq but worked as IGLHRC's communications coordinator until the MENA Program was launched in 2009. Alizadeh held graduate degrees in international relations and international peace studies. As he observed, this inclined him to situate LGBT advocacy in a wider context, which often meant thinking beyond sexual rights to broader geopolitical dynamics.

My work was initially based in New York. With Coman's departure, I worked most closely with Rebecca Clarke, the communications and research director, who joined IGLHRC in September 2007. Clarke was born and raised in the United Kingdom and studied at Cambridge before getting her doctorate in political science at Columbia. Clarke had written on a number of feminist and LGBT issues (including adoption and LGBT families), had been an adjunct faculty member, and had previously worked at an organization that focused on voting rights. Clarke was the only parent in the office, but was frequently the first person in the office and the last to leave. She was extremely well liked, especially by those she managed, and was an understanding figure in an environment that could feel tense and tumultuous.

The Communications and Research Department had two other staff at the beginning of my fieldwork. The research and policy associate, Sara Perle, was twenty-five years old. As a law student, she interned at IGLHRC in 2007, interned at the Center for Reproductive Rights in 2008, and returned to IGLHRC to work full time in 2009. Perle identified as bisexual or queer and was deeply interested in technology, social media, and advocacy at the UN. The web designer, Laura Thomas, had not primarily worked in LGBT or human rights advocacy, but was referred by her cousin, who had worked for IGLHRC in San Francisco. We also spent a lot of time together during my fieldwork, as she began working at IGLHRC the week before I arrived and our desks were initially stationed next to each other.

Other brokers in New York were less involved in programmatic work. The operations manager, Frank Gilmore, was hired in August 2007. IGL-HRC's fundraising and finances were also managed in New York. The deputy director of development, Tanya Ampatuan, had been at IGLHRC since Ettelbrick's tenure. Ampatuan, a Filipina American, had worked with Ettelbrick at the National Gay and Lesbian Task Force, where she was a research fellow, before accepting her position at IGLHRC in May 2006. When I arrived, Ampatuan oversaw Jennifer Adams, IGLHRC's development associate. Adams joined IGLHRC after graduating from college, and had been on staff since July 2008.

Within the New York office, some relationships were evidently strong when I arrived. The younger communications, development, and operations staff were all similar in age, and socialized outside of the office. Thanks to their physical proximity in the office and their personalities, the brokers in Communications and Research in general formed a tight-knit group.

The ties among brokers were reinforced in the first few weeks of my fieldwork, when Johnson announced that Clarke was leaving the organization. Clarke was one of the most well-liked people on staff. Shortly after a financial staffer was downsized when an external accounting firm was hired to run IGLHRC's financial department,[5] the decision to let Clarke go upset many brokers in New York. When I arrived, brokers complained about

IGLHRC's past dysfunctions, but after this incident, brokers registered their complaints in the present tense.

Thus, for the first four months of my fieldwork, IGLHRC lacked both a full-time program director and a full-time communications and research director, distorting a hierarchy with virtually no middle management between the executive director and the program staff, researchers, and interns. Schultz was in two or three days a week as interim program director, and Perle, who had been employed at IGLHRC for less than six months, became acting director of communications and research. The development staff was cut in half when Adams, who was particularly incensed by the downsizing, found a job at a nearby suicide-prevention NGO and put in her two weeks' notice in early December.

As the year progressed, some of this volatility subsided. Adams helped hire her replacement, Robert Smith, a recent graduate who became active in intersectional race, class, gender, and sexuality politics through his involvement with Brown University's Third World Center. After moving to New York, Smith had volunteered with a number of queer organizations, including the Audre Lorde Project and the Ali Forney Center for homeless youth. He applied at IGLHRC when he moved to New York after college, but thought he might ultimately go back to school to become a historian.

Other positions were also filled over time. In the fall, Emily Jones was brought in as a consultant to help with a fundraising proposal for the MENA Program, and was ultimately hired as program director, a position she assumed in January 2010. Around the same time, Sam Cook was hired as director of communications and research. Cook, who lived in New York but was a South African citizen, was unable to start until February 2010 as the work permit process dragged on.

Both Jones and Cook were particularly influential in IGLHRC's advocacy, as they managed brokers in their departments but also held sway with Johnson in a way that few brokers did. As program director, Jones worked most closely with regional staff. Notably, she was the only broker at IGLHRC whose professional background was squarely in the field of LGBT human rights. Jones had received a master's degree in human rights from the London School of Economics, then became the first full-time researcher for HRW's LGBT Rights Program, where she worked with former IGLHRC program director Scott Long. As a consultant, she had advised other human rights NGOs on LGBT issues as well.

Despite this background, Jones was among the most critical of the human rights framework, and attuned to its limitations. In our interview, she commented:

> I don't believe in a one-size-fits-all human rights approach, I don't believe in a one-size-fits-all internationalist approach. . . . One of the challenges I always have with the human rights framework is how to go beyond its emphasis on arbitrary arrests and violence and talk about the *huge* range of economic, social, and cultural rights that influence our lives. I'm also very concerned with inequality within the LGBT community itself. All too often, LGBT movement agendas are too narrowly constructed around the priorities of a funding base that is privileged based on class, gender, race, etc. But if I wanted to work for normativity, I shouldn't be working in human rights.[6]

Jones's acknowledgment of the limits of human rights approaches was influenced by her queer and feminist politics; she was skeptical of the willingness of powerful institutions to deliver meaningful justice to the most marginalized. Cook also took a measured approach to the human rights framework, which was equally influenced by her personal and professional background. Cook held law degrees from the University of Cape Town (UCT) and Columbia, and was one of the only brokers at IGLHRC with formal legal training. Previously, she had been the director of the Peace-Women Project at the Women's International League for Peace and Freedom (WILPF), where she worked on UN advocacy and issues of women, peace, and security. She had also worked with groups that addressed gender and violence using different frameworks, including Rape Crisis; the Law, Race, and Gender Unit at UCT; and the Women's Legal Center. In general, however, Cook's ideas about identity politics and human rights were formed in a very different sociopolitical context than many of her colleagues. As she recalled in an interview:

> I have a very fierce and clear sense of what I think is just and not, and about my being entitled and almost obligated in some circumstances to pull things out. I think growing up as a white South African, and my father being very clear on the need to recognize your own privilege—it's not enough to say racism is wrong. It's also important that you recognize where you've been privileged. . . . All of the many, many conversations and fights and really

quite awkward situations in student politics have, one, toughened me up, and also, taught me that if I'm doing something because I believe in a principle, and not because I'm trying to "help" other people, and not because I'm being condescending, then I should speak. And I know that that voice has been appreciated.

Cook was strong in her convictions, and tended to be more direct than most of her colleagues. At the same time, she disliked hierarchy and placed a premium on the well-being of those she supervised, two things that quickly endeared her to those of us in her department. Although this reflected her principles, she recounted that it was also shaped by her own burnout:

> Everyone I know in activism who's good at saying, "I can't, and I've made a decision ahead of time that I can't do x or y," and sticks with it, you dig around in their past, and they've got to a point where they're physically a mess, where they're at the doctor all the time, they have some serious illness, they can't sleep, they've put on weight, lost weight, whatever, and they're a mess. And you're like, ah, yes.
>
> [Have you ever hit that point?]
>
> Yeah. Hence, my very good boundaries.

Cook was especially pragmatic about brokers' limitations. She was frequently the first to say that a project was not feasible or that staff were stretched too thin. She was also acutely aware that Perle, Thomas, and I would readily stay late to finish projects given to us at the last minute, and gently insisted that we develop better boundaries. As I discuss below, this sometimes proved definitive in deciding which projects brokers undertook.

The last major hire during my fieldwork was Chris Saldana, the executive assistant. Saldana had recently graduated from Yale, where he was involved in queer activism but turned his academic and activist attention to drug policy reform. Saldana found that IGLHRC "feels like it's very much a culture of inefficiency," and as "a big efficiency kind of guy," he sought to enhance IGLHRC's effectiveness in his role. Upon his arrival, he also functioned as an intermediary between Johnson and the staff. Along with the arrival of Jones and Cook, this greatly streamlined the ad hoc system for managing projects that was operating when I arrived.

All of these brokers worked at IGLHRC and collaborated on its operations and programs, but they were far from homogenous. Each arrived at IGLHRC at a different time; brought different backgrounds, relationships, and priorities to his or her work; and had a different style of interpersonal interaction. In the context of IGLHRC's history, however, there were some characteristics of the workplace that meaningfully shaped its work during my fieldwork.

The first was the rate of staff turnover.[7] When I arrived at IGLHRC, nobody had been there longer than five years. After Clarke departed, the three brokers in Communications and Research collectively had fewer than eight months of work experience at IGLHRC. Brokers sometimes left with little advance notice, which could be disruptive when they took their knowledge and contacts with them and left unfinished projects with colleagues. (In a particularly memorable incident, Perle, who had spent a year working on IGLHRC's ECOSOC accreditation, was frustrated to discover that a whole series of files related to the project not only existed, but had been stored, unbeknownst to her, inside her desk.)

The high turnover created a steep learning curve for new hires. During my time at IGLHRC, it was rare for outgoing employees to train their successors, and there were few codified instructions detailing IGLHRC's priorities, terminology, or tactical arsenal. As Saldana commented about his training:

> You would expect that there would be the rules: come on time, you have this many sick days, or these are our goals, this is what everyone's working on, this is what this person is supposed to do. I have no idea. I've kind of been osmosing it little by little.

My experience was similar; I was asked to start writing updates for the website on my first day. Although it was particularly acute for younger staff, brokers at all levels observed that much of their work was learned by simply doing. I figured out how to write action alerts and letters to governments by copying older examples, and only bothered to look at the strategic plan because I was ethnographically interested in it. Knowledge was conveyed to new employees through practice and replication, and often not through explicit, formalized models that could be questioned, contested, or refined by brokers.

A second characteristic of brokerage at IGLHRC was heterogeneity. Critics have charged that transnational LGBT organizations are "dominated by white Western males."[8] Taken literally, this was dubious at IGLHRC, which has never been run by a white Western male. Of the twenty-one brokers employed full time by IGLHRC at various points during my field-work, nine might be considered white, ten were "Western" in the sense that they were from the North, and ten identified as male. The only brokers who were white, Western, and male were Gilmore and me, a visiting anthropologist.

Even these categorizations, however, tell us little. How should one classify Argentinians, who may be raced differently in different spaces? Or the child of a Filipina domestic worker, who moved to the United States when her mother's employer paid her university fees? Or an Iranian asylee settled permanently in New Jersey? Or a male-identified activist who also identifies as a transgender lesbian?

Identity-based categories are necessarily schematic, and ill-equipped to capture the richness of individual lives. Critics who charge that IGLHRC is white, Western, or male typically mean that its operative *ideology* is white, Western, or male. Many aspects of IGLHRC's advocacy are legacies of a human rights tradition developed in the West. Brokers typically presumed that SOGI are meaningful aspects of personhood and that all people should be able to enjoy certain rights by virtue of their humanity. This was true even when brokers were cognizant that the "LGBT" moniker does not reflect the full diversity of sexual subjectivities, or knew that the human rights framework has its limitations.

Here, too, generalizations obscure the richness of brokers' politics. During my fieldwork, few brokers had worked primarily in LGBT advocacy, particularly at the international level. Most had worked in other movements, some of which heavily overlapped with LGBT work and some of which were quite distinct. Brokers were involved, for example, with antiracist work, voting rights, public health, suicide prevention, rape counseling, reproductive rights, homelessness, drug policy, and academia.[9] This diversified the staff, but also informed brokers' capacity to think expansively about justice.

As a result, intersectional analysis was not uncommon at IGLHRC. It shaped IGLHRC's response to reports of men being hanged in Iran on rape charges, for example, which many activists in the North read as being hanged for being gay. The complex interplay of political commitments held by various brokers was influential in shaping IGLHRC's public response to the situation. As Poore recalled:

> Paula, Hossein and I worked on it, and I had to say, we're saying that the
> government is wrong to hang these people, frame them, even if they did what

they did. But there's somebody else's voice that we're not looking at. If these young men *are* rapists, their victims—who speaks for them? And I don't think I'm going to be able to write an article supporting them without also speaking for their victims. Because what, we're suddenly going to just ignore it? Yeah, it's true that they may be framed—I mean, Hossein kept saying, they're framed, they're framed. Yes. But in the event that this is not a frame-up, we need to at least acknowledge that as an organization, we do not condone rape. As an organization, we *do* want to say that victims of rape are always silenced, and they can't come out, because they may be penalized. We at least need to say that, before we say we're totally against the fact that these guys are being penalized.

Brokers publicly expressed these concerns.[10] As with the hate crimes discussion, this intersectional approach often meant that mainstream LGBT issues were scrutinized under a social justice lens. Cook, who spent years focusing on women, peace, and security, was understandably diffident about movements spending time, money, and energy so LGBT people could serve in the military, calling the demand "militarist and patriarchal." Jones, a signatory of the "Beyond Marriage" manifesto and board member of QEJ, expressed skepticism about marriage as an institution but spoke supportively of inclusion as program director.[11]

Focusing on race, geography, and gender might also elide socioeconomic and educational homogeneity, which the trend toward professionalization exacerbates. The most consistent commonality among IGLHRC's brokers was that they were middle class, something that is less often remarked on in critiques of transnational LGBT advocacy. Brokers at IGLHRC tended to think of themselves as professionals as well as activists, and most had postsecondary degrees, often from elite institutions. Brokers' educational backgrounds made them fairly critical of rigid identity politics and assimilationist demands, but also shaped the tactics they (and I) thought to adopt. IGLHRC's model was fairly legalistic, for example, and brokers tended to seek legitimation by institutional actors, like UN agencies, regional mechanisms, or Country Coordinating Mechanisms (CCMs) and governments designing National Strategic Plans (NSPs) to combat HIV/AIDS. This was a very particular kind of advocacy, which brokers problematized but reproduced in their interventions.

A final characteristic of brokerage at IGLHRC was fluidity in roles and projects. In practice, urgent tasks, diverse skills and interests, and staff travel or departures meant that the small staff was regularly tasked with projects that could not always be predicted. When I first arrived at IGLHRC and reviewed the contract I had negotiated months earlier, a senior broker told me in all seriousness that I should rip it up, since a different set of projects had become institutional priorities. I was a research fellow, but found myself picking up activists at the airport, co-organizing a protest, and liaising with a coalition of faith-based groups for LGBT rights. Perle, who was technically in Communications and Research, spearheaded a good deal of IGLHRC's UN advocacy.

Often, brokers expressed frustration that roles and organizational hierarchy were not clearly defined. The oxymoronic tension at the heart of professional activism made this a constant source of consternation. In human rights activism, resourcefulness and self-sacrifice are often valorized as signs of commitment to a larger cause. Yet as professionals, brokers repeatedly demanded clear procedures and job descriptions, which few had in any codified form. Those in Cape Town expressed frustration about what they perceived as mixed signals about the chain of command in New York, and felt torn between programmatic work and the writing and fact-checking that was also part of their job. While brokers resented tasks they considered peripheral to their job or found the chain of command unclear, they also balked at the imposition of bureaucracy and hierarchy.

The high turnover of the staff, their backgrounds and politics, and the fluidity of their roles all set the stage for the scenes that played out daily at IGLHRC. Against this backdrop, brokers came to offices, interacted with each other, and carried out projects. Understanding the settings they inhabited and how they acted in them offers a much richer picture of what IGLHRC's advocacy actually involves.

IGLHRC's Office Environment

During my fieldwork, IGLHRC's headquarters and the revamped MENA Program were based in New York. The Africa office was in Cape Town, and the LAC office was in Buenos Aires. The API Program was run by Poore outside of Washington, D.C., and Cristobal in Quezon City, an area of Manila, and each worked from home.

IGLHRC's headquarters was housed in an aging skyscraper in New York's financial district, just a stone's throw from Wall Street. It shared a floor with two domestic NGOs, the Trevor Project and the National Gay and Lesbian Task Force. Visitors were greeted by an etching on the door depicting

IGLHRC's logo, a globe with continents made up of tiny human silhouettes. After buzzing in, they passed into a small sitting area with a rack of publications. When I left in 2010, the rack still proudly displayed newsletters from 2008, when Archbishop Desmond Tutu accepted IGLHRC's Outspoken Award. To the left was a small kitchen where staff made coffee, reheated lunch, and tried to inconspicuously hide cakes on office birthdays.

Ahead was an open-plan office, with desks for ten people running along pastel yellow walls. A bank of file cabinets occupied the center of the room, draped by a rainbow flag and littered with a stereo, magazines, and the snacks that Alizadeh often brought for the staff. The space was lit by fluorescent fixtures and a bank of windows along one wall, with cabinets holding old files, publications, and supplies mounted above the desks. Along the interior wall were a small office shared by Jones and Cook, a larger office for Ampatuan and consultants working on finances, and a midsize office occupied by Johnson. On the far end was the conference room—a cool, muted space humming with recycled air where brokers held meetings, met visitors, and made private or sensitive calls.

In its layout, decor, and the way it was inhabited, the office felt like an NGO. Saldana offered a telling impression shortly after he was hired:

> I walked in and immediately I was like, okay, I'm in a nonprofit office. There are wheelie chairs, people use them liberally, there's a pot of old coffee, the beat-down fridge, the three computers that nobody wants to use but sometimes have to, the one nice computer. You know? People walking around laughing and joking, confusion, vague chaos.

Despite tense moments, the atmosphere was generally informal. The layout facilitated camaraderie among junior staff, who were spatially segregated from senior staff with semiprivate offices. Brokers freely came and went with various commitments, for example, meetings at the UN, other NGOs, or universities in the city; coffee or lunch with activists passing through New York; or medical appointments. With the fluorescent lighting and the distractions of the shared workspace, some brokers preferred to work elsewhere when something demanded intensive, sustained attention. This flexibility gave brokers a sense of independence and agency in their work, but it could also prolong or delay decisions and outputs until relevant people could meet or sign off on them.

The Africa Program was situated on the top floor of a small office building in Cape Town's central business district. Upon climbing the stairs, visitors entered a shaded conference room, which opened into a kitchen and bathrooms on one side and a large, airy open-plan workspace on the other. Brokers had desks facing the walls in their respective corners, and worked with their backs to the center of the room. I occupied an empty desk under a bulletin board with years-old notes pinned to it, working between Mukasa and Ukwimi. It was not uncommon for only one or two of us to be in the office. Brokers in Cape Town regularly traveled to meet with activists, attended regional and international meetings, or worked from home.

The LAC Program had space in a suite of LGBT NGOs in Buenos Aires, but used it sparingly. Ettelbrick had insisted that IGLHRC retain a physical office, but Ferreyra and D'Elio preferred to work from home. In an interview, Ferreyra estimated that they only used the space about twice a month.

IGLHRC's physical spaces shaped interpersonal and professional dynamics in myriad ways. The open plans made conversations semipublic, which changed the tenor of constructive criticism and encouraged brokers to seek validation after the fact from their colleagues. In a workplace that dealt heavily with sex and sexuality, even offhand remarks and familiar teasing could sometimes surprise or offend colleagues who overheard them out of context.[12]

The spaces also facilitated cooperation among particular brokers. The open plan encouraged bonding among junior staff who lacked semiprivate offices, but also enabled gossip and discontent to spread beyond management's earshot. Jones was often on the phone with activists off-site and preferred to work with the door closed so she could hear across poor Skype and telephone connections; Cook, who shared that office, preferred a more open workspace, and frequently wandered out to visit with those she supervised: Perle, Thomas, and me. The physical arrangement of the office in Cape Town, where brokers worked in silence with their backs to each other, did little to help relieve any tensions that arose among colleagues.

Being dispersed was also complicated. The LAC Program worked extremely well together, but for other brokers, working together from a distance could produce tension. When connectivity was limited, messages were misinterpreted, or a project was put on hold until someone returned or responded, distance and absences rippled through the many types of advocacy brokers undertook.

IGLHRC's Advocacy and Outreach

Within IGLHRC, brokers defined and divided their work in particular ways. The program staff worked most directly with local partners, providing assistance, turning to them for information, and collaboratively promoting LGBT human rights. The communications staff researched issues facing LGBT people globally, publicized human rights violations, and called for supporters and governments to take action. The development staff promoted IGLHRC's work and ensured there were funds to underwrite and expand its programs. Within these broad mandates, brokers with distinctive priorities designed advocacy and programming carried out in IGLHRC's name.

Program Work

Over half of the staff was tasked with program work, and the rest assisted with their projects in various ways. Brokers juggled a multitude of short- and long-term projects, which were subject to the vagaries of funding, unexpected crises, and the calendars of bodies like the UN, IACHR, ACHPR, and various human rights commissions. Nonetheless, some projects were focal points for program staff during my fieldwork, and hint at the political and tactical differences among the regional offices.

The Africa Program primarily supported local activists in a series of prominent cases that arose in late 2009 and early 2010. Brokers were involved in different ways with the Anti-Homosexuality Bill in Uganda; the proposed criminalization of same-sex activity in Rwanda; the arrest of Tiwonge Chimbalanga and Steven Monjeza and the harassment of human rights defenders in Malawi; mob violence and the constitutional reform process in Kenya; trainings and HIV/AIDS work in Zambia; and emergency responses to raids, arrests, and detentions in Tanzania, Rwanda, and Zimbabwe. Kilonzo regularly engaged with the ACHPR, promoting LGBT inclusion, monitoring hostile activity, and networking with other civil society groups. Ukwimi coordinated presentations by LGBT and MSM activists at the Eighteenth International AIDS Conference in Vienna, and worked with partners to ensure same-sex practicing people were represented in CCMs and NSPs. Mukasa was heavily involved in supporting LGBT refugees, repeatedly returned to Uganda to assist activists, and helped spearhead the first conference of transgender activists in Lusophone Africa, held in Mozambique in the summer of 2010.

The API Program was involved in responsive work as well as a number of more proactive, larger-scale projects. Cristobal primarily worked with movements in the Philippines on the renewed push for an antidiscrimination bill, the accreditation of the LGBT political party Ang Ladlad, and the recovery efforts after Hurricane Ondoy. Poore was responsive to incidents in China and restrictive laws proposed in Aceh, Indonesia, but was also finishing a documentary about the Yogyakarta Principles and Asian LGBT advocacy, *Courage Unfolds*, released to commemorate IDAHO in May 2011. Both also had initiatives they wanted to undertake. Cristobal, who worked in a country that sent massive numbers of overseas foreign workers abroad, planned to explore how LGBT migrants dealt with multiple marginalizations. Poore was eager to develop a cross-regional project on fundamentalisms after witnessing an escalation in antigay religious rhetoric in the Philippines, Japan, and Indonesia.

The LAC Program protested a number of localized cases of homophobia by police and state agents. With local partners, brokers issued action alerts drawing attention to attacks against a transgender man in La Matanza, Argentina; the arrest of LGBT people in Caracas, Venezuela; the murders of trans people in Guatemala; the murder of a young activist, Walter Tróchez, and three travesti women in Honduras; discrimination against students in Belize; and the abduction of a lesbian in Paraguay. Brokers held IGLHRC's first-ever strategy workshop with trans activists in the Caribbean, and participated in a fact-finding mission to Haiti in April 2010. They also lobbied intergovernmental bodies, continuing their coalitional advocacy at the Organization of American States (OAS), IACHR, and Mercosur.

The MENA Program had just begun, and was in a fairly exploratory stage. Alizadeh was deeply skeptical of aggressive advocacy in the region, and emphasized listening to movements and identifying constructive ways to support them. This was supplanted by media monitoring, and Alizadeh tracked when and where relevant issues were being raised in the media and politics. Where movements were actively engaging the government, IGLHRC and partners advocated more openly. Alizadeh worked closely with activists in Turkey on multiple interventions, urging officials to change the vague Law of Misdemeanors, overturn an order to close Black Pink Triangle in Izmir, and protect trans people at heightened risk of violence.

Brokers' work was frequently driven by circumstantial needs, but it was also heavily shaped by the backgrounds of brokers themselves. Personal ties to movements in particular countries—for example, Argentina, the Philippines, and Uganda—deepened the work that IGLHRC was able to do in those contexts.[13] Brokers also brought thematic priorities to their work. Poore and Cristobal focused on women, migrants, and sexual rights, for example, reflecting their own commitments and those of the movements in which they operated. The same was true of tactics; Alizadeh, whose background was in politics and international relations, was skeptical of conventional human rights tactics in his region, while Ferreyra, who had been at IGLHRC for a decade, used action alerts far more than other brokers. Poore, a filmmaker, used visual media to produce *Courage Unfolds*. These preferences were regularly apparent in brokers' programmatic work, including emergency response, movement building, and public education.

Emergency Response and Movement Building

The most unpredictable and reactive form of program work was emergency response, which often put long-term interventions on hold. This took various forms—for example, wiring money for safe houses; giving material or political support to activists to get passports, visas, or transportation; visiting detainees; strategizing with activists; helping to procure lawyers; or intervening with sympathetic authorities. Typically, regional staff worked with in-country activists to assess their needs and formulate any response. When necessary, requests for material support were forwarded to New York for approval.

The pressure to say or do something about high-profile emergencies was often acutely felt by brokers. As Jones observed, this was exasperating for those who were also conscious of more systemic marginalization:

> People want to talk about the arrest that just happened in x city and they want to talk about the horrible bill that was introduced in y city, but they don't necessarily want to talk about systematic issues like employment discrimination, traditional gender roles, and legal documents, issues that you can never work on solely in an emergency framework.

Brokers in every region echoed this frustration, and consciously tried to stage proactive interventions through advocacy and trainings.

The Africa Program's convenings in particular generated declarations, networks, and research projects.[14] As Johnson, the former senior regional specialist, recalled in an interview:

I think we played a really important role in catalyzing the African LGBT movement. A lot of the convenings around which people started getting a sense of themselves and their power and their potential, I think, we convened. . . . Convenings don't always have concrete outcomes, but I think they are spaces in which people develop political community, and know each other, and know where to go for help, and develop a sense of what the possibilities are.

During Johnson's tenure, IGLHRC held convenings on advocacy at the ACHPR, defining a transgender movement in Africa,[15] and blackmail and extortion of LGBT people. In these spaces, brokers catalyzed exchange and discussion, typically resulting in projects where IGLHRC played a central role.

Brokers also hosted human rights trainings, albeit less often than in the 1990s, when movements were younger and LGBT human rights discourse was less widespread. The largest took the form of Activist Institutes, which brought activists in a region together to strategize around a topic or issue. During my fieldwork, Poore and Cristobal hosted an institute on violence against LBT people in Asia, which built on a previous consultation to launch a multiyear research project around the issue. In an interview, Poore remembered that first meeting:

At that consultation, we were basically trying to figure out, look, we've heard repeatedly that violence is a big issue, and that groups don't have the resources to do the level of documentation, and again and again, people have said, you know, we want to do documentation, and we need to get trained, and we need the resources so that we can provide hard data so that people can take our claims of violence seriously. So the consultation was to find out what people were finding out in their countries about the problem—what kinds of research they had already done, what were the models of research that they had either experienced or had participated in and hated, you know? And all the problems with it, and why.

Brokers accepted applicants from five countries, who gathered in Manila for the institute. As Poore recalled, the criteria for participation in this three-year, multicountry project were a matter of live discussion:

Ging felt that we needed to build the capacity of our partners while they were doing the research. I felt that we couldn't afford to do that. I felt that the people who were going to be undertaking the research needed to be people who could deliver, so we would be building their capacity in other things—for instance, doing a level of documentation that maybe they didn't do before, or doing the kind of outreach that they were not comfortable doing, pushing them beyond the comfort zone, or grounding them in the human rights framework, or helping them to think about end use so that they can develop the advocacy project. So yes, we were building capacity, but not at the one-on-one level. I felt like we needed to be at a higher level, you know? We needed to start at a level where, these are people who knew what research and documentation was. They may not do analysis and they may not do research, but they certainly had done documentation in their groups and stuff.

In the context of IGLHRC's history, Cristobal and Poore's positions illustrate how the immediate demands of human rights advocacy and movement building can sometimes operate in tension. On one hand, advocacy required rigorous, complete documentation. On the other hand, requiring particular skills threatened to exclude some movements from the project entirely.

Trainings and institutes were places where IGLHRC did utilize a particular model of human rights, along with all of the political and ideological presumptions that entailed. As Poore recounted, the institute triggered skepticism about the utility of the human rights framework for documenting violence, and a broader understanding was negotiated:

Except for one group, one country, I think everybody else said these are our objections, but we realize that for practical purposes, we need to use the human rights framework, because of the end use for the data. Many of them were wanting to use the data with lawyers who would want that kind of human rights documentation. They were going to use it with legislators. So they felt that to be taken "seriously"—which is kind of sad, you know, to be taken seriously—they needed to use the human rights framework to do their documentation.

Given their past work, Poore and Cristobal readily grasped the limitations of the human rights framework, which is ill-equipped to deal with violence in the private sphere that is not immediately attributable to the state. As Poore explained, this recognition explicitly informed the project:

What we did was, we said, so let's acknowledge what are the weaknesses of the human rights framework, and let's figure out how we are going to be expansive. . . . So given that we were feminists who believed in the sexual rights framework, we basically said that we're going to meld both, so that we're going to use the sexual rights framework, expand the human rights framework, for this project, because it makes sense to do so. And so it was fine. It worked. I don't know what other people do who don't have a sexual rights framework, or the women's framework. Because the human rights framework is very limiting. It is extremely limiting.

Indeed, as the API Institute suggests, interventions were often built around topical issues in a region—transgender and intersex issues, religious fundamentalisms, or violence against women—that troubled the limitations of a traditionally state-centric human rights framework. In these movement-building activities, brokers did not only explain the human rights framework to activists. Instead, they embarked on collaborative projects that creatively drew on human rights frameworks to develop compelling cases against the marginalization that activists witnessed in context.

Communications and Research

In collaboration with the program staff, the Communications and Research staff in New York primarily worked on IGLHRC's public, written materials. Brokers produced a diverse array of outputs, including action alerts, letters to governments, and reports, which each had specific purposes. While I explore IGLHRC's role in producing knowledge in chapter 5, it is worth reviewing here how brokerage shaped the development and use of these tools.

Action Alerts

From IGLHRC's earliest days, action alerts have been used to call public attention to an issue and mobilize a response. During my fieldwork, IGL-HRC had e-mail addresses for twenty-two thousand people; twelve thousand had responded to one or more alerts. Alerts have existed in various incarnations over time, yet there was no formal template for how they should be designed.[16] Typically, they followed a semi-standardized format that brokers learned by copying previous alerts—a short subject line, the right or rights that had been violated, a description of the incident and any relevant information, a requested action, a list of contacts to whom appeals should be sent, and a sample letter.

The utility of action alerts was a topic of frequent discussion at IGL-HRC, and their use varied under different brokers. Johnson told me that alerts "need to be about issues that rise to a certain level . . . or they need to be about a pattern." He felt IGLHRC should release no more than two alerts per month; brokers in New York were conscious that flooding supporters with e-mails would be counterproductive, and thus weighed disparate incidents in different countries to decide where they would speak out.

Fluctuations in the focus and number of action alerts suggest how much discretion individuals can exercise in IGLHRC's advocacy. In the two months from early September to early November, for example, Clarke and Schultz approved three alerts. In the three months from early November until early February, Perle issued nine alerts, a particularly sharp increase since the office closed for the holidays during this period. And in the eight months from early February until late September, Cook and Jones issued just one alert, regarding a lesbian from Paraguay who was abducted and assaulted by family members with no response from the government.

Some programs were deeply skeptical of action alerts, and rarely used them. Alizadeh expressed concern in an interview about how to determine their impact:

> We ask people to send an e-mail to the president of Uganda . . . and five hundred people e-mail him. How do you measure the changes? Does it really change things, or is it to make people feel good about themselves? And if so, how is that impacting our partners? Are we blowing smoke up their ass, or doing something that is really changing things for them?

Other programs enthusiastically embraced alerts. The LAC Program, in particular, proposed a number of alerts that were viewed skeptically by brokers in New York. The issues they tackled were not obviously systemic—for example, a single person being murdered or facing expulsion from school—and brokers doubted that global pressure would be a proportionate and productive response. Nonetheless, regional staff and partners felt these calls to action were helpful, and brokers in New York often acquiesced.

Even so, questions remained. One was depth. Some brokers, particularly those concerned with response rates, felt alerts should be brief, straightforward, and compelling enough that people would write to policymakers. Others, particularly those with a human rights background, argued that alerts needed to explain what had specifically happened and detail the rights that had been violated. Questions of length and depth were in part linked to assumptions about the primary audience for alerts. If it was supporters, the goal was to get them to read the alert, learn what IGLHRC was doing, and send a message. If it was the policymakers to whom faxes, e-mails, and letters were being directed, the goal was to describe what had happened in such a way that the human rights violation was obvious and irrefutable.

In general, brokers felt alerts were most appropriate when they were requested by partners on the ground and publicized abuses that might otherwise be ignored. But at times, brokers acknowledged other motivations: to feel like something was being done, to make IGLHRC's donors and mailing list feel included in its work, and to balance advocacy so sparsely covered countries (like China) received attention. While brokers downplayed any motivation other than efficacy and impact, they frequently referenced other pressures in their deliberations.

The role of other actors also shaped IGLHRC's practice. The decline of action alerts toward the end of my fieldwork may have been linked to the imminent launch of All Out, which was created by a founder of Avaaz.org, a campaigning website. In February 2010, Avaaz's petition against Uganda's Anti-Homosexuality Bill was signed over 450,000 times in just two weeks. IGLHRC's own alert from October 2009 had generated fewer than one thousand faxes to Ugandan officials. Avaaz's petition revived internal discussions about whether alerts were the best use of IGLHRC's time and resources, and whether IGLHRC might produce alerts that were substantively deeper than All Out's. IGLHRC's public campaigns were thus influenced both by internal debates and by external actors with new tools and the expertise needed to do large-scale advocacy more effectively.

Letters to Governments

A less visible type of advocacy was IGLHRC's letters to governments. These were usually sent privately, although some were public or discreetly posted on the sidebar of a country's page on IGLHRC's website. Brokers sent letters when they believed a direct appeal to the government would improve a situation or signal that somebody was paying attention, and suspected a letter would be more strategic than publicly pressuring the government with an alert.

In early 2010, the flexible process used for writing letters was evident over a three-week period when a letter was being written to Malawian president Bingu wa Mutharika. IGLHRC opted for a letter for various reasons. State

and intergovernmental representatives were vocally protesting the detention of Tiwonge Chimbalanga and Steven Monjeza, a couple arrested for
participating in a commitment ceremony. Brokers were worried about other
violations that were receiving less press, and for which the state could be
held directly accountable. Coverage of the couple rarely mentioned, for
example, that an LGBT-friendly NGO, the Centre for the Development of
People (CEDEP), was raided just weeks before their arrest. There was only
fleeting coverage of an activist reportedly arrested for putting up posters
proclaiming that "Gay Rights are Human Rights," an elderly woman allegedly expelled from her village for lesbianism, and a man reportedly charged
with sodomy. IGLHRC itself had been largely silent on these issues; I saw
scattered reports of the incidents and Jones heard of them from a colleague
in Europe, but Ukwimi said CEDEP had not raised them with him.

When CEDEP did raise concerns about violations that went beyond
Chimbalanga and Monjeza's imprisonment, it was over a conference they
held on HIV and the human rights of MSM. Police arrived to question participants during the first day of the two-day conference, intimidating many
participants enough that they did not return. The raid and police questioning suggested the state was deliberately cracking down on homosexuality
and its defenders, and arguably, more so than with the arrest of the couple,
which only occurred after the media sensationalized their ceremony as a
gay wedding.

Brokers were obviously concerned for the well-being of the couple. They
also worried about the precedent their sentencing could set. If Chimbalanga and Monjeza were sent to prison despite the lack of evidence against
them, pretrial abuses they suffered, and strong intervention from the international community, it would set a dangerous precedent elsewhere in the
region. This was especially true because wa Mutharika was the head of the
African Union (AU) at the time, giving him added credibility to speak for
the region on the controversial topic of LGBT rights.

For all these reasons, IGLHRC opted to write to wa Mutharika directly,
signaling that NGOs were tracking events in the country beyond the well-
publicized trial of Chimbalanga and Monjeza. The process of writing a
letter was not well defined; Jones and Cook both felt these communications should be produced by regional staff rather than those in New York.
In this case, the process involved me in New York and Ukwimi in Cape
Town, who had just joined IGLHRC and was quickly thrust into advocacy
around the arrests. Jones was also involved in the process, overseeing our

work, often simultaneously, to finalize a version that could be sent relatively quickly.

After Ukwimi sent the first draft of the letter, Jones asked if Communications and Research had a template for writing letters to governments, or if I could find past letters I considered exemplary. There was no template; as with other outputs, the process was a form of institutional knowledge acquired by mimicking past letters and refining the final product with feedback from other brokers. A survey of past letters, however, revealed some common features. Letters typically described the situation; specified the rights that were being violated and the domestic, regional, and international commitments that were being breached; and offered clear recommendations to government officials to remedy the situation.

These finished products showed little of the processual work that went into writing letters to governments, which became apparent as Ukwimi and I exchanged multiple drafts. Ukwimi composed the first draft, which Jones forwarded to me as part of the vetting process. My draft described wa Mutharika decrying homosexuality as "disgusting" and "un-Malawian," the harassment of conference participants, and the incarceration of Monjeza and Chimbalanga in more detail, and argued that Articles 19–21, 32–35, and 38 of Malawi's constitution were all violated by the incidents that had occurred. I then invoked the African Charter, ICCPR, ICESCR, and *Toonen* in the broadest of terms. Finally, I made specific requests, writing, "We ask you to swiftly and publicly reaffirm the human rights of all Africans—including LGBT Africans—to life, privacy, and freedoms of assembly, association, opinion, and expression. We also ask that you demonstrate your commitment to those rights by investigating police harassment of the recent conference in Liwonge, reprimanding any wrongdoing by the police, releasing Monjeza and Chimbalanga, and repealing all discriminatory laws which target LGBT Malawians and deprive them of their fundamental rights."

My draft was then edited by Jones, who added information on prison conditions reminiscent of the detailed documentation produced by HRW, where she previously worked, and clarified the condition of Monjeza's health after misconceptions were circulated by another activist. Although wa Mutharika's comments were made on April 23, 2010, the dialogic editing meant that the letter was not released until May 11, 2010—a lengthy period that was not uncommon as drafts bounced between brokers who were liaising with partners, brokers who identified relevant laws and finessed messaging, and brokers who were ultimately responsible for approving outputs. While Jones outlined a series of steps for producing letters in the future, this process remained fairly ad hoc.[17] As a broker in Communications and Research observed, brokers were good at formulating guidelines, but far worse at actually applying them as exceptional circumstances, time constraints, or other justifications arose. Although the dialogic process could frustrate staff and delay immediate interventions, it also ensured that outputs were vetted by multiple actors at IGLHRC and were as accurate and comprehensive as possible, striking some balance between the competing concerns of a U.S.-based NGO weighing in on abuses abroad.

Reports

One of the most iconic outputs of human rights organizations is the human rights report. The construction of a report involves an economy of knowledge all its own, which blends partnership, research, and advocacy. Reports vary by organization, and their design and presentation legitimates particular kinds of knowledge. As Richard Wilson has argued, human rights reports tend to reduce intimate violations of the person to "bare 'facts,'" stripped of social embeddedness and authorial interpretation.[18] AI, for example, traditionally produced reports with a factual, dispassionate feel, which described atrocities in the most straightforward way possible. To appear authoritative, few adjectives or adverbs were used to convey the suffering of those whose experiences were presented. I was told by a broker at HRW that their reporting protocol is far less formulaic than outsiders usually suppose, but they almost always include documentation as well as recommendations for stakeholders to remedy alleged violations. As ethnographic work by former staffers has vividly described, these too are ideological in their terminology, paradigms, and tacit inconsistencies.[19]

IGLHRC's reports were varied in their origins, process, and purpose even within the organization. A number had been proposed, partially finished, and left in different stages of development. All the reports in the pipeline were developed by brokers prior to the arrival of Cook, Perle, Thomas, or me, who were charged with revisions, editing, and what Johnson termed "getting them out the door." Like *Words of Hate, Climate of Fear: Human Rights Violations and Challenges to the LGBT Movement in Senegal,* discussed in chapter 5, these projects often spanned multiple years and multiple researchers. Just before my fieldwork began, IGLHRC released *Equal and Indivisible: Crafting Inclusive Shadow Reports for CEDAW,* a guide for groups submitting shadow reports on LBT issues to the CEDAW Committee. In addition to *Words of Hate, Climate of Fear,* which was conceptualized, researched, and partially drafted before Joel Nana, from Cameroon, left the Africa Program, six reports remained in the pipeline. They focused on trans people in poverty in LAC, trans people in sub-Saharan Africa, LGBT community centers in Africa, blackmail and extortion of LGBT Africans, human rights violations in Cameroon, and the challenges facing LGBT people in postdisaster contexts, based on interviews conducted during a week-long trip to Haiti in April 2010.

The history of each publication illustrates how personnel changes, institutional priorities, and probable reception all shape the development and deployment of human rights reports. The first report, initially issued in Spanish and titled *Trans Latinoamericanas en Situacion de Pobreza Extrema,* was released in May 2009. Under the title *Transgender People Surviving Extreme Poverty,* the English version was the subject of lengthy discussions with partners, who felt strongly about particular terminology (for example, "trans" rather than "transgender") and asked to have their names removed from the translation if their suggestions were not incorporated.[20] The project had been originally conceptualized as a submission to the UN's Independent Expert on the Question of Human Rights and Extreme Poverty, and brokers felt far more primary documentation needed to be done before it would be at a publishable standard as a credible human rights report. Given the difficulty of completing and translating it, brokers opted not to prioritize it as a full-fledged publication. Perle, who was immersed in UN advocacy, was reluctant to scrap the report altogether because its introduction had been written by the Independent Expert. Perle believed the introduction was an important tool that could lend prominence and legitimacy to the concerns the report raised. Jones and Cook echoed this sentiment and pledged to find ways to use the introduction, but felt there was no obvious way to publish it.

Another report on transgender issues, *Voices from Trans Africa,* also encountered difficulties, though there were plans to release it throughout my fieldwork. The report initially emerged from a convening to define and plot a path forward for the burgeoning transgender movement in Africa. It included stories from trans individuals in Africa and sought to analyze the conditions they faced. By the time Cook and Jones arrived and encountered the project, the interviews were felt to be outdated, but Mukasa, who helped collect the stories and was a friend and colleague of many of those who contributed, felt IGLHRC needed to publish it for the sake of those interviewed. New interviews, which were to be conducted at the training in Mozambique, never materialized. When Mukasa left IGLHRC, brokers were unsure how to proceed.

Johnson, who initiated many of the reports in the Africa Program, was eager to see them published. The bulk of the work had been done, and as the person who secured funding for the reports, he was eager to show finished products to funders. Other brokers doubted whether the reports remained relevant. The report on community centers, for example, was initiated in 2008, when brokers arranged for activists from GALCK to tour centers in South Africa. Following the study tour, five community centers participated in two conference calls about their operations. IGLHRC hired a consultant to send follow-up questions to participants about the work they were doing, the design of the centers, the populations they served, the programs they offered, and the challenges they faced. A draft was produced by Johnson and two consultants, and discussions around it continued for a year before I was tasked to complete it as a research fellow. By 2010, however, the consultant was no longer working with IGLHRC, and her notes, recordings, and other documentation had been lost. My own edits were mostly cosmetic, and reorganized the report into thematic discussions of advocacy, service provision, and community building. After inconclusive discussions about whether the report could be safely launched, given its detailed descriptions of the centers involved, the report was privately sent to participating centers in October 2010 but never publicly released.

The report on blackmail and extortion was also the result of a consultation, one which Johnson had organized in Johannesburg in October 2007. The consultation brought lawyers, academics, and activists together to define blackmail and extortion, to survey what was known and what groups were doing to respond, and to commission studies to get a sense of the scope of the problem and how it might be addressed. Chapters were commissioned from researchers in Zimbabwe, Ghana, Cameroon, Malawi, and Nigeria, most of whom had close ties to IGLHRC's partners in the region. The pieces were collected by brokers at the Africa Program, and the report, like the others, was added to the backlog of publications entrusted to Clarke and then Cook. Some of the chapters needed editing, rewriting of parts, and standardization before they could be published, but this work had stalled since the initial submissions were received. I inherited this as my primary assignment while in Cape Town, and the volume was eventually published as *Nowhere to Turn: Blackmail and Extortion of LGBT People in Sub-Saharan Africa* in January 2011.

One could deconstruct the terminology and frameworks used in the report, but it is impossible to do this well without also understanding the structural pressures under which it developed. The funneling of half-finished and unedited reports from the various regions to New York placed tremendous pressure on Cook and other staff who were tasked with follow-up interviews, research, and fact-checking on a variety of topics; editing what was already produced; getting feedback from reviewers, board members, and partners who participated in the research; arranging for the design of PDFs and the printing of the final reports; and setting up the press releases, publicity, or advocacy that would accompany each release.

In practice, it was difficult to get widespread consensus on any language other than "LGBT" in these reports. Johnson and Jones both disliked the term "sexual minorities" because it implied a correlative "sexual majority" they found problematic. Johnson avoided "LGBTI," feeling it was merely symbolic given the minimal attention IGLHRC paid to intersex issues. The phrase "LGBTI and same-sex practicing," which I proposed for *Nowhere to Turn*, was changed to "LGBT" shortly before the volume went to print. This was partially because it was the formulation used at the original convening, but also because it was not a gloss that researchers themselves had used when conducting their surveys and interviews.

I was not involved with two of the reports, which I nonetheless read at different stages. The first was on SOGI-related human rights violations in Cameroon, and was coauthored by HRW, IGLHRC, Alternatives-Cameroun, and L'Association pour la Défense des Droits des Homosexuels (ADE-FHO).[21] The NGOs released the report as *Criminalizing Identities: Rights Abuses in Cameroon Based on Sexual Orientation and Gender Identity*, published shortly after my departure in late 2010.

The final report—which was eventually published instead as a briefing paper—had been conceptualized years earlier. In my interview with Ettelbrick, she recalled wanting to write a piece on the way that LGBT people fared after major coups and upheavals, spurred by reports of targeted killings of gay men in Iraq following the U.S. invasion. This was a project that she, Johnson, and a research fellow had planned to write together, but the research fellow had not ultimately gotten involved, and it failed to materialize.

The concept was revised after the January 2010 earthquake in Haiti, when Johnson wanted to explore how members of a partner organization,

SEROvie, had been affected by the earthquake and overlooked in the humanitarian response. The plan faced strong pushback from Cook, who argued that the backlog of reports was unmanageable, and that more thought needed to be given to which ideas became reports and why. The extant reports had all been commissioned, researched, and drafted years earlier, and brokers questioned their ongoing relevance to IGLHRC's work. During Cook's first year, her priority was completing or ceasing work on these existing, half-finished reports so brokers could fully assess the rationale, methodology, and advocacy strategy for future publications.

At the end of my fieldwork, the report was in limbo. Johnson visited Haiti and wanted to release some tangible output from the trip, whether in the form of a report or a briefing paper. The intern who accompanied him, Samara Fox, was also invested in seeing the research published. Fox planned to focus on health and human rights at Harvard Law School, and was invested in publishing work in that field. To bring IGLHRC's reporting work fully up to speed, Cook held the organization to first completing the community centers report and *Nowhere to Turn*. The production process for *Criminalizing Identities* was also somewhat fixed, as it was being produced in conjunction with other NGOs. Under those circumstances, it was not until March 2011 that IGLHRC released the briefing paper in conjunction with SEROvie. The history of this document, like others, hints at the complex interplay of personal, institutional, and logistical demands that shape when and how brokers publicize human rights violations.

Development

The other aspect of brokers' work was development. IGLHRC's work was funded by a $2 million budget, and a great deal depended on the performance of the two full-time brokers who fundraised for its work.

As noted in chapter 1, IGLHRC's revenue has increasingly been raised through foundation grants, which made up 77 percent of the budget for fiscal year 2011. This sparked lengthy internal conversations at IGLHRC. On one hand, foundation grants made IGLHRC's budget somewhat regular and predictable. Many donors funded a range of LGBT organizations, and some actively strategized with recipients. On the other hand, some brokers and board members felt that more attention needed to be paid to IGLHRC's supporters, who remained largely untapped as a donor base. Brokers used direct mail appeals, house parties, and other tactics to reach individual donors. Ampatuan and Smith also sought to rebuild a grassroots base with the Global Dignity Fund, where donors could contribute a monthly sum of $10 or more to support IGLHRC's work.

In general, however, the shift toward foundation funding was such that forgoing it would be impossible in the short term, and brokers continued to pursue large grants to fund their work. Brokers regularly sought to leverage existing relationships for new initiatives like the MENA Program. At times, however, they pursued untapped sources of funding and proposed new programs. In these instances, IGLHRC's projects were partially or wholly contingent on the success of funding proposals. At least two of these, a project to address SOGI-related persecution as a form of torture and a training packet on LGBT rights and HIV/AIDS, were proposed during my fieldwork. Both were unsuccessful, and the projects were unrealized as a result. While support from foundations meant IGLHRC did not have to chase money to operate, the skill of development brokers and availability of funding for particular projects still meaningfully shaped IGLHRC's substantive programming.

CONCLUSION

Critics and supporters alike often treat human rights NGOs as agentive entities that carry out an ideological project. In IGLHRC's work, however, advocacy was not simply the mechanical pursuit of a political agenda. Instead, it was highly dependent on the dynamics of an organization and the backgrounds and priorities of the brokers who animated it.

To understand how and why brokers do what they do, it is helpful to conceptualize the NGO as an arena populated by human actors who inhabit space, interact with each other, and grapple with successes and failures. The dynamics of that arena all affected IGLHRC's advocacy and, in some small way, how the broader category of LGBT human rights has taken shape. IGLHRC's work still heavily depended on the strengths and weaknesses of brokers negotiating the routine challenges of a small NGO with a large mandate but relatively little power. How they constructed, promoted, and institutionalized LGBT rights under those circumstances is critical, and is the focus of the remaining chapters.

3 Fusing Human Rights and Sexual Politics

Advocating for LGBT Human Rights Worldwide

Brokers routinely referred to IGLHRC as an "LGBT human rights organization," a formulation that also appeared in its promotional and advocacy materials. The description seems self-evident, but the conjunction of these two qualifiers—a focus on LGBT people on one hand, and the use of the human rights framework on the other—set IGLHRC apart from most other NGOs. While NGOs like AI and HRW engaged LGBT issues, that was only part of their larger commitment to human rights. Conversely, the Human Rights Campaign in the United States, Stonewall in the United Kingdom, and other domestic LGBT NGOs invoked rights, but did not use human rights instruments in any meaningful way. IGLHRC remained the largest transnational NGO calling itself an LGBT human rights organization and working on issues affecting LGBT people through the human rights framework.

By specifying a constituency and an approach, this hybrid framing subtly circumscribed advocacy at IGLHRC. Brokers expressed frustration with the narrowness of gay and lesbian identity politics and, at different times, acknowledged the limitations of the human rights framework. Often, brokers adopted a sexual rights framework, which looked beyond identity politics and highlighted the culpability of nonstate actors.[1] As a result, some of their advocacy challenged hegemonic understandings of Euro-American LGBT politics and human rights. At other times, however, brokers instinctively fell back on dominant, familiar models, narrowly focusing on LGBT populations and promoting the most basic and widely accepted human rights.

IGLHRC publicly demanded "Human Rights for Everyone, Everywhere." In practice, however, brokers had to determine who their partners would be; which cases merited attention or intervention; and where resources, time, and energy would be spent. To do so, they were simultaneously guided by the experiential needs of LGBT people and the possibilities of the human rights framework, which were not always easily reconcilable. The practice of advocacy forced brokers to navigate these tensions and creatively incorporate, adjust, and resist aspects of LGBT and human rights advocacy in their work. Ultimately, this not only shaped brokers' own projects, but subtly shaped the construction of LGBT human rights as a category.[2]

NEGOTIATING THE COMPLEXITY OF HUMAN RIGHTS

IGLHRC touted itself as promoting "Human Rights for Everyone, Everywhere." The claim seems ambitious, but recalls the core ideological and political foundations of the human rights regime. A foundational tenet of human rights is universality, which grounds human rights–based arguments even when these diverge in their understandings of what rights can and should be protected. With the UDHR in 1948, diplomats articulated a set of rights that all people were to enjoy by virtue of their humanity.

Among early skeptics of this approach were anthropologists, who emphasized the specificity of purportedly universal legal norms. In 1947, the Executive Board of the American Anthropological Association (AAA) issued its "Statement on Human Rights," principally authored by Melville Herskovits. Written in response to the drafting of the UDHR, the statement objected to the notion of universal ethical or moral principles by which all cultures could be judged and governed:

> Ideas of right and wrong, good and evil, are found in all societies, though they differ in their expression among different peoples. What is held to be a human right in one society may be regarded as anti-social by another people, or by the same people in a different period of their history. . . . The rights of Man in the Twentieth Century cannot be circumscribed by the standards of any single culture, or be dictated by the aspirations of any single people. Such a document will lead to frustration, not realization of the personalities of vast numbers of human beings.[3]

A commitment to universality necessarily underlies human rights—that is, the entitlements persons enjoy by virtue of their humanity. The AAA questioned the very foundation of this project.

The recognition that human rights are products of specific historical trajectories, and resonate more strongly in some contexts than others, has generated increasingly nuanced understandings of their universality.[4] Strong proponents insist that human rights are normatively desirable, and provide a standard to which states should be held legally and morally accountable. Others have sought universal or near-universal foundations for human rights in the commonalities of different traditions of ethics and justice, from retribution and proportionality to human dignity.[5] Still others acknowledge cultural specificity, but insist that very basic rights cannot be abrogated in the name of cultural difference in any nominally democratic polity.[6] Each approach articulates core entitlements that are owed to persons by virtue of their humanity.

Efforts by and for women; children; indigenous persons; disabled persons; migrants; refugees; ethnic, national, and religious minorities; and, of course, LGBT persons have had complex repercussions for the universality of human rights. On one hand, these claims have bolstered universality by looking to supranational mechanisms for legitimation. The willingness of human rights defenders to circumvent their community or state demonstrates the power of standards that transcend citizenship and rest instead on one's humanity. On the other hand, these claims have caused skeptical governments to balk at what they regard as human rights gone amok. As advocates affirm the rights of aliens, criminals, prisoners, terrorists, sex workers, and LGBT persons, officials have forcefully distinguished between what they consider legitimate and illegitimate claims.

The category of LGBT rights remains among the most politically controversial in contemporary human rights debates. Skeptics routinely cite LGBT rights to illustrate how absurd or unprincipled human rights discourse has become.[7] LGBT rights not only call into question governments' authority to regulate morality for a purported social good, but challenge beliefs and norms that are deeply rooted in a wider social fabric. As Jack Donnelly has observed, "homosexuality is widely considered—by significant segments of society in all countries, and by most people in most countries—to be profoundly immoral."[8] Unlike *jus cogens* norms which met with widespread approval prior to their institutionalization in global human rights agreements, the protection of SOGI has often preceded, or been only tentatively grounded in, public opinion. The seeming specificity of SOGI has fostered the belief that LGBT persons demand "special rights" or "new rights," framings that have proven persuasive in debates in the North and South alike.[9] By implication, the rhetoric of new or special rights contrasts LGBT rights with universal human rights, making it seem selfish or trivial for advocates to spend time, energy, and resources securing them.

Brokers have therefore made a subtle distinction between "LGBT human rights" and "the human rights of LGBT people." While the former suggests rights that are specific to LGBT people, the latter evokes a framework of universal rights that LGBT people, like others, must enjoy.[10] Brokers stress that they are not demanding *new* rights, but simply seeking to ensure that the human rights of all persons, as articulated in widely ratified agreements, are extended to those marginalized on the basis of SOGI.[11]

Yet since 1948, a vast range of rights have been located under the umbrella of the human rights project. What brokers opt to foreground as the "human rights of LGBT people" is determined both by brokers' own politics and by opportunities to be recognized in the human rights arena.[12] To make inroads with reluctant governments and curb the worst abuses, brokers stressed those human rights that were least controversial and most firmly established in international law. Brokers did not ignore socioeconomic rights, but in international forums, they typically foregrounded decriminalization and nondiscrimination, especially as the latter related to freedoms of assembly, association, and expression. Conscious of the potential for backlash, brokers were not particularly vocal about the right to marry and form a family of one's choosing, which is increasingly demanded in Euro-American contexts.[13]

The persistent emphasis on decriminalization and nondiscrimination had two political implications. First, it situated the vast majority of IGL-HRC's campaigns outside of the North, where the most glaring violations were less frequent and were addressed by domestic groups who often had recourse to responsive judicial mechanisms. Second, it permitted very little ambivalence or recognition that the human rights of LGBT people might be subject to qualification. The focus on gross violations and the politicized terrain on which arguments were set forth meant that IGLHRC's public statements were unequivocal. Brokers had little space to engage in conversations about balancing rights or acknowledge situations where two rights, or two rights as they are understood in a particular context, may meaningfully conflict.[14] Like others in this field, brokers at IGLHRC downplayed regional and international provisions that allow for exceptions to or qualifications of rights.[15] The ICCPR, for example, repeatedly qualifies rights for purposes of "national security, public order *(ordre public)*, public health or morals or the rights and freedoms of others," and Article 27(2) of the African Charter states that rights should be exercised "with due regard to the rights of others, collective security, morality, and common interest."[16]

Instead of engaging accusations that the human rights of LGBT people are an affront to wider communal concerns, brokers tended to dismiss or pointedly ignore them.

While this is understandable and legally defensible, it creates tensions insofar as the rights of queer individuals are perceived to (or actually) conflict with the norms of a wider community. The African Charter, for example, specifically recognizes a duality of rights and responsibilities, and does so more explicitly than other regional and international charters. The emphasis on responsibility was evident in discourses on sexual rights in Uganda and Malawi. In Uganda, where Article 37 of the constitution protects the right to culture, tradition, and religion, LGBT activists were challenged by opponents who cited the freedom of speech of those calling for violence, the freedom of religion of those seeking to ban homosexuality, and the rights of children who were said to be duped or seduced into homosexuality. In Malawi, this rhetoric took a more balanced tone, but was similarly prevalent. As Deputy Minister of Finance Frazer Nihorya remarked, "This is a tricky matter because issues of rights have corresponding responsibilities.... It is the popular opinion of Malawians which will influence government's position on the matter."[17]

The idea that rights are predicated on, and intertwined with, responsibilities to others is recognized within transnational NGOs, but it is difficult to articulate these nuances in the middle of crises where they are reliably redeployed against defenders of LGBT human rights. The stakes rose with the passage of a resolution at the HRC affirming "the traditional values of humankind," promulgated by states that have been hostile to any recognition of LGBT human rights.[18] In highly polarized settings, brokers have been reluctant to engage in discussions about balancing rights. Instead, they insist that rights can be simultaneously enjoyed, often in such a way that individual rights implicitly take precedence over the norms of the wider community.

This does not mean brokers are unaware of these dilemmas. Following a round of questioning during IGLHRC's application for consultative status with ECOSOC, Johnson repeatedly wondered aloud if a project grappling with the issue of conflicting rights might be worth undertaking. Amid other priorities competing for time and resources, however, there was little impetus to look critically at whether rights may necessarily trade off with each other, and no moment where doing so would not potentially endanger other advocacy efforts with partners or governments.

Paradoxically, IGLHRC's focus on particularly egregious violations during my fieldwork may therefore build support but also validate critical assessments of the LGBT human rights project. By focusing on violations that largely occur in the South and that allow for very little acknowledgment of complexity, brokers make a strong case to those who are potentially supportive, but appear uninterested in dialogue to a bloc of states that are hostile to their claims.

NEGOTIATING THE COMPLEXITY OF LGBT POLITICS

Calling an organization a gay and lesbian human rights commission not only specifies a particular approach, but foregrounds a particular constituency. IGLHRC's name identifies its core constituents as gay and lesbian. It makes no mention of bisexual and transgender persons—an omission characteristic of many U.S.-based gay and lesbian nonprofits in the 1990s—or other forms of sexual subjectivity.

Yet as I describe in chapter 1, the boundaries of this category have been fairly plastic. For years, brokers at IGLHRC have used the "LGBT" acronym in their work and factored trans issues into their programming. And even "LGBT" is not fully inclusive of the forms of sexual subjectivity brokers have sought to represent.[19] As Khan recalled of the early 2000s:

> We understood that the identities, that framework of LGBT does not resonate around the world. So we were increasingly using a sexual rights framework that was one that encompassed the LGBT identities, but also would include people who didn't use that identity, but maybe identified themselves as men who have sex with men, or women who have sex with women, but did not think of themselves as lesbian or gay.

Johnson reiterated this point, recognizing that adherence to rigid identity categories would fail to capture the complexity of actual lives:

> I think the important thing is that we don't believe . . . that the only people that we're working for or talking about are LGBT people, there's a whole bunch of people on whose behalf we need to be concerned who aren't LGBT. To give you a quick example, I was in a bar in Joburg one night with a guy who's from Nigeria, married to a woman in Nigeria, married to a woman in South Africa, mainly for his papers, engaging in sex work with men, you know, engaging with men for sex for fun, in a bar, that is ostensibly gay, but would probably never identify itself as a gay bar so that it can stay open in

that part of Joburg without too much violence. And I said to myself, what's the relevance of calling this guy gay, or bi, or anything like that? It's irrelevant in this circumstance. And today, he's involved in one set of behaviors, next year, he may be involved in a completely different set, based on choice, necessity, finance, you know, political realities, location. Our main stakeholders and those with whom we work might be those people who choose to define as LGBT, you know, those are likely to be the activists, the people who run organizations, but not even always in that case.

And indeed, during my fieldwork, IGLHRC's programming and advocacy was not always self-evidently about LGBT people. Instead, brokers' work focused on violations people experienced because they transgressed gender norms, engaged or were suspected to engage in same-sex activity, or simply advocated for the rights of LGBT people.

Yet in subtle ways, IGLHRC's LGBT constituency persistently defined its work. Jaya Sharma has persuasively highlighted how efforts to mobilize under the sexual rights banner have routinely lapsed into identity-based organizing; although they are theoretically expansive, sexual rights are typically invoked to specifically address the needs of women, LGBT people, and sex workers.[20] To understand how and why sexual rights activists might define their focus in these particular ways, however, attention to the actual practice of human rights is critical. Some brokers made efforts to expand IGLHRC's focus and work in solidarity with other movements, but amid resource constraints and competing priorities, these efforts were at times deemed peripheral to, or outside the scope of, the mandate of an LGBT organization. Precisely what IGLHRC's mandate implicitly included is illuminated by looking at the terminology brokers used, the ways they attempted to be broadly inclusive, and the ongoing debates where the boundaries of their advocacy were enforced.

"LGBT" and the Origins and Specificity of Sexual Identity Politics

A number of scholars have traced the genesis of LGBT politics to the North, particularly the United States, and charted their global diffusion. As these politics travel, particular discourses, events, and symbols have become readily recognizable hallmarks of LGBT movements. Among the most basic underpinnings of "Global Gay" subjectivity are identity politics and the presumption that SOGI are stable, meaningful parts of human selfhood.[21] The power of these assumptions is evident even where they take on local specificity—for example, the idea of "coming out" is embraced in local idioms like "unmasking" or "unfurling one's cape."[22] Pride marches, which began as a commemoration of the Stonewall Riots in New York, have globalized to the extent that most major metropoles now host an annual march, which prominently features symbols like the pink triangle or the rainbow.[23] While sexual politics have been vernacularized by activists in different contexts, they have also contributed to the perception and visibility of a transnational LGBT movement.

Yet this assemblage of discourses, events, and symbols is the product of a particular history, and its adoption can foreclose sexual and political possibilities elsewhere. Critics decry the risky assignation of labels like "gay" and "lesbian" to those who may not adopt them themselves,[24] the use of tactics or strategies that backfire in context,[25] and the pursuit of goals that are likely to reinforce other social inequalities.[26] Reproducing Northern LGBT agendas is not only controversial because they emphasize identity politics, but because they replicate and legitimate particular political projects.

The words "gay and lesbian" in IGLHRC's name conjure up this assemblage of U.S.-based discourses and tactics. Brokers did focus primarily on LGBT people, sought recognition from governmental and intergovernmental bodies, and fought for familiar goals like decriminalization, freedom from persecution and violence, nondiscrimination laws, and freedoms of expression, assembly, and speech. For brokers, the most resonant models of human sexuality and sexual politics were ones that originated in the North and widely globalized. Nonetheless, brokers were conscious of the limitations of these models, and actively sought to expand them in their work. Where brokers positioned themselves in this milieu—being familiar with the terms of LGBT identity and community, but consciously embracing an open-ended understanding of sexuality and sexual politics that was not so firmly rooted in the North—was considerably more complicated than their identity politics might suggest.

While brokers used the "LGBT" acronym and viewed this as an expansive and flexible, if not neutral, umbrella term for those marginalized because of their sexual identity, practices, or affiliations, there was also a shift away from identity politics that was evident at IGLHRC. It was rare for brokers to refer to a person as "gay" unless that person was known to be publicly self-identified as such. While this was not always the case in private conversation, this principle was taken very seriously where public statements were concerned. Brokers occasionally referred to people as "LGBT" if they were in some way queer but their particular self-identification was unknown, and often talked about the LGBT *movement* in a particular country, regardless of how the known leaders of organizations in that country self-identified. Brokers might not have been comfortable identifying a particular person as LGBT, but presumed that there were LGBT persons around the globe, and that those persons were at risk of human rights violations.

The "LGBT" moniker was regularly used by every broker at IGLHRC and tended to be the identifier of choice in public outputs. Potential alternatives were considerably more controversial and sporadically used. In some instances, however, these were employed to limit adherence to identity politics and maximize the neutrality and transnational applicability of IGLHRC's reach, a move fraught with political implications of its own.

Constructing a Basis for Universality: Sexual Minorities, SOGI, MSM and WSW, and Intersex and Queer People

While "LGBT" had become the standard gloss for the constituencies of most U.S.-based organizations, brokers at IGLHRC worked across many national and regional political domains and found alternative framings useful at different times. As Perle commented to me with a shrug one afternoon, "Sometimes, it's about identity, and sometimes it's really not." Brokers frequently worked on cases where the persons involved did not necessarily identify as LGBT or queer, but were persecuted for behaving or organizing in ways others deemed unacceptable. It proved difficult, if not impossible, to do transnational LGBT work using a single lens for understanding sexuality.

The limited applicability of identity politics spawned many strategies transnational NGOs used to be maximally inclusive. For a period, the term "sexual minority" was used to describe those who were marginalized because of their sexuality. As those who use it point out, the term is broadly inclusive, "being open to any group (previously, now, or in the future) stigmatized or despised as a result of sexual orientation, identity, or behavior," and by using the language of minorities, it "explicitly focuses our attention on the issue of discrimination, and at least the possibility of political action to eliminate it."[27]

During my fieldwork, however, Johnson, Cook, and Jones were reluctant to use the term and actively edited it from press releases and outputs. As Jones put it in an interview:

> We could use another framework, but any framework has its limitations and needs qualifications. For a while the term "sexual minorities" became more

popular, but I hear less of it today. To me, it's not particularly appealing. I don't want to be reduced to simply sexuality when gender identity and expression are also so related to how we navigate the world. I also don't want to emphasize a minority identity, which suggests there is a majority set of behaviors upon which rights could be based—which actually, when you talk about sexuality, is a debatable point. There are a lot of shades of grey, at the very least.

When the term was used, it was with reservations. When Johnson referred to sexual minorities in a discussion at the U.S. Congress, for example, he made pointed air quotes around the term.

In human rights networks, a popular alternative was to talk about those marginalized on the basis of SOGI. The concepts of sexual orientation and gender identity are categorical; like race, religion, sex, nationality, or other enumerated categories of nondiscrimination law, they encompass majorities and minorities alike. "SOGI" presumes universally relevant aspects of personhood—that everybody has a sexual orientation and a gender identity—but allowed brokers to tactically avoid ascribing any *specific* orientation or identity. By discussing a person's "real or perceived" SOGI, brokers could remain agnostic about a person's actual attractions or identifications.

While "SOGI" was helpful, it often proved unwieldy in practice. First, "SOGI" was difficult to use in shorthand references to actual people. It was categorical, and had to be couched in formulations like "people marginalized on the basis of their sexual orientation or gender identity." This was perhaps plausible at the UN, but far clumsier in press releases or interviews. Second, "SOGI" primarily functioned in the negative. It was easy to talk about those marginalized on the basis of SOGI, but much rarer to hear people talk about those *united* by SOGI, or to identify forms of commonality among them. The term was not particularly descriptive of the day-to-day efforts of activists and brokers working to build domestic and transnational communities. Finally, "SOGI" was open to misinterpretation, some of it deliberate. As Eve Kosofsky Sedgwick observes in *Epistemology of the Closet,* sexual orientation is conventionally understood to refer to the gender of one's sexual or romantic object, not other characteristics or things to which one might be sexually oriented.[28] As I describe in chapter 6, Egypt regularly insisted at the UN that recognizing SOGI would protect so-called sexual orientations like pedophilia, necrophilia, and zoophilia.[29] Brokers vocally disagreed, but some frustrated supporters began suggesting that states might be more supportive of a narrower, more familiar category of "LGBT people."

To avoid intractable debates over the cross-cultural meaning of sexual identities and categories, some have suggested that transnational advocacy should instead focus on sexual behavior.[30] This has been partially realized by public health practitioners who use "MSM" and "WSW" to highlight contingency and avoid the connotations associated with "homosexuality" or "LGBT." In doing so, they centralize sexual practice, not sexual desires or identities, at the heart of their work.

The wholesale adoption of "MSM" and "WSW," or even the gender-neutral "same-sex practicing," was difficult at IGLHRC. Most obviously, brokers rarely knew with any certainty whether a person experiencing human rights violations was sexually active, or who that person was sexually active with. (Nor did they care; whether a person actually engaged in same-sex activity was usually incidental to the fact of their persecution.) Often, brokers also did not know the gender identity of the person in question, or whether they identified as a man or woman at all, which was particularly difficult where transgender movements were young or nonexistent. In many contexts, "gay" was locally understood to include biologically male persons who were effeminate or female-identified, where "lesbian," "tomboy," or other terms were understood to include biologically female persons who were masculine or male-identified. For public health professionals who dealt with sexual behavior, "MSM" and "WSW" described relevant behaviors. For human rights professionals who did not always know who they were working with or how they and their partners identified, such terms were rife with problematic assumptions. Some behavioral terms also failed to resonate with brokers as a result of their own cultural contexts; in one discussion, Jones remarked that she instinctively disliked the archaic, clinical connotations of "homosexual," and other brokers agreed.[31]

Brokers also expressed concern that terms like "MSM" and "WSW" erased forms of identification that activists in particular *did* find meaningful, including their ability to be recognized as LGBT.[32] Tactical use of behavioral terms has been particularly widespread in sub-Saharan Africa, where activists have used the prevalence of HIV among MSM to press for decriminalization of same-sex activity and improvement of services to same-sex-practicing persons.[33] As Kilonzo noted in an interview:

A discomfort has been voiced, and I share it deeply, that HIV resources are stripping people of their identity, because you end up using words like MSM or WSW instead of LGBT for various political reasons. . . . At the end of the day, if countries still fail to recognize that the rights of LGBT are at stake, and they're only interested in men who have sex with men, then you're reduced to sex, and your life is oriented around having sex. Or as men, or as women, so what happens to the trans people? Even to gay people or lesbian people, their lives are not just sex only. There's a lot more in the package. It's your whole identity. It's your visibility. . . . It's being hidden now within the discussion of MSM, and for me, that's a bigger loss than not having MSM at all, or not having the resources at all. The working of governments has been to acknowledge that there is a certain degree of resources that are needed to address HIV in terms of men who have sex with men, but they have totally refused to acknowledge that there is an LGBT community in their country, which, to me, is the worst loss.

As Kilonzo suggests, "MSM" and "WSW" have limitations of their own, including dependence on a binary gender system that has been roundly criticized by trans activists. As bisexual and trans people have mobilized to expand the focus of gay and lesbian advocacy, "LGBT" has come to connote a wide range of genders and sexualities that make it more expansive and provisional than "gay and lesbian" alone. The acronym can be expansive enough to include indigenous subjectivities as well. As one Filipina activist, Naomi Fontanos, has remarked, "'It's so impossible to break away from the LGBT moniker, because it's so widely used. I think a more profitable way of going about it is to talk about LGBT as [including] *bakla, bayot, tomboy,* and transgender.'"[34] These are among the reasons that, despite its Northern roots, "LGBT" has become the de rigueur term in transnational advocacy.

Other movements globally have expanded this acronym, which IGLHRC has been reluctant to do. Particularly in Latin America and Africa, "LGBT" has been replaced by "LGBTI" in recognition of intersex people. The term "queer," which paradoxically functions as both an anti-identitarian adjective for subversive behavior and an umbrella term for subversive identities, has also been used independently or appended to make the acronym "LGBTQ."

Brokers at IGLHRC use these terms conversationally, but have resisted their institutional adoption for various reasons. Brokers occasionally appended "I" when it was immediately relevant or when working with self-identified LGBTI groups, but because intersex issues were rarely the explicit focus of IGLHRC's work, Johnson maintained that it was disingenuous to promote IGLHRC as an LGBTI organization. IGLHRC was not oblivious or hostile to intersex issues; it produced internal discussion papers on trans and intersex advocacy, and the LAC Program devoted its Activist Institute to trans and intersex advocacy in 2005. Still, brokers rarely gave intersex issues the attention they gave to gay, lesbian, and transgender issues. While most brokers in New York used the term "queer" quite frequently—and many identified as such—they rarely appended it to the LGBT acronym. It was scarcely used by the NGOs and governments that IGLHRC worked with in the human rights arena, and brokers saw little point in appending it to an acronym that was already felt to be flexible and provisional.

In light of these alternatives and their limitations, brokers at IGLHRC primarily operated on behalf of a constituency they glossed as "LGBT." They understood the strategic necessity of alternatives; brokers used "MSM," "WSW," or "SOGI" in contexts where behavioral or categorical classifications were preferable. They recognized that "LGBT" was identity-based and historically specific, but considered it more inclusive and empowering than the alternatives. "LGBT" had the benefit of being widely recognizable to partners around the globe, who overwhelmingly used the acronym or variants thereof in their own work. Following their lead, brokers used "LGBT" to describe movements, but were cautious about ascriptive terminology when talking about specific incidents, groups, and individuals.

THE BOUNDARIES OF "LGBT HUMAN RIGHTS": ADULTERY, SEX WORK, AND PUBLIC SEX

In interviews, every executive director of IGLHRC, from its founding to the present, emphasized the importance of a sexual rights framework that is not predicated on identity, but on the dignity and bodily autonomy of all persons. As Johnson observed:

> We used to refer to ourselves much more as a sexual rights organization, and I don't know if you've noticed this, but I try to keep that language alive. But we don't really subscribe to it the way we used to. And I think that was one of the ways in which we rose up above our name, and above LGBT identity, by identifying with a much broader and inclusive sexual rights movement.

Feminist advocates theorize sexual rights as a subset of human rights that takes issue with, and seeks to correct, the presumptive maleness of the human rights project. The concept has been elaborated to include a wide range of rights over one's own body, sexuality, and reproductive capacity. Sexual rights advocates highlight violations of basic freedoms and capabilities by families, communities, and other nonstate actors, as well as differential access to resources and control over bodily integrity through laws and norms that disproportionately affect women and girls.[35] Brokers have situated the human rights of LGBT people within this framework, stressing that sexual autonomy and gender expression should be understood as part of the sexual rights project.

Brokers at IGLHRC, especially those who had been active in feminist or women's rights movements, found sexual rights approaches helpful for two reasons. First, they offered a corrective to limitations of the traditional human rights framework. Ettelbrick, for example, emphasized how sexual rights overcome a narrow focus on state actors:

> I think feminism has brought a really important piece to the idea of human rights, and defining them in the context of sexual rights, in which there are traditions and cultures around sexuality in particular that tend to abuse people based on certain aspects of their lives. . . . That, I think, is a framework we needed to create to get out of the state versus the individual action and get more into the social norms that define the lives of women and gay people, et cetera.

Second, they provided a platform to find common cause with other movements.[36] The broad resonance of sexual rights and bodily autonomy was perhaps best described by Alizadeh:

> [With human rights, you] are talking about a very specific framework that works in the West, and in some contexts also may be relevant, but in others is not. So there are countries in the [MENA] region, they decided they don't want to talk about gay rights, they want to talk about civil society, personal space, basically. That's the hot debate in Morocco; they want to talk about "personal rights," because they feel that this is a better framework. There are models they prefer to talk about—basically, sexual rights, but not LGBT rights. There are other countries where you talk about punishments for crimes and what that means, like legal reforms. And then you have other activists who have chosen to go use a medical framework. Whatever works for them, this is my view.

This kind of flexibility was not uncommon; brokers often incorporated expansive understandings of human rights or alternative frameworks into their advocacy. The sexual rights framework in particular helped brokers find common ground with movements working on women's rights, HIV/AIDS, sexual health, reproductive rights, and sex work.

In their day-to-day work, however, brokers drew subtle distinctions between sexual rights that fit within their understanding of IGLHRC's mandate and those they felt unable to deal with. These were not laid out in writing, but were often insisted on in practice.

Most obviously, brokers almost always focused on violations against people who were LGBT or queer. Laws regulating heterosexual ages of consent, premarital sex, restrictions on partners within marriage, adultery, polygamy and polygyny, divorce, and the rights of widows or widowers were not IGLHRC's primary concern, either privately or in public outputs. Whether brokers dealt with LGBT persons in particular or SOGI more broadly, they did not meaningfully battle restrictions on cisgender heterosexuals.[37]

At times, a wider perspective was possible. One example was IGLHRC's response to the revised adultery law in Aceh, Indonesia, in September 2009. IGLHRC's update represented a rare instance of other forms of sexual rights violations being raised as cause for concern.[38] In large part, this was due to Poore, who crafted the statement and consciously sought to go beyond the issues directly affecting LGBT people. As she recalled in an interview:

> When you look at that law, it's a horrible law. True, they have now included homosexuality as an act of adultery, therefore punishable under sharia. And they consider it premarital sex, because you're having—I don't know *how* they come up with this stuff—*pre*marital sex, so therefore, you will come under the category of heterosexual *pre*marital sex, which is whipping, and jail, and fines. A hundred lashes with a cane. But if you're heterosexual, and you commit adultery, forget about the caning and all of that, you get stoned to death.
>
> And so, you know, it became a little frustrating for me when I was working on that thing, to get all, to get so focused on homosexuality. Because I'm like, heck, if you're a heterosexual, you're going to be stoned to death! We should be actually fighting with them to get rid of the law! And that's what they were doing in Aceh. . . .
>
> I was really troubled. . . . I never wanted to work on gay rights, you know. In fact, I feel a bit strange. And the way that I do my work is to not think about it as gay rights. I'm not working on SOGI rights, I'm actually working

on all of the rights. I'm working on the fact that all these other rights are taken away, simply because somebody at the very basic level is not given this right. That's how it makes sense to me. That you feel entitled to take away housing, and take away safety, and discriminate, and violate, and do all kinds of stuff, simply because you feel this person is not human and therefore has no rights. That's it. That makes sense to me. But in this country, for instance, in the U.S., this whole push for these identity-based rights, that is very, a little bit sickening to me, actually.

Poore's reticence about narrow identitarian frameworks was one that virtually everybody at IGLHRC voiced to some extent. When asked about the personal politics of brokers at IGLHRC, Poore agreed that the sexual rights framework was one that people considered helpful, but failed for various reasons to put into practice:

I think IGLHRC has the framework, but we don't practice it so much. We don't have it in our culture, in our organizational culture. We're a little too focused on the LGBT stuff. And then, when you bring it up, people will say, well, that's because we're an LGBT organization. And I'm like, but we're not. We're a human rights organization. Yes, we're defending the human rights of LGBT people, but does that mean that we're an LGBT organization? I find that there's a distinction there.

So then the whole thing is, well, we can't be everything to everybody, and we can't do everything, and we can't—you know, this is what our funders fund us for. It's like any kind of justification to not think cross-issue, to think intersectionally. . . .

I don't know, for some reason, we, as an organization, as a board, as funders, we seem to fall back on that whole identity-based kind of organizing, which is so old-fashioned. People of color communities in [the United States] have walked away from that, have realized that, hey, you want to fight police violence, you better start doing cross-movement work. And we're still holding on this old way of doing it. . . . I feel like we, who are at the front line of knowing how this works—because we're not a traditional old-fashioned human rights, male-dominated organization. We use different frameworks.[39]

I quote Poore at length because her comments canvass many of the reasons brokers offered for focusing on issues directly targeting LGBT people. Some pointed to IGLHRC's name, saying that it is, by definition, an

LGBT organization. Others cited accountability to funders; resources for LGBT human rights are miniscule relative to funding for other human rights, and many of IGLHRC's funders specifically provided support for LGBT advocacy. Poore's reflections also hint at brokers' tendency to fall back on established tactics and assumptions about their constituency, especially when pressured to act quickly by the board, their supporters, the media, or other NGOs with which they competed for publicity, funding, or relevance.

The issue became more complex when LGBT people's human rights were threatened, but the violations themselves were not immediately because of SOGI. This was apparent when lines were drawn regarding sex work and the rights of sex workers. In general, brokers voiced strong support for sex workers, and recognized that they also faced criminalization, marginalization, and violence on the basis of sex and gender norms. There were a number of instances where IGLHRC institutionally supported demands for sex workers' rights—for example, when brokers posted a call from Akina Mama wa Afrika to support the right to meet at the African Women's Leadership Institute for sex work activists in East Africa.[40] In other instances, brokers privately placed relationships with governments on the line by refusing to repudiate or distance themselves from LGBT activists who engaged in sex work because of their precarious social position.

Nonetheless, sex work was not specifically incorporated into IGLHRC's mandate in a proactive way. This posed a difficulty where LGBT people were engaged in sex work or where LGBT movements drew explicit connections between violations faced by individuals because they were LGBT and because they were sex workers.[41] Brokers grappled with this in particular in Turkey, where activists explicitly connected the structural and material marginalization they faced as LGBT people, particularly as trans women, with the pressure to enter into sex work for survival.

As Alizadeh pointed out, this raised complex questions about agency and structural violence for a human rights organization:

> We have this politically correct attitude—oh, if they are sex workers, that's their choice, we'll respect that. I'm all with you on that. But if there's structural violence that's happening in a society that does not allow individuals to have any other option but being sex workers, then I have a problem with that, you know. So you have to start thinking about how you want to address this issue and highlight the fact that even the sex workers, which is the lowest

kind of job in that society that you can get, you still don't have that guarantee. Even among sex workers, you're being discriminated against because of who you are.

While brokers thought critically about these issues, many were frustrated by a perceived inability to translate their commitments into practice. In an interview at the end of my time with the Africa Program, Kilonzo specifically bemoaned the inability to make common cause with other movements, pointing to LGBT groups' limited advocacy around sex work during proposed revisions to Rwanda's penal code:

> Every time I'm attending an African Commission session, LGBT activists, we all keep to ourselves. . . . I see other groups like indigenous people, they're all over, they're in all thematic groups. I see people with disabilities, they're in all thematic groups. When you're discussing HIV, when you're discussing the environment, they're in all groups. You end up being labeled that group, the LGBT group that only seeks their own rights but not supporting other people when they're articulating their agenda.
>
> And this was more pronounced when we responded to the crisis in Rwanda, when Parliament was about to review the penal code to include same-sex relations. Right now, it's not criminalized; Parliament wanted to review the law to make it criminal. The sex workers' movement came on board and supported the LGBT movement very well. Very well. But soon after that succeeded, we retreated to our own safe spaces. And when the sex workers needed support, because their article was next, was following soon after the article against LGBT, we were nowhere to support them. And that taught them a bad lesson . . . that we want everybody around to support us, but when it's our turn to give support to other people, we are not there.

At the same time, brokers in Cape Town drew lines in their own work, and did not always err on the side of maximal inclusion. On one occasion, they were contacted about an incident in an East African country where there had been a spate of arrests of LGBT people, and were informed that two trans or gay sex workers had been arrested and detained. The pair was requesting financial help from IGLHRC, but did not want brokers to intercede with the government on their behalf for fear of repercussions. In a discussion of the case, a broker in the African Program not only stressed that IGLHRC was not an emergency funder for individuals, but suggested that if they were arrested for violating laws against sex work and not on SOGI grounds, their arrest arguably fell outside IGLHRC's ambit.

This was not merely a decision by program staff, but one that was reiterated at different times by the executive director. As Johnson noted in one interview:

> I think we need to use our history and our affinities as our filter. I don't think we should work broadly on the rights of female sex workers who are engaged mainly in heterosexual transactional sex. That's not what I think we should do. But when the human rights challenges that female sex workers are experiencing overlap, and are emblematic of the kinds of challenges that MSM sex workers are involved in, and we can bring added value to the struggles of those female sex workers, then I think we should be doing it. I mean . . . do we bring something to it? We have a community, I don't ever want to, like, deny that, or be ashamed of it. We have a community that we embrace, and that embraces us, and so that's who we're working for. I think we need to be broad and understand the connections between what happens to us and how we live our lives and ways in which *all* other people live their lives and are circumscribed around their sexuality, or challenged around their bodies and their sexual choices, and their gender expression. We need to make those connections, but we're still . . . we're unabashedly queer.

Johnson's quote reflects the kind of pragmatism about cross-sectional struggles that Poore appeared to find frustrating. Brokers were readily able to draw connections between disparate forms of sexual policing, but were not always able to devote limited time, energy, and resources to issues that were not demonstrably about SOGI.

Other tactical considerations weighed in as well. As Oliver Phillips has pointed out, same-sex sexuality, sex work, and other affronts to regnant norms pose a difficult challenge for those appealing to the human rights regime for protection. The most sympathetic claimants in human rights advocacy are those who can be portrayed as innocent victims, particularly those who are targeted based on something they cannot change.[42] It is considerably harder to advocate for LGBT people, sex workers, and others who fall outside of what Gayle Rubin calls the "charmed circle" of sexuality, or that which is "'good,' 'normal' and 'natural.'"[43] The boundaries of the charmed circle and what is inside or outside of its circumference vary cross-culturally, but the principle remains the same. Given the political sensitivity of sexual rights issues, practical opportunities for an aggressive, expansive defense of sexual autonomy varied considerably across countries and movements. Where local LGBT groups actively worked in coalition with sex workers, brokers at IGLHRC had more opportunities to voice support for sex workers' rights. In contexts where local LGBT groups and sex workers did not work closely together or distanced themselves from each other, there were fewer instances where intervention from a U.S.-based LGBT NGO would be helpful for either population.

The difficulty of articulating a robust defense of sexual freedom also affected a final category that brokers grappled with privately but rarely foregrounded publicly. Many brokers at IGLHRC were sympathetic to those who engaged in public cruising or were arrested for public sex, understanding that a lack of private space, social hostility, and moral rigidity all pushed same-sex activity into the so-called public sphere and then demonized it when it was discovered.

In practice, however, public sex was subject to similar qualifications as sex work. It rarely seemed helpful or strategic to forcefully decry laws against public sex as unjust; when brokers critiqued these types of arrests, they typically stressed that they were detrimental or counterproductive from a health and human rights approach. One such arrest for public sex between two men in Dakar was brought to my attention during the production of *Words of Hate, Climate of Fear,* IGLHRC's report on homophobia and transphobia in Senegal. On November 12, 2009, two men were reportedly arrested for publicly engaging in same-sex activity on the grounds of Amadou Barry Stadium. When I mentioned reports of the arrest to a supervisor in New York, I was told not to put it on the website, as the two were technically arrested for public sex and not same-sex activity. While IGLHRC had been actively involved in other cases of arrests in Senegal—assisting with asylum claims and resettlement, securing legal representation, and visiting arrestees in prison—this particular case was neither publicized widely nor further investigated by staff.[44]

This is not to say that brokers were indifferent to invasive controls on heterosexual sexuality, were unsympathetic to sex work, or were uncomfortable with public sex. To the contrary, most brokers seemed quite sympathetic to these issues and were far more sex-positive than IGLHRC's public advocacy might have suggested. Despite these sympathies, brokers at times felt compelled to more narrowly specify the constituencies that they were able or supposed to serve as an LGBT human rights organization. What kept them from speaking out more forcefully on other sexual rights at particular times was the sense that these were not part of their mandate, that they were too scarcely resourced to adequately cover them, or that it would be strategically unwise or detrimental to partners to aggressively advocate for a broader range of sexual rights. As a result, the sexual rights framework that emerged at IGLHRC remained focused primarily on violations that were tangentially linked to the targeting of LGBT persons— for example, the expansive law in Aceh, the proposed restrictions in Rwanda, or the persecution of transgender sex workers in Turkey—and brokers less often campaigned on other sexual rights issues in a proactive way.

HYBRIDITY AND THE PROBLEMS AND POSSIBILITIES OF LGBT HUMAN RIGHTS ADVOCACY

The incidents that brokers felt demanded a response rarely invited long-term, strategic development of the human rights framework for LGBT persons. Amid incidents that garnered high-profile attention, however, brokers were also involved in thoughtful and theoretical projects that sought to shape how LGBT issues were treated within a human rights framework and how human rights mechanisms were utilized by LGBT communities. Indeed, much of the intellectual and programmatic work at IGLHRC carried on the tradition Dorf began when brokers pressured AI to address SOGI-based persecution. This and other early campaigns drew attention to the myriad ways that LGBT persons were denied recourse to the full range of universal human rights. At the same time, brokers called attention to unique forms of persecution that LGBT people face, and fought to get them taken seriously in the human rights arena. In this proactive work, IGLHRC's identification as an LGBT human rights organization allowed brokers to tack between two frameworks—LGBT politics and human rights—that other advocates mobilized separately. The juxtaposition of these two frameworks enabled work that would not be possible in either one alone.

IGLHRC as an LGBT Human Rights Organization

Brokers were quite conscious of the limitations of different frameworks, and many valued that their approach differed from human rights NGOs that were not LGBT-identified. Jones, whose background was in the human rights arena, noted:

There's something to be said for working for an LGBT organization. It gives you a different kind of access to the community, and also, IGLHRC, for better and worse, can be scrappy, and I actually think that's what movement-based work requires a little bit of. You need to be flexible enough to have lots of different strategies, and recognize that when you're working with community-based organizations, just focusing on documentation and reporting is not going to be enough.

By virtue of being an LGBT organization, there are times when it's also easy to distance ourselves from the human rights framework, because part of the relationship with queers seeking rights is to say let us in. And that can be a challenge in using the human rights framework, and it's certainly a challenge when you're trying to talk about nonstate actor violence. But it's also a strength that we have.

For as often as they used the human rights framework as a tool, it was notable that many brokers at IGLHRC were not wed to it ideologically or in their advocacy. In an interview, Johnson was frank about this point:

The average person, I'd say, doesn't enjoy their human rights. The average person in Africa doesn't . . . and I don't think it matters, rural or urban, but in general, human rights are a luxury in most people's lives. And so to use them as an argument, to use that framework as a place to start when trying to explain to your neighbor why you should be free as an LGBT person, I don't think it's the best approach. I think it's an approach. It's certainly an approach you take with government, with government institutions.

By identifying as an LGBT organization, brokers felt able to use approaches that might not necessarily be used by mainstream human rights organizations. Rather than proceeding from the rights enshrined in international law, brokers at IGLHRC often took their cue from the forms of marginalization experienced by LGBT people globally, and only then fit these into a human rights framework as best as possible.

Many of the best examples of this emerged from convenings and Activist Institutes, which brought activists together to discuss salient issues for LGBT populations. Explorations of religious fundamentalisms, violence against women, and blackmail were not projects that would have obviously derived from a traditional human rights framework. They focused first and foremost on nonstate actors—for example, looking at persecution by religious groups, violence in the home or community, and extortion by coworkers, family, and neighbors. Of course, they were likely to conclude that state-sponsored criminalization of same-sex activity and indifference to complaints of mistreatment exacerbated nonstate persecution, and to encourage various kinds of legal reform as part of a proactive solution. Still, at their core, these projects took the lived experiences of LGBT persons as their primary impetus, then sought to fit these into the human rights framework by creatively invoking its guarantees. Three projects illustrate how sexual politics provided an entry into working creatively with the human rights framework: the publication of *Nowhere to Turn*, a funding proposal on torture and the persecution of LGBT persons, and IGLHRC's disaster relief after the earthquake in Haiti.

The example I was most familiar with during my time at IGLHRC was the research on blackmail and extortion and eventual publication of *Nowhere to Turn*. As part of my fieldwork with the Africa Program, I edited chapters by researchers who explored how blackmail and extortion impacted LGBT people in Zimbabwe, Nigeria, Malawi, Ghana, and Cameroon.

What was notable about the collection was that it emerged from the felt needs of LGBT groups on the continent, who stressed that blackmail and extortion were among the most prevalent abuses their constituencies faced. This has since been confirmed by studies that found that 18 percent of respondents in Malawi, 21.3 percent in Namibia, and 26.5 percent in Botswana had been blackmailed because of their sexuality.[45] The proportion of respondents across all three countries who had been blackmailed (21.2 percent) was larger than those who were afraid to walk in their community (19 percent) or seek health services (18.5 percent), had been beaten up by a government or police official (12.2 percent), or were denied housing (6.9 percent) or health care (5.1 percent).[46] Another study suggested that 23.1 percent of respondents in Abuja, Nigeria, had been victims of blackmail.[47] Even in South Africa, where same-sex activity is not criminalized, 10.5 percent of MSM respondents reported being blackmailed in periurban townships outside of Cape Town.[48] The recognition that this was an unaddressed problem for LGBT people provided the impetus for IGLHRC's research, rather than the sense that blackmail was self-evidently a human rights issue.

Indeed, a major portion of the work I was tasked to do on the report was research on where blackmail and extortion might be creatively fit *into* the human rights framework. There is relatively little writing about blackmail and extortion from a human rights perspective; these crimes are frequently committed by nonstate actors and are at least nominally addressed by domestic criminal law in most jurisdictions. A survey of UN documentation for the report revealed that the rare references by treaty bodies mostly raised concern about the use of extortion to target vulnerable groups.[49] The topic had been referenced by a small number of Special Procedures, but only the Special Rapporteur on Torture and Other Cruel, Inhuman, or Degrading Treatment or Punishment specifically referenced blackmail or extortion on SOGI grounds.[50] The occasional references expressed concern about these crimes, but rarely articulated why they might constitute human rights violations.

As a result, the conclusion of *Nowhere to Turn* specifically looked at the justifications that might be used to treat blackmail and extortion as human rights issues, including the deprivation of dignity, privacy, and autonomy; the impunity of state and nonstate actors complicit in these crimes; and the violation of the right to equality that LGBT persons suffer when they are denied formal redress.[51] The publicity surrounding the launch focused heavily on the ways that blackmail and extortion impinge on fundamental human rights, taking the realities of LGBT lives as a starting point to elaborate on the human rights framework.

Notably, projects like the report were often supported by donors who funded LGBT advocacy and were not adamant that it be undertaken within a human rights framework. While donors are often criticized for influencing organizational agendas, IGLHRC's attempts to obtain support from human rights funders also demonstrates the generative aspects of these relationships, which encouraged creative redefinitions of what might be considered a human rights violation.

A good example of this was a proposal IGLHRC developed, which was considered but not ultimately funded, on LGBT people and torture. The funding body in question was a series of Northern governments seeking proposals from human rights NGOs working on torture and other forms of cruel, inhuman, or degrading treatment. IGLHRC's proposal sought to define, document, and seek redress for repeated persecution of LGBT persons as a form of torture.

A similar strategy had been used in the 1990s, when feminists and women's rights advocates made concerted conceptual moves to define violence against women as a form of torture under existing international law.[52] The strategy was controversial for some human rights activists and theorists, who saw this as inefficacious or as potentially diluting the potency of a human rights violation that is widely met with grave opprobrium.[53]

Similar ambivalence was present among brokers, who were conscious of the complexity of this approach. A debate about the proposal took place one afternoon in New York after a broker finished a call with a colleague at a generalist human rights NGO. They had been drafting a joint press release on the abuse of transgender women by police in Turkey, which he had described as "torture." He noted with alarm that she had balked at the word, and made it clear that her institution was not able to use the term in that context.

The difference of opinion between the two brokers, and the positions of their respective organizations, revolved around whether "complicity" in torture required active participation or simple inaction when systemic persecution was brought to the attention of state agents. The other NGO, which worked on a range of human rights issues, including the torture of political and social dissidents, aligned itself with the former position. IGL-HRC, which was then seeking to frame the systemic persecution of LGBT persons as a form of torture, opted for the latter.

Cook noted the similarity to debates about violence against women as a form of torture. She expressed sympathy with both positions, noting that she felt uncomfortable when terms like "genocide" and "apartheid" were used loosely to describe killings and discrimination, but also pointing out that the OAS had established precedent for a more expansive understanding of torture.[54] Perle added that the Convention Against Torture also left the distinction open to interpretation, establishing that "consent or acquiescence" could constitute torture under international law.[55]

Brokers ultimately avoided using the term "torture" in the joint press release, with everyone present agreeing that a case for their novel interpretation needed to be carefully made. If approved, the project would give them space to advance their claim more thoughtfully.

The proposal had been developed by senior brokers at IGLHRC in conjunction with NGOs with experience documenting and prosecuting torture cases, who would have been co-grantees if the proposal had been successful. Brokers were aware of the perceived gravity of the distinction between torture and other abuses, but were open to the idea that the project could generate much-needed material and symbolic support to deal with the very real persecution of LGBT persons. The proposal was ultimately rejected by the funding body, and brokers did not plan other initiatives at the time to advance the more expansive understanding of torture.

While *Nowhere to Turn* and the torture proposal grappled with the expansion or elaboration of human rights from an LGBT perspective, there were also campaigns at IGLHRC that simply fell outside the boundaries of the human rights framework but were felt to be urgent and necessary. When a massive earthquake devastated the Haitian capital of Port-au-Prince on January 12, 2010, it decimated the headquarters of one of IGLHRC's in-country partners, an MSM group called SEROvie. The earthquake destroyed SEROvie's space, killed fourteen people who were present at a support group, and left MSM in Port-au-Prince without an intact organization that provided them with healthcare, essential medications, and safer-sex supplies.

As news of the earthquake spread, brokers met and quickly agreed to prepare a fundraising drive to raise money for rebuilding efforts and the restoration of SEROvie's services. The appeal was foregrounded on IGLHRC's webpage and promoted in an e-mail blast to supporters, and raised thousands of dollars for earthquake relief. The funds were used to purchase a number of items identified and prioritized by SEROvie, including safer-sex supplies, office equipment, and tents to be used as temporary headquarters for the organization.[56]

In these efforts, IGLHRC rapidly shifted into a disaster relief role with relatively little discussion that I witnessed. What was important was that a partner was in need. Although brokers later went to Haiti to deliver supplies and explore the vulnerability of LGBT people in the wake of disasters, their rights-based analysis was introduced late in a campaign that was primarily about securing the immediate needs of an MSM population at risk.

In all three of these initiatives, brokers responded to the felt needs of LGBT persons in ways that troubled the traditional human rights framework. By translating marginalization and discrimination into the language of human rights, or by eschewing human rights justifications entirely, brokers engaged in advocacy that a generalist human rights organization might have considered beyond their mandate. As I explore below, the converse was also true, and the human rights framework counseled brokers to embrace positions that LGBT organizations without that framework often eschewed.

IGLHRC as a Human Rights Organization for LGBT People

Brokers' LGBT affinities allowed them to work beyond the constraints of the human rights framework, but they also used human rights to think beyond identity politics. Many brokers stressed that the ideological expansiveness of human rights appealed to them, particularly because of the linkages it created with other social movements. Jones echoed the sentiment of a number of these brokers when she recalled:

> I started doing human rights work because I was looking for a way of connecting seemingly disparate issues. I felt like I was working in identity-based silos, and human rights was a way of demanding that if I was working on women's rights, I was also thinking through poverty, I was also thinking through race. And so it was a framework I was really drawn to despite its limitations of being very legalistic, and very alienating to a lot of people.

To some extent, this set their advocacy apart from other LGBT NGOs whose approach was not specifically grounded in the human rights framework. As Clarke observed shortly after her departure:

> Conceptually, there are big differences between the civil rights framework that a lot of the LGBT organizations use domestically and the human rights framework. . . . At a certain level, even though they're situated within a social justice framework, equality is the end goal for many domestic organizations. There was a differentiation between that and what we're doing. I think in part—in fact, I know in part—this comes from [Ettelbrick], who is a feminist scholar herself. When she was writing early on in the LGBT movement, she really wrote of a transformative vision of a movement which was much more akin to radical feminist desires for a transformed universe.

Throughout IGLHRC's history, there have been numerous instances where a holistic conception of human rights fostered a more expansive understanding of social justice than mainstream LGBT NGOs expressed in the United States. As Khan, who was executive director when the United States began bombing Afghanistan, recalled:

> I think the thing I was particularly proud of was that IGLHRC took a very early and vocal position that was antiwar. And that was something that happened fast, because *all* of that happened so fast. I mean, we woke up one morning and there were the buildings going down. We were among the first LGBT groups in the country, if not the first, to take an antiwar position. And we were criticized for that by conservative elements of the gay movement, and I think we were held in very high regard by others for taking such a vocal

position when other national LGBT groups were not doing the same thing.....
We were a human rights agency, and in times of war, people who are vulnerable already become increasingly vulnerable, and those are certainly LGBT
people, and that was our analysis.

A similar view was expressed by her successor, Ettelbrick, who even drew
a distinction between IGLHRC and one of the more progressive LGBT
NGOs in the United States:

> One of the things I loved about working at IGLHRC is that it was much easier
> working from a human rights perspective to convince colleagues and our
> donors and our board that things beyond strictly gay and lesbian issues, and
> trans issues, were important for us to be engaged in. In the U.S., it's so nar-
> row, and *so* identity-based. For instance, when I was at the Task Force, I kept
> pushing, pushing, pushing, saying the Task Force should have a position
> against the death penalty. And people kept saying, how is that a gay issue?
> Well, internationally, let me just say that there's no question it's a gay issue.
> You need to look at Iran, you need to look at Nigeria and the sharia states
> there, and you need to look at where people can be stoned because they're
> gay, and in a nanosecond, you see that. But also, as a human rights thing, we
> work—instinctively, and by structure—with a broader set of principles.

Khan and Ettelbrick's views are not anomalous; Johnson proudly told visiting students that IGLHRC was strictly abolitionist with regard to the death
penalty. In conversations and interviews, brokers expressed strong reservations about a number of priorities—for instance, the passage of hate crimes
legislation or the demand for same-sex marriage—that were heavily cham-
pioned by mainstream U.S.-based LGBT organizations.

For myriad reasons, the human rights framework legitimated interventions that would be unimaginable or difficult in LGBT advocacy in the
United States. The human rights framework sets an absolute baseline of
treatment that sidesteps epistemological questions; a notable hindrance in
U.S.-based LGBT advocacy has been the question of whether sexual orientation is as innate as race or sex. This has not only shaped whether sexual orientation receives heightened scrutiny from the courts, but has been
pivotal in shifting public sentiment. In both legal and popular advocacy,
the advancement of LGBT rights has heavily relied on the insistence that
SOGI are innate and immutable aspects of personhood.

While IGLHRC occasionally implied that sexuality is immutable in its public outputs, its advocacy hardly depended on this assertion. Brokers insisted that all persons are entitled to the enjoyment of human rights, regardless of SOGI, and defended those rights even when it was unclear how an individual identified. Campaigns for decriminalization and the inclusion of MSM and WSW in public health programs, which often explicitly stress that same-sex practicing persons are not innately gay, lesbian, or even LGBT, are examples of demands for human rights protections regardless of the origins of same-sex sexuality.

Above all, the human rights framework offered a platform that supports but transcends LGBT issues. It places a heavy emphasis on the indivisibility and interconnectedness of rights, providing a strong basis for intramovement and intermovement solidarity. As IGLHRC's stances on issues like war, the death penalty, and Israeli occupation suggest, this has enabled broader coalitions to be constructed within LGBT movements and among other human rights movements—something that domestic LGBT organizations have found challenging within a more circumscribed frame.

The Limits of Hybridity

By tacking between their LGBT constituency and a human rights approach, brokers were able to formulate priorities and interventions that would be unlikely to develop through either framework alone. While this choice of frameworks could be freeing, brokers also struggled with the limits of hybridity.

By identifying as an LGBT organization, for example, making a case for human rights, or even sexual rights, often became more difficult. The introduction of subgroups into the wider rubric of universal human rights immediately invited charges that IGLHRC was campaigning for special rights, and sometimes endangered allies who cooperated with the group. As Alizadeh noted, the use of the term "gay and lesbian" in IGLHRC's title had potential consequences that could not be dodged by emphasizing one framework over another:

> In many countries, if you start with LGBT, you alienate people and you endanger your partners in countries, by just saying, oh, we work with a gay and lesbian human rights commission. The Middle East is a prime example where you have to be very careful, even about the name.... There are people I know for sure won't approach us, and they told me so, because of our name. They have no problem working with gay people, but if you bring a U.S.-based

organization that's called gay and lesbian, that's like the kiss of death for them. They're not going to work with me, and they made it clear, they said, oh, we'll work with Human Rights Watch or Amnesty International, not because they're inherently more capable, but because of the name, you know? And I understand that, and I respect that.

Although the human rights framework provides a theoretical basis for cross-movement work, the reality was that self-identifying as an LGBT organization meant that some groups could not or would not work with IGLHRC, despite the best intentions or politics of its staff.

The converse was also true. Although the human rights framework helped brokers transcend the identity-based advocacy that is so prevalent in the United States, it also imposed its own ideological strictures, which could be off-putting in contexts where human rights were viewed with suspicion. The expansion of rights discourse alongside persistent failures to deliver tangible justice to the world's most marginalized groups has left a deep-rooted skepticism toward rights in much of the South—and perhaps especially toward those, like LGBT people, who appear to be the beneficiaries of special rights and whose suffering attracts swift responses from NGOs and world leaders. As a result, the discourse, mechanisms, and geopolitical affinities of human rights organizations deterred potential supporters who might embrace more transformative kinds of queer organizing. Alizadeh observed that this could be a limitation for advocates using an overtly rights-based approach:

The problem with [human rights activists] really is that we already have a framework, and that's international treaties and international conventions. And nobody gives a damn about what those treaties are where I'm working, the region I'm working on. So you really need to find other means, other ways to approach those people. If you really want to go there, you need to invest, basically, to understand what the cultures are. That cultural understanding requires some study. Like anything else, you need to be smart about it. You have to understand what they say, what they mean. The listening is half of the solution, and that never comes across. . . . As long as you stick to language that nobody understands, you won't have an ally, you know?

While brokers were committed to transcending the limitations of the human rights framework, most of their interventions nonetheless reflected faith in the idea that rights were worth defending and promoting, and most of the tools they could offer to activists were created with human rights advocacy in mind. To the extent that the human rights project itself was viewed with skepticism or hostility, there was little that hybridity could offer to circumvent its limitations.

CONCLUSION

As a result of IGLHRC's name and history, brokers were conscious that their work was directed toward a particular constituency and situated within a particular framework. Throughout my fieldwork, brokers grappled with the limitations of LGBT politics and human rights. While IGLHRC's affinities limited brokers' work in some ways, its dual focus could also be hybridized or held in productive tension to produce innovative interventions in LGBT human rights advocacy.

In the following chapters, the work that brokers carried out under this banner is explored in more detail. While brokers demonstrated a remarkable ability to flexibly navigate LGBT politics and the limitations of the human rights framework, these moves had implications for their work with partners in the South; their production and dissemination of knowledge about gender, sexuality, and human rights transnationally; and their advocacy with the UN and regional mechanisms. As brokers constructed particular understandings of LGBT human rights, the choices they made had repercussions for the promotion and institutionalization of these rights transnationally.

4 LGBT Human Rights Advocacy and the Partnership Principle

As a wider field of NGOs incorporated SOGI into human rights advocacy, brokers faced pressure to distinguish IGLHRC from groups doing similar work. IGLHRC's staff retreat in September 2010 not only revisited organizational goals and the tactics necessary to achieve them, but also sought to identify what was *not* helpful for brokers to pursue. Part of this involved defining a theory of change for the organization, which would determine what actions staff would or would not take.

When I asked what set IGLHRC apart, Johnson outlined two aspects of its work:

> I can give you the stock answer, which is that we highlight and foreground the voices of local activists, and work in partnership, and it's all true. But if I got really honest about it, I'd say what really makes us distinct is that we're broad and comprehensive. You know, I'm very proud, we have programs in four regions of the world at this point, and staff on the ground, and so I don't think *anybody* knows comprehensively what is going on, not in every single country at every single moment, but a sense of what the current overall, overarching situation is for LGBT in Africa, and how to respond. In Asia. In LAC. The Middle East is a new one, and a tricky one. I think that's what we bring, and if we keep finding ways to funnel all this information and then bring it back out, then I think that's really where we're unique.

In the following two chapters, I look at these forms of promoting human rights in turn—first, at IGLHRC's partnerships with groups around the world, and second, at IGLHRC's role in producing, disseminating, and validating knowledge about LGBT issues. Both involve complexities that trouble simple dichotomies between North and South or even global and local advocacy. Brokers and regional programs negotiated these complexities in their own ways, which reflected their political priorities as well as the demands of the networks and sociopolitical systems in which they operated.

"Do No Harm" and the Partnership Principle at IGLHRC

Over time, a number of principles became de facto tenets of IGLHRC's work. Brokers recognized that interference from a U.S.-based LGBT NGO could be counterproductive for activists on the ground, and Johnson maintained that IGLHRC's primary responsibility was to "do no harm" in its advocacy. The principal means by which brokers ensured they did no harm—and sought to make IGLHRC's advocacy consonant with local realities and priorities— was a rhetorical and programmatic commitment to "partnership."

The emphasis on partnership took place against a backdrop of wider transnational trends. Globalization has increasingly enabled Southern movements to agitate globally, which is powerfully evident in the Zapatista movement, opposition to dam and deforestation projects, and other campaigns that skillfully use media and information technologies to develop networks, raise awareness, and rally global supporters.[1] As Southern activists speak for themselves, "NGOs that participate in transnational advocacy networks are likely to be challenged to justify their activities, to explain what makes them legitimate advocates."[2]

In this context, the rhetoric of empowerment and capacity building has gradually replaced messianic promises to save or protect Southerners.[3] Since the 1970s, the notion of partnership has been widely employed by development NGOs as a structuring principle for North–South relationships.[4] For NGOs that do not directly represent a constituency, "it is the transnational nature of their activities, their capacity to link micro-level grassroots operational work to more macro-level advocacy work through cross-border networks, that gives them their legitimacy."[5]

The ubiquity of "partnership" has led to closer scrutiny of its power dynamics. Critics contend that concepts like "partnership" and "empowerment" are empty, and primarily function to mask meaningful inequalities in resources, capacity, and power.[6] Practitioners have responded that partnerships provide space for agendas to be negotiated, however imperfectly, among a network of actors, and must be evaluated empirically.[7] Both perspectives are partially accurate; partnerships can make transnational work more palatable but can also make it more thoughtful.[8] Where partnerships are seen as self-evidently good, closer examination offers a richer understanding of power in transnational advocacy networks.

Partnership has been scrutinized in development anthropology, but the concept has also shaped public health, human rights, and social justice interventions. The growth of transnational women's rights advocacy, for example, has raised critical questions about power differentials within networks and their consequences for political agendas.[9] The formation of transnational LGBT rights networks have generated similar concerns about neocolonialism and paternalism in advocacy.[10] Brokers at IGLHRC were attuned to these critiques of transnational work, which they regularly struggled with in their advocacy.

Although external critiques of transnational LGBT advocacy are well known, brokers also struggled with North–South tensions *within* IGLHRC. In the mid-2000s, the increasing focus on the UN and abandonment of direct services to asylum seekers, as well as internal tensions over leadership at IGLHRC, left many feeling that the organization was growing disconnected from the grassroots. Dissent within IGLHRC went public; disgruntled brokers created an anonymous blog describing their grievances and the LGBT press reported the mass resignation of a number of staff.[11] Many brokers left IGLHRC, including Sardá, who departed after a decade and publicly announced: "The reasons that motivated this decision are my disagreement with the political vision implemented by the current Executive Director and my need to prioritize my work in a South-South context."[12]

Partnership with Southern groups offered a defense to charges of neocolonialism, but it also provided a means to do work effectively and responsibly. As Ettelbrick suggested in an interview, partnerships were central to IGLHRC's efficacy as a U.S.-based NGO: "I think wherever you come from in the world, if you can build solid relationships, build working relationships with activists, and build the trust, that's key." Brokers genuinely believed in mutuality and North–South cooperation, a position informed both by academic theory and by their activism.[13] (One staff member recalled that, in a previous position, she began automatically rejecting internship applicants who talked about "saving" women from sex trafficking or genital cutting.) For brokers, the idea that local movements should advise and direct any transnational intervention simply went without saying.

The confluence of transnational trends, internal pressures, and the politics of brokers themselves made an ethic of partnership central at IGLHRC.

In development, it meant working with local or regional groups when submitting proposals to funders or implementing projects. In communications, it meant consulting in-country activists before producing any calls to action, sharing and verifying information, and foregrounding local groups' materials on IGLHRC's website. In programs, partnership was realized in myriad ways, but was often expressed in terms of capacity building and technical assistance. Kilonzo explained what that practically meant:

> With capacity building, different countries are at different levels. Some are just emerging and young. Some have had previous trainings and work with us. [It's] how to organize, to even start off, get support, do a proposal, fundraise, how to document human rights. Sometimes it may require you to help people with documenting skills, or if there is a legal issue required, working with lawyers, advising with the various options, even the lawyers themselves having a particular strategy that is sensitive to LGBT issues. At a different level, groups may [need] to issue a press statement, or an alert, or different mechanisms to respond to media, so they may need you to even help them with drafting, putting the ideas together. There are different technical supports, people at different levels in different countries.

Brokers thus had considerable leeway to meet the distinctive needs of partner organizations.[14] Indeed, what partnerships would practically entail was never fully known at the outset. As in development, partnering on a project "does not mean carrying out an already-planned programme but is a constant process of negotiation."[15] What brokers provided to partners, what they expected of them, and how they responded to conflicts were all negotiated processually. A commitment to partnership still left a great deal to be negotiated in practice.

Despite daily references to "partners" and "partnership," these concepts were not monolithic, and took different shapes as they applied to different actors and regions. As Johnson pointed out to me, "Partnership is a very broad term, and we don't have formal partnerships, either, so the people with whom we engage in strategic relationships are many." As scholars look beyond partnership to theorize "political responsibility," negotiations that occur within partnerships are critically important.[16] Who were brokers referring to when they spoke of partners and partnership? What did they feel was owed to them, and what was expected in return? When did partnership define the work that brokers undertook, and when were the wishes of partners qualified or overridden by other priorities? Brokers routinely confronted these questions, and their responses decisively shaped their advocacy.

DEFINING AND DEVELOPING PARTNERSHIPS

IGLHRC's partners were not homogeneous, and brokers worked with them for distinct reasons that the singular gloss of "partnership" elides. As Jones reflected:

> There is the partnership with another organization that shares our politics as well as respects and appreciates our work. There is the partnership with an organization that is the only LGBT game in town, the sole LGBT organization that we know in a particular place. And then, we also partner with incipient activists and organizations all the time.

A number of considerations were taken into account in forming, developing, and terminating partnerships. Jones's assessment neatly summarizes three key reasons brokers partnered with Southern groups: a history of collaboration and trust, pragmatic utility, and the desire to build movements where they were young or unconnected to transnational networks. Although these rationales frequently shifted or blurred together, they were all used to justify partnerships at IGLHRC.

Partnerships Based on a History of Collaboration and Trust

Many of IGLHRC's partnerships were strengthened by the longstanding personal and professional ties of its staff. From their previous work, many brokers were in contact with activists around the globe whose advice and collaboration they sought on a regular basis. As Ettelbrick recalled, "The IGLHRC staff has always been very diverse. . . . We had people from so many different places—different degrees of connection, I guess, to their countries of origin, but many still very much connected, and able, then, to bring in different perspectives to our work."

The Africa Program provides a good illustration of the significance of these lasting ties. From her previous work with the ICJ, Kilonzo had strong relationships with lawyers, human rights defenders, and human rights groups in Africa whom she continued to draw on and work with at IGLHRC. These were particularly helpful in her advocacy in regional mechanisms like the AU, the ACHPR, and, to a lesser extent, blocs like the East African

Community (EAC). Kilonzo, a Kenyan, was particularly close to members of GALCK, and served on their board. Ukwimi drew heavily on relationships formed during his time at PSI in Zambia, and worked closely with Friends of Rainka and AMSHeR. Similarly, Mukasa was a founder of SMUG, and an iconic figure in Uganda's LGBT movement. He figured prominently in landmark successes in the country, including *Ooyo and Mukasa v. Attorney General of Uganda,* which established that rights in Uganda's constitution extend to LGBT and *kuchu* persons. As the only publicly identified transgender broker at IGLHRC, Mukasa was a key liaison with transgender and intersex groups like Gender Dynamix in Cape Town. The centrality of personal relationships was also evident among brokers themselves; Kilonzo helped with legal strategy for *Ooyo and Mukasa,* and was hired as Mukasa's supervisor two years later.

Relationships were critical in a movement dominated by visible figureheads. In sub-Saharan Africa, activists, their organizations, and the movement in a given country could sometimes function almost synonymously. (In a telling instance, an activist visiting the office in Cape Town was half-jokingly introduced to me as "the LGBT movement in Lesotho.") When brokers were close to these figureheads, IGLHRC was often intensely involved as a collaborator and supporter of their work. When brokers distanced themselves from these figureheads because of political, managerial, or interpersonal differences, it could at times strain advocacy with their NGOs or limit work in their country.

In many cases, established relationships gave brokers a place to turn when information and guidance were urgently needed but contacts in a particular place were lacking. When international media reported that an Uzbekistani man had been jailed for his HIV/AIDS outreach, for example, nobody in New York could think of Uzbekistani groups they had partnered with in the past. In the absence of a direct contact, they turned to other trusted figures in central Asia who could confirm the incident and advise whether advocacy might be helpful.

Brokers relied heavily on these established relationships, and the trust they placed in them decisively shaped IGLHRC's advocacy.[17] From mid-2009 to mid-2010, the work of IGLHRC's Africa Program, executive director, and Communications and Research staff was dominated by the tabling of Uganda's Anti-Homosexuality Bill, the proposed prohibition of same-sex activity in Rwanda, the arrest of Tiwonge Chimbalanga and Steven Monjeza in Malawi on charges of "unnatural offenses" and "gross indecency," and sporadic arrests and violence in Kenya, Senegal, and Tanzania. These incidents were time sensitive, volatile, and sensationalized by local and international media, and IGLHRC's interventions in all of them were shaped by relationships established with in-country partners before the crises arose.

The Only Game in Town: Pragmatism, Necessity, and Strategy

Although IGLHRC preferred to work with trusted partners, it was not possible for eighteen people to maintain deep, lasting relationships with activists in every country around the globe. When brokers felt they *had* to respond to egregious or high-profile incidents, they also worked with groups that did not have established relationships with IGLHRC, but were perceived as the most credible voices for LGBT people in the country in question.

The imperative to respond is in many ways a Northern impulse, with historical, professional, and moral underpinnings. IGLHRC promoted "Human Rights for Everyone, Everywhere," so it was difficult for brokers to justify inaction on incidents brought to their attention by activists, other NGOs, journalists, donors, and the board. The imperative to respond was also internalized by brokers; debates about what IGLHRC should say or do about an incident allowed for deliberation, but often presumed that *something* had to be said or done. To recognize a gross violation of human rights and do nothing seemed morally unacceptable. As Cook argued, brokers—especially young brokers—felt this moral obligation acutely:

> You're like, if I can do something, I'd rather do something, because I'm scared that if change doesn't happen, I'll look back and go, if only I had stayed up all night once and written the Argentinean CEDAW report, and then all those trans activists in Argentina would be happy because their agenda was achieved. But we have to let go of some of that, because some of it is not our own personal egos, necessarily, but like these kind of meta-activist egos, for social justice activists, where we get into this whole "we can change the world" kind of thing.

With the most egregious and heavily publicized incidents in particular, brokers felt pressure to actively seek out and assist NGOs that were leading local responses. In keeping with their commitment to partnership, brokers felt it was better to work with in-country LGBT organizations than to ignore a crisis or work without them. As a result, some partnerships were forged from perceived necessity rather than any lengthy process of collaboration and trust.

In these instances, brokers frequently partnered with groups they considered "the only game in town." Brokers used this phrase to explain why they worked with groups that did not have deep ties to IGLHRC, and did not necessarily share their own commitments. In the phrase, the "game" in question was advocating for LGBT rights, and the relevant "town" was typically the nation-state where an incident had occurred. Notably, the latter criterion mattered a great deal. To avoid being or appearing imperialist, brokers reflexively looked to national groups for guidance in emergencies rather than local groups, groups from neighboring nation-states, or transnational networks.

These pragmatic partnerships were strongest during times of crisis and decreased in intensity when tensions abated, but they could always be maintained and revived. Groups considered "the only game in town" that showed promise for long-term cooperation were subtly but gradually encouraged to become stronger partners through engagement and capacity building. As I discuss below, brokers took movement building seriously, and it was primarily when groups were ethically suspect that brokers kept them at a distance and minimally invested in their growth.

Reaching Out and Building Movements Globally

As outlined in chapter 1, the idea of movement building has become increasingly central to IGLHRC's mission. Brokers made concerted efforts to expand the network of supportive groups with which they worked—not simply to make contacts, but to integrate those groups into a global movement. Brokers linked activists to funders, sponsored their participation in conferences and trainings, and involved them in exchanges where nascent groups were paired with established groups in neighboring countries. Partnerships were further strengthened by joint work on grant proposals, research projects, legal challenges, emergency responses, presentations at supranational forums, and shadow reports where NGOs presented information to UN treaty bodies.

The concept of movement building was heavily promoted at IGLHRC. In an interview, Johnson recalled how he developed networks through the Africa Program:

> I think the very first convening we did after I became Africa Program coordinator was at the African Commission. And it was a big convening, I think we had twenty-five people. And I didn't know all of them, so I did a lot of

calling around, talking to people. Do you know this person? Does she do good work? Does she really represent queer communities? Who's in her orbit? And it's interesting, because if I go back and I look at that list of who came, a lot of them were people I didn't know, but it was a good list.

In outreach to young or nascent movements, the question of who *became* a partner was an open one. A complex interplay of structural and ideological factors primed brokers at IGLHRC to interact with, and partner with, specific groups. Some related to ideology and self-identification, and some related to the ways networks legitimated particular actors.

First, groups were most visible to brokers when they framed their work in terms that were cognizable to transnational NGOs. Groups were particularly likely to come to IGLHRC's attention as potential partners if they self-identified as "gay" or "LGBT" in their name or their advocacy. Partnership was also facilitated when groups operated with a human rights–based framework, or were capable of doing so when necessary.

Yet not all partners were explicitly LGBT or human rights groups. Particularly in MENA and Africa, where illegality and stigma posed real challenges for organizations, brokers regularly worked with groups that were neither LGBT-identified nor solely focused on human rights. Notably, IGLHRC's closest partners during my fieldwork did not use "gay" or "lesbian" in their titles.[18] Both SMUG in Uganda and CEDEP in Malawi, for instance, operated under different frameworks—the former used "sexual minorities," and the latter used "MSM" and "most-at-risk populations" (MARPs). Many partners were public health NGOs, particularly where same-sex activity was illegal or heavily stigmatized and appeals to rights rang hollow.

What these groups could do, however, was speak the language of transnational LGBT human rights advocacy. They could deploy terms like "MSM," "WSW," "LGBT," and "SOGI" to articulate what kind of advocacy they planned to undertake, and to frame that advocacy for IGLHRC and others using a human rights framework. When registering with the government, lobbying politicians, or advertising services, however, these groups might be more cautious in characterizing their programs and priorities in order to minimize potentially hostile responses.

Organizationally, transnational NGOs are best equipped to support groups that are recognizable as NGOs, with a name, website, and bank account.[19] To the extent this was true at IGLHRC, it was both for logistical reasons and because partners were supposed to be representative of a larger community. The benefits of partnership—establishing legitimacy, avoiding neocolonialism, and doing work effectively—dissipated if IGLHRC took its cues from individuals who were not trusted and respected locally. By turning to established, organized groups, brokers sought to ensure that the most authoritative collective of LGBT activists was guiding their work.

Of course, informal networks and unaffiliated individuals remained invaluable sources of guidance, particularly for the regional programs. As Johnson noted:

> When folks are in trouble, that's who they go to, the *doyenne* of the community. And sometimes, they're not the people who transition into becoming formal leaders, because that's not what they're good at. They're like the mothers. And those people are really important in terms of really knowing what's on the ground, knowing when the situation is getting tricky, knowing how to put security issues into play. . . . And then there are the allies, the lawyers, the medical personnel, just the folks who really care and make their resources available.

These people were often difficult to identify through formal channels, and identifying and working with them required long-term, deep engagement in a region. IGLHRC's deliberate hiring of activists and retention of regional personnel made a meaningful difference in that regard. The extent to which brokers were familiar with (or part of) networks in a region strongly influenced their ability to tap into unofficial channels for guidance. With a small staff, the arrivals and departures of particular activists reshaped IGLHRC's relationships to movements in particular countries.

Second, potential partners became visible by traveling in the same circles as brokers. The world of transnational LGBT human rights advocacy is growing, but is still powerfully shaped by tight-knit personal and professional relationships. The identification of new partners was powerfully aided by networks of activists, NGOs, and funders that collectively legitimated certain groups as credible representatives of LGBT populations in a given locale. Ukwimi explained how new partnerships could be formed:

> Some of them we've met at conferences, maybe some time back, and then we just realize, I'm going to Guinea, oh, I actually met somebody from Guinea at a conference, okay, let me look up the business card and get in touch with them when I go to Guinea, and they'll probably connect me with somebody.

Or some of our already-existing partners will kind of point us in the right direction. "Oh, you're going to Mongolia, okay, these are the kind of people there and let me do an introductory email and you can start talking."

In a number of virtual and physical spaces, Northern activists were especially likely to encounter Southern activists and form relationships on which partnerships were based. Most brokers at IGLHRC were on two mailing lists—a semiprivate list for LGBT activists and Euro-Queer, a public list for updates from Europe and beyond. One way for incipient groups to assert their presence in LGBT human rights networks was to post on these lists, making themselves visible to key players and alerting them to their work. Over time, budding relationships and attendance at conferences, convenings, and summits mutually cemented the place of particular activists and groups.[20]

Other groups emerged incidentally, often at regional and international conferences where gender and sexuality were discussed. Brokers met activists at the CSW, discussions sponsored by New York–based groups like the American Foundation for AIDS Research and the American Jewish World Service, and events at Columbia, CUNY, NYU, and the New School. Connections were made at summits like ICASA in Dakar in 2008 and the Eighteenth International AIDS Conference in Vienna in 2010. In these venues, activists encountered brokers who expressed interest in their work.

In one paradigmatic example, brokers were invited to a brown-bag lunch sponsored by a funding body that had just given a grant to an NGO from West Africa. The funder was eager to link Johnson with a representative of the NGO, and I watched as the three strategized about conditions in the country where the group operated, exchanged business cards, and pledged to stay in touch. Thanks to shared membership on key listservs, I stayed appraised of the grantee's work as he participated in transnational discussions. A little over a year later, I ran into him at a conference in Johannesburg, where I was part of the launch of *Nowhere to Turn* and he was presenting his group's programs and networking with funders and NGOs on the continent. In these various spaces, transnational relationships were both forged and reinforced.

Brokers also had individual preferences that affected whom they trusted, with whom they preferred to work, and where they sought out groups to support. In LAC, Ferreyra had the benefit of broad-based democratic social movements that made it natural to work in coalition with labor, feminist, and indigenous peoples' movements.[21] Kilonzo had worked for the ICJ when there was widespread skepticism about whether mainstream human rights NGOs should take on LGBT issues. She preferred to build alliances within civil society, and was critical of the tendency to work exclusively on SOGI issues. In a region where visible partnerships with self-identified LGBT NGOs were controversial and risky, Alizadeh was open to working with those who were reluctant to publicly associate with IGLHRC, including religious hardliners opposed to its work. He noted that "there is a strong desire to choose who the partners are, and I have a tendency to see the other side of the argument." By contrast, Poore, who had worked in women's rights, was skeptical of working with hardliners, finding little common cause in their priorities. Instead, she preferred to work with feminist groups, particularly LBT groups, to create space for women under the rubric of sexual rights.

All of these preferences oriented the regional programs toward particular partners in their work. Brokers in New York were generally comfortable with this diversity of tactics, deferring to program staff on what was or was not strategic in their regions. Combined with the geographical remove of most programs from headquarters in New York, that allowed a considerable degree of heterogeneity in IGLHRC's partnerships.

THE PARTNERSHIP IDEAL IN PRACTICE

Although brokers valued partnership and the egalitarianism implied by the term, at times various factors prevented this ideal from being fully realized in practice. Working transnationally meant that it was sometimes difficult to get answers or opinions from partners who were busy, were traveling, had weak Internet or phone connections, or could not or would not respond to e-mails or telephone calls. When partners did respond, if their answers were ambiguous or halfhearted and there was not a sufficiently thorough conversation about the efficacy of transnational support, brokers would typically opt not to proceed.

In many cases, however, stumbling blocks to partnership were more regular and predictable. In the following section, I consider how the partnership ideal was complicated in practice: when there were no clear partners; when partners were unable or unwilling to be visible; when partners had different values, politics, and standards; when there were multiple or competing partners; and when partners were self-sufficient. While each partnership was unique, these stumbling blocks complicated a best-case scenario and forced brokers to think critically about what meaningful partnership required.

When There Were No Clear Partners

Organizational commitments are not only evident in frontstage advocacy and outputs, but in what brokers opt *not* to do. This was evident with *Words of Hate, Climate of Fear: Human Rights Violations and Challenges to the LGBT Movement in Senegal,* which was researched, written, and printed before brokers embargoed it on the eve of its launch. The demise of the report occurred in a field where brokers no longer had identifiable partners, leaving IGLHRC vulnerable to criticism by other stakeholders in Senegal. When those stakeholders objected to the release of the report, brokers felt they had to shelve it indefinitely.

Completing the report was complicated. It had been the primary responsibility of Joel Nana, IGLHRC's program associate for West Africa, who left in 2009 without an organized transfer of files. Given the small size of the Africa Program, IGLHRC's firsthand knowledge about Senegal (and West Africa) was largely lost with Nana's departure. Records of who had been interviewed and how to reach them were missing, as were many of the citations and any advocacy strategy for the report. The report passed to Clarke in New York, who assigned the project to me shortly before her departure. I had no contacts in Senegal, did not speak Wolof, and had limited reading comprehension of French. With Clarke's departure, the project was supervised by Johnson and Schultz, who had numerous demands on their time in the office.

Yet brokers felt pressure to release the report. The pattern of abuses had escalated in Senegal, with anti-LGBT rhetoric from politicians and religious leaders increasing steadily.[22] Donors had committed to the project, and brokers had already commissioned None on Record: Voices of Queer Africa to record audio profiles of LGBT individuals. Brokers had a rough draft with firsthand testimony, including narratives from same-sex practicing women who were typically absent from research on SOGI in Senegal. Brokers also knew that HRW was working on its own report on the topic, which could render theirs obsolete. While there were recognizable shortcomings in the project, a great deal of time, energy, and resources had been invested in its completion. The proposed solution was to conduct additional interviews using Johnson's contacts, to update and revise the text, and to release the report and turn to other drafts in the pipeline. The project continued throughout the fall.

In December, IGLHRC sent an e-mail to individuals who were consulted or interviewed for the report. It included a four-page executive summary, which contained key findings and recommendations for the government of Senegal, neighboring governments, human rights NGOs, and religious leaders. In February, a final message was sent asking about friendly press in Senegal who might be willing to run a story on the report when it was released the following week.

That Thursday, a white foreign national living in Senegal contacted IGL-HRC to express concern that the report's release between two religious holidays would reignite the anti-LGBT fervor that had put same-sex-practicing persons at risk. None of the Senegalese partners had registered objections, but brokers coordinating the launch of the report—Johnson, Jones, Kilonzo, and I—discussed scaling back any media outreach within Senegal and Francophone Africa.

By Friday, however, I received a message from a Senegalese HIV/AIDS service provider who had been interviewed for the report, expressing concern that an international LGBT group's criticism of the government was likely to do more harm than good. Over the course of the morning, HIV/AIDS groups in the United States, Canada, and France contacted IGL-HRC to let brokers know they had heard about the report, and to request that it not be released at that time.

Doubts piled up as the business day ended. Johnson was away at the Creating Change conference in Texas. Jones had started work as IGLHRC's program director that week; Cook, who would normally oversee report launches with Jones and the relevant regional program coordinator, had been unable to start work because of her visa; and Kilonzo, who would typically be in charge of the launch as the Africa Program coordinator, had not been deeply involved with the production of the report. I had contacted almost fifty news outlets, and six of them, including the Associated Press and Voice of America, were planning to run features on the report on Monday. Thomas had spent countless hours crafting pages with interactive timelines, MP3s of Senegalese interviewees telling their stories, and a PDF of the report, all of which were about to go live. A launch event was scheduled the following week at CUNY; I had advertised it widely, invited speakers and coordinated travel, and organized a reception.

Nonetheless, it was unanimously agreed that the launch had to be post-poned in light of the security concerns being raised by Senegalese groups and their transnational networks. Brokers decided to postpone the release until after the religious holidays. Later, it gradually became clear that stake-holders preferred the report not be released at all.

Some stakeholders objected to the content of the report, which they felt clumsily described religious and political dynamics and was obviously not written by a Senegalese researcher. (In fact, substantial portions of the final version were written and edited by me, an anthropologist who was horri-fied when Alizadeh offhandedly remarked that the situation bore striking similarities to Massad's critique of transnational LGBT work.) Others hinted at a more pragmatic calculation; activists were making inroads on HIV prevention for MSM, and worried that any overt advocacy by an LGBT-identified organization, even if it focused on public health and HIV pre-vention, would make them targets for political and religious authorities. Even if the report did not upset officials, the perception that Senegal was persecuting LGBT people and imprisoning HIV/AIDS activists could jeop-ardize the large sums of HIV/AIDS funding that had poured into the coun-try in the belief that it was liberal and stable.

The report, which cost upward of $15,000 to produce, was embargoed, and brokers were instructed to not let copies leave the office. In the follow-ing weeks, brokers debated what diffuse but insistent skepticism meant for their advocacy. The original partners were no longer key players; the Sen-egalese LGBT organization And Ligeey had disbanded, its leader had died, and many of its members were in exile.[23] The primary author of the report, too, was no longer at IGLHRC to liaise with Senegalese stakeholders, and Johnson, who had been involved with the project from its inception as the former senior regional specialist for Africa, was now preoccupied with other matters as executive director.

IGLHRC was instead confronted with a chorus of voices, none of which fit the mold for a conventional partner. The individual who registered the initial objection was a foreign national who was not Senegalese. He wor-ried the report would disrupt the work of a loose network that was trying to conduct advocacy through a Senegalese lens, and sought to turn the debate toward public health rather than human rights or the decriminal-ization of homosexuality.[24] He was backed by a service provider who *was* Senegalese, but did not identify as LGBT or same-sex practicing. Both had strong ties within and beyond Senegal that made their voices impossible to ignore. By contrast, IGLHRC's strongest partner from And Ligeey had moved to Belgium as a refugee. Another interviewee, a West African who was based in Senegal, angrily e-mailed IGLHRC arguing that the report should be released and that violations against LGBT people, not simply MSM, should be publicized. One individual who was Senegalese, MSM-identified, an activist and community leader, and in Senegal had worked closely with IGLHRC on the report, but in light of the pressures facing Senegalese LGBT and MSM communities and the cacophony of voices counseling against the release, he ultimately did not endorse the release when presented with others' concerns.

IGLHRC was not contacted by an MSM, LGBT, or queer-identified Senegalese person in the HIV coalition that spoke for those groups. This spoke to the difficulty of reconciling partnership with a consciousness about power within networks, as Jones reflected:

> It appeared to me that IGLHRC had been talking with some of the key gay activists and community leaders in Senegal, but they were working primarily underground and/or at the community level. They were not setting national advocacy agendas, though some straight allies in the public health sector were. So, though the people IGLHRC was speaking with were in many ways the most credible because of their lived experience, talking to them alone was not enough. To do good human rights work, I think one must actually map movements to understand who has the power, and what kind of power, and what kind of access.

One challenge of mapping movements was accounting for voices that were *not* heard. None of the voices objecting to the report were women. Codou Bop has argued that in the sexual politics of Senegal, MSM get legal, material, and symbolic protection by declining to confront the government. Women's organizations, by contrast, have been far bolder in criticizing sexism and heterosexism, challenging religious fundamentalism, and calling for LGBT rights in the country.[25] At IGLHRC, brokers were frustrated by the perceived paternalism of HIV organizations led by white men and straight men who had no incentive to advocate for LGBT rights, and the fact that the testimonies of queer women in the report would not be heard as a result.[26]

In light of concerns about safety, security, and potential backlash, and aware that some individuals in Senegal had publicly registered objections, brokers readily concluded that the report could not be released. In Johnson's words, "We did great work on Senegal, but we dropped the ball because we weren't having that kind of communication on a deep level. . . . And it came back and bit us in the ass." Many brokers were frustrated that those who advised, endorsed, and helped with the report expressed concerns just days before the launch, or had not vouched for it when it came under fire.[27] Citing partnership, however, they concluded they could not responsibly release the report.

When Partners Were Covert

A second complication with partnership arose in instances where partnership required being covert. This was especially challenging in the MENA region, where few groups wanted to openly associate with a U.S.-based NGO promoting LGBT human rights. This led to the formation of covert partnerships, wherein brokers communicated privately with groups to understand their needs, develop strategy, and link activists in politically hostile contexts.

Partnerships where NGOs work with one another covertly are relatively undertheorized in scholarship on transnational advocacy networks. In the classic "boomerang" model, domestic actors use global networks to leverage external pressure and win concessions from their government.[28] The model works well when exposing abuses produces moral, political, or economic leverage.[29] In places where that leverage does not exist, or agents of the state *gain* political power by denying rights to LGBT persons, the model is of limited utility and can easily backfire.

Many of IGLHRC's tactics were premised on the utility of the boomerang model. The bulk of the outputs from Communications and Research were, at their core, tools to name and shame states that committed or permitted violations against LGBT persons. Using that model, IGLHRC's model of partnership worked fairly well, as brokers consulted local groups about the efficacy of action and the content and targeting of any interventions.

In relationships where visibility was a liability, however, brokers had fewer tools at their disposal. Some criticized the lack of support for partnerships where naming and shaming had to be avoided, and where long-term material support would likely have more impact. As Alizadeh noted, advocacy in the MENA region required a very different set of strategies, which cautioned against any singular approach:

> Everybody knows more or less what the needs are in the region. But the problem is that nobody wants to accept responsibility for them. Some

organizations just simply say, oh, well, this is not what we do. . . . The problem with many internationals is that they already think they know what the problem is. They rarely listen to people. Regardless of what your sickness is, they already have this cure, this pill that cures all sorts of ailments.

In these partnerships, IGLHRC's role was difficult to determine. Partners generally did not want IGLHRC to lobby for LGBT rights or openly criticize governments. For their part, brokers did not see IGLHRC as a funder, as an asylum or refugee agency, or as a source of documentation and reporting in the region. Without its traditional tactical arsenal, IGLHRC's role in the MENA region was exploratory. Alizadeh had just launched the program; its first year, which coincided with my fieldwork, mostly involved privately linking activists to each other, consulting colleagues, researching and media monitoring, and campaigning in contexts like Turkey, where groups invited international pressure.

Covert relationships were also challenging when brokers faced criticism from those who were privy to frontstage advocacy but not backstage arrangements they privately made. Often, this occurred when brokers appeared to act without the consent of local groups. Interventions by transnational LGBT NGOs into alleged human rights violations in the Middle East have been criticized for catalyzing backlash against populations they render hypervisible.[30] To outsiders, it seemed IGLHRC still risked this from time to time. Brokers periodically issued alerts or press releases without identifying a partner, giving the impression that they were operating unilaterally. This typically happened when partners felt it was helpful to bring violations to light, but *not* helpful to expose activists working to counter them locally. During my fieldwork, at least two high-profile interventions appeared to lack local support, but were privately shaped by local partners.

Brokers also faced criticism when they apparently *failed* to intervene. A high-profile example was when Michael Lucas, a gay pornography mogul, was vocally critical of IGLHRC in *Out* magazine after the Celebration of Courage gala in 2010. Registering displeasure at IGLHRC's lack of visible advocacy in the MENA region, Lucas said, "They're so afraid to say that it's the Islamic countries in the Middle East and Africa that are responsible for all these death penalties. It's ridiculous, this little piece of shit organization. If you want to speak the truth, speak all the truth."[31] What Lucas failed to realize, and what nobody could say, was that two brokers from IGLHRC were absent from the gala precisely because they were quietly meeting activists across the Middle East, identifying ways that IGLHRC could be a better partner and working to develop a strategy that would be sensitive to regional needs. More obviously, Lucas's criticism failed to appreciate that condemnation from a U.S.-based gay and lesbian group was unlikely to cow governments in the MENA region into protecting LGBT persons; to the contrary, it was far more likely to heighten the salience of SOGI and invite persecution.

Juxtaposing criticism from postcolonial theorists like Massad and neoconservatives like Lucas illustrates how difficult it was for brokers to espouse partnership and then intervene when partners were unable or unwilling to be named. IGLHRC was so avowedly committed to planning its interventions with local groups that exceptions demanded explanation, but these exceptions were precisely where tacit silences were critically important.

Furthermore, visibility was not static, and even overt partnerships were strained by public scrutiny. These tensions were evident in IGLHRC's work in Malawi. IGLHRC had worked with CEDEP since May 2007, when Johnson and CEDEP's Gift Trapence attended a meeting to launch Pan-African ILGA. Brokers from the organizations cooperated on presentations at ICASA, advocacy at the ACHPR, research for *Nowhere to Turn,* and lobbying around PEPFAR (President's Emergency Plan for AIDS Relief) funding from the United States. They continued working together after December 9, 2009, when CEDEP's offices were raided by police and a staff member was arrested on dubious charges of possessing pornography. It was while IGLHRC's offices were closed for the holidays on December 29, 2009, however, that staff from CEDEP contacted brokers at IGLHRC with news that two individuals had been arrested following media reports of a same-sex engagement ceremony.

Over the following months, brokers at IGLHRC primarily liaised with brokers at CEDEP, with whom they had collaborated in the past. CEDEP believed that "improving the welfare of minority groups, including prisoners, sex workers, and those in same-sex relationships, is crucial to the health and well-being of all peoples."[32] Although their mission was broad, IGLHRC worked with them on LGBT issues, and regarded them as the most credible local organization working for LGBT Malawians during that period.

As the couple's arrest made headlines, however, journalists and activists regularly referred to CEDEP as an LGBT rights organization. This was not simply presumptiveness on the part of Northern actors. Trapence was vocally supportive of LGBT rights, and spoke out for them in Malawi and abroad. Throughout the duration of Chimbalanga and Monjeza's imprisonment, CEDEP's website focused almost exclusively on the couple and MSM issues, with only a passing mention in its mission statement of prisoners, sex workers, or other MARPs. CEDEP appeared to be an LGBT or MSM organization, and Northern NGOs that were committed to partnership had come to rely on its authority.

Many rank-and-file members, however, allegedly balked at CEDEP's visibility as an "LGBT" NGO. As Kilonzo noted:

> All the press alerts, releases, and briefings, were like, we are consulting with the only LGBT organization in Malawi. And the members were like, who told these people we were an LGBT organization? Okay, people have known them to be supportive, but . . . the media was busy out here in the world outing them, and you know, they did not take it well, and for different reasons. Some of them have moved into government positions. Some are members of Parliament. And nobody sat back to ask, who are these individuals we are calling CEDEP? . . .
>
> The community in Malawi, for fear of being victimized, they first of all shied away from the stories. They did not want to be quoted directly, and even the one organization that people knew to be supportive of LGBT, they were internally conflicted—do we do public health, or do we address LGBT?

During Chimbalanga and Monjeza's detention, the work CEDEP had done on public health and human rights in calmer times became reconfigured by the crisis. Suddenly, actors in Malawi and around the globe were focused on CEDEP's work, publicly defining it in a way that few members were in a position to dispute.

Covert partnerships are rarely discussed in analyses of transnational advocacy around women's rights, the environment, or human rights, although groups in these networks may be more or less explicit about their transnational affiliations.[33] Where groups were unable to publicly affiliate with IGLHRC or grew uncomfortable with their affiliation during crises, however, secrecy was sometimes essential for functional advocacy. Brokers recognized that partnerships that did not leave some room for adaptation and informality were unlikely to make headway in countries where work with Northern groups was risky.

When Partners Had Different Values, Politics, and Standards

A third complication with partnership arose when brokers' values, politics, or standards differed from those of their partners. Brokers believed in local leadership, but had other ideological investments as well. When partners did not share commitments to values like inclusivity or accountability, these investments became highly salient.

A core function of partnership was to minimize Northern imperialism by ensuring that in-country activists and NGOs retained the ultimate say on political strategy. The association of partnership with self-determination offered little guidance to brokers who found they philosophically disagreed with partners' approaches, and elided the real difficulties of negotiating disagreements when they occurred.[34] The idea that respect for self-determination can sit uneasily with other values is not new,[35] but is rarely acknowledged when nondirective partnership is touted as a structuring mechanism for transnational work.

One of the most routine sticking points in partnerships was inclusivity. Brokers at IGLHRC advocated for populations across the LGBT spectrum, not only representing gay men, but also lesbian, transgender, and bisexual persons. Not all partners had the same constituencies. CEDEP, for example, focused on MSM and HIV, and seemed to do little with WSW or self-identified trans populations. Although CEDEP was the best-placed organization for brokers to liaise with regarding Chimbalanga and Monjeza's trial, that partnership was not necessarily an investment in outreach to LBT women in Malawi.

IGLHRC's partnership in Haiti sparked active discussions about inclusivity and the limits of the nation-state as a frame for intervention. On January 13, 2010, brokers arrived at work to blanket coverage of the previous day's earthquake in Haiti. Just four months before, Johnson had visited Haiti and met with SEROvie, an NGO promoting HIV prevention, treatment, and care to MSM in the country.

The earthquake destroyed SEROvie's office in Port-au-Prince and killed a number of its members and clients. In response to a query from Johnson, SEROvie's executive director replied:

> We were having our usual support group meeting on a quiet Tuesday afternoon when the worst happened. The sound is unforgettable. I can't even describe the horror as the ceiling and the wall of the conference room started to fall and the chaos started.[36]

Although disaster response was not part of IGLHRC's mandate, brokers met that morning and discussed how they might respond. Because IGL-HRC had a relationship with SEROvie and, importantly, considered it a partner, there was a palpable sense that something had to be done.

SEROvie was IGLHRC's established partner in Haiti, but brokers were conscious that it worked specifically with MSM. Many brokers suggested directing funds to Colectiva Mujer y Salud, a feminist group in the Dominican Republic that could ensure that aid reached women, including LBT women, in Haiti. Crucially, at the time, there were no known LBT or LGBT organizations in Haiti with whom brokers at IGLHRC could build partnerships.

A compromise was reached that was widely supported by brokers in which some financial support would be immediately sent to both SEROvie and Colectiva Mujer y Salud. An appeal for funds would be placed on IGLHRC's website and "e-blasted" to its mailing list, and those funds would be directed to SEROvie. The appeals had to be worded carefully; IGL-HRC would be legally obligated to provide the funds to the promised partner organization, and brokers would not have discretion to redirect funds to organizations that might be more capable of reaching particular populations as circumstances changed.

In April, Johnson, Ferreyra, and Fox, a French speaker, delivered tents, supplies, and safer-sex materials to SEROvie. In an interview after the trip, Fox highlighted how the partnership with SEROvie shaped which communities IGLHRC reached out to following the disaster:

> I think the fact that SEROvie was an established partner of ours made it easier to connect with the MSM side of this issue. Once we were on the ground, I don't think we did enough legwork in terms of getting in touch with feminist organizations or LBT individuals. And so once we were there, we only ultimately ended up meeting with three LBT civil society individuals, and one OSI staff member who sort of spoke about the feminist and LBT side of the earthquake.

Partnership shaped IGLHRC's response to the earthquake in myriad ways. Because SEROvie was an established partner, brokers swiftly began raising funds for its recovery. They expressed a contemporaneous commitment to equality and inclusivity across the LGBT spectrum by wiring money to feminist activists. When SEROvie was better equipped to receive funds, however, it was SEROvie, as a partner and a Haitian organization, that received IGLHRC's larger donation and hosted its visit to Haiti. SEROvie and IGLHRC's subsequent publication on LGBT persons in postdisaster contexts featured the testimony and experiences of MSM, but also incorporated research into challenges facing LBT women.[37]

The emphasis on inclusivity was one of many of ideological commitments brokers held. They were suspicious of sexism, racism, classism, and nationalism, and, in New York, were largely secular. They voiced support for reproductive rights and a range of sexual rights, including sex workers' rights and access to abortion. They decried assimilation, with many of their domestic commitments rooted in more radical queer politics. Some of their most respected partners were those who shared those commitments.

Brokers were also committed to organizational values that informed their partnerships.[38] They were reluctant to work with activists who were suspected of misappropriating or misusing funds. NGOs with a reputation for good financial management were often better able to weather funding changes than those whose reputations were mixed.[39] Concepts of accountability, representativeness, transparency, and good governance—which Kate Bedford calls "the new common sense of our times" in development work[40]—were all standards to which partners were held, and self-aggrandizement, patronage, and other practices were viewed with disdain.

All of these challenges highlight the limits of partnership as a structuring device for transnational work. Because IGLHRC's partnerships were largely along national lines—with SMUG in Uganda, CEDEP in Malawi, or SEROvie in Haiti—they provided a helpful tool to level North–South power disparities, but sometimes prevented brokers from insisting on their own values, intervening on behalf of marginalized populations, or imposing standards to which they expected partners to be held accountable. The renunciation of imperialism, expressed through a staunch commitment to partnership, often made these sorts of complex interventions more difficult.

When There Were Multiple and Competing Partners

A fourth stumbling block arose in countries with multiple NGOs, where potential partners—and their viewpoints—were varied and frequently in conflict. This diversity of actors and agendas can prove difficult to navigate, particularly when the politics of transnational NGOs steer brokers in contradictory directions.[41]

It is increasingly common for multiple groups to advocate for LGBT rights in any given country. Brokers typically turned to partners with whom they had worked in the past or, in the absence of such groups, those who were most visibly identified with LGBT issues. As new groups emerged, these preferences could function to keep brokers from working with alternative partners with different assessments, priorities, and strategies.

During my fieldwork, IGLHRC's responses to two high-profile incidents illustrated how brokers navigated a field of possible partners. One of these was the tabling of Uganda's Anti-Homosexuality Bill, which contained numerous provisions that not only targeted LGBT people, but human rights defenders and civil society more generally. Both male-male and female-female sexual activity are legally prohibited in Uganda under the Penal Code Act of 1950, using language that remains virtually standardized in former British colonies.[42] The draft Anti-Homosexuality Bill further prescribed life in prison for anyone who "touches another person with the intention of committing the act of homosexuality." It permitted the imprisonment of anyone who "aids, abets, counsels, or procures another to engage in acts of homosexuality," "promotes homosexuality," or fails to report violations of the law within twenty-four hours. The bill drew fire from human rights defenders for proposing to void Uganda's adherence to any treaty or agreement that contradicted the law, and rejected any recognition of the concepts of sexual orientation, gender identity, sexual rights, and sexual minorities within Uganda.[43] It was the death penalty, however, that was most often highlighted internationally. Activists and journalists dubbed the legislation the "Kill the Gays Bill" because of a provision to punish "aggravated homosexuality," including same-sex activity by a person who is HIV positive or a repeat offender, with death.[44]

The legislation, which David Bahati introduced as a Private Member's Bill, galvanized a wide network of human rights and civil society NGOs. Brokers at IGLHRC, however, had been working with Ugandan activists for years. Thanks to Mukasa's deep ties to the country's movement, IGLHRC raised concern about increased homophobia in Uganda as early as March 2009—seven months before the bill was tabled—after American evangelicals traveled to Uganda to hold a three-day seminar on homosexuality. At the seminar, Scott Lively, Don Schmierer, and Caleb Lee Brundidge described the threat that LGBT persons posed to the social fabric and suggested they could be cured and saved. Activists from SMUG monitored the conference, and SMUG and IGLHRC publicly warned of the likelihood that anti-LGBT sentiment in Uganda would rise.[45]

Thanks to their prior work in Uganda, IGLHRC and other human rights organizations became aware of the bill before it was tabled, and were able to obtain details of the draft legislation. As a result, IGLHRC, HRW, AI, ARC International, and other NGOs were ready to immediately respond to the tabling of the bill by releasing a prepared statement condemning the legislation and warning of its adverse effects, which was endorsed by Akina Mama wa Afrika and the Uganda Feminist Forum. Within days, IGLHRC and SMUG issued an action alert. Ugandan groups were busy responding to the bill as well, forming the Civil Society Coalition on Human Rights and Constitutional Law. The Coalition provided a united front for domestic groups who approached the issues raised by the bill in different ways.

IGLHRC worked with the Coalition, but SMUG, a long-standing partner in Uganda, guided most of IGLHRC's advocacy. One of SMUG's earliest requests was for a day of concerted international action against the bill, designed to raise awareness in the North and convey opposition to Ugandan missions around the globe. The request received some pushback from brokers at IGLHRC, who worried that the date was too soon to organize a large, safe, and well-publicized protest. SMUG altered the original request; it maintained its call for international pressure, but extended the period for the actions. With the African Services Committee, Health GAP, and ACT-UP Philadelphia, I helped coordinate a protest outside of the Ugandan Mission to the UN while other groups protested in Washington, D.C. Additional protests were hosted by groups in San Francisco, Chicago, London, Pretoria, Beirut, and elsewhere.

Throughout the bill's lifespan, brokers instinctively turned to SMUG for guidance. When right-wing pastor Lou Engle planned to visit Kampala to hold a rally dubbed "TheCall: Uganda," a network of U.S.-based pro-LGBT faith groups launched a campaign called "Stop TheCall to Violence." Engle was known for his militant rhetoric decrying homosexuality in the United States, and brokers worried that a rally in Kampala, preceded by weeks of fasting, would trigger a lethal backlash. As IGLHRC's representative in the network, I was asked if Ugandan groups thought a campaign in the United States would be helpful or whether publicity would do more harm than good. Rather than reaching out to the Coalition, faith leaders in Uganda, or prominent figures like Sylvia Tamale of Makerere University, I was advised by Johnson to contact SMUG for their opinion. Ultimately, I worked with

SMUG throughout the campaign to coordinate publicity and messaging, and conveyed their preferences to faith-based groups in the United States.

The preference for trusted allies in a field of possible partners was not limited to Uganda. In Malawi, early statements supporting Chimbalanga and Monjeza did not only come from CEDEP, but from the Centre for Human Rights and Rehabilitation (CHRR), a mainstream human rights NGO in Malawi. Yet throughout the arrest, detention, and trial of the couple, CEDEP remained IGLHRC's trusted source of information about their well-being, Chimbalanga's preferred name and gender identity, and the desirability of possible interventions. It was CEDEP who called for a letter-writing campaign to the couple in prison; brokers at IGLHRC obliged by launching a postcard campaign at the annual Celebration of Courage gala.

The partnership with CEDEP was particularly notable because other alliances might have called for different strategies. After Chimbalanga and Monjeza were pardoned, many members of CEDEP were eager to shrug off the notoriety they endured during the trial and return to their work with MARPs. As Johnson stressed in a posttrial statement, however, the pardon was only a partial victory.[46] The conviction itself was not overturned, and same-sex activity remained illegal in Malawi. Structurally, nothing had changed to make LGBT people better off in the country. (Indeed, months later, the government criminalized same-sex activity between women.) Some activists and lawyers in Malawi echoed Johnson's assessment, and argued that NGOs should press ahead with a legal challenge to have the law against same-sex activity ruled unconstitutional. Others noted that this not only could backfire in the form of a negative judgment but could prolong or exacerbate anti-LGBT sentiment and security concerns. Deferring to CEDEP, brokers at IGLHRC opted not to pursue a legal challenge, and to focus on the well-being of activists at risk.

In crowded fields of active NGOs, partnership was necessarily selective. In Uganda, brokers at IGLHRC had worked with SMUG for years and considered it a strong, trusted representative of Ugandan LGBT communities. In Malawi, IGLHRC had worked with CEDEP on a number of projects, and acquiesced to its strategic advice. In both cases, brokers worked most closely with known partners they considered part of a larger LGBT movement rather than civil society or human rights organizations that were just emerging on their institutional radar.

What this means for "partnership" as a principle is complex. As supportive networks grew, IGLHRC's preference for trusted partners meant these groups typically guided its advocacy. At times, this gave brokers leeway to use tactics they preferred, as long-standing partners were usually most familiar and comfortable with the types of pressure they typically employed. As young NGOs flourish, however, questions about who IGLHRC's partners are, whether they represent a wider movement, and under what conditions brokers might break with them—or allow input from alternative partners to guide their work—become increasingly urgent.

When Potential Partners Were Self-Sufficient

When partners are disbanded, covert, or multiple, coordinating advocacy can be complex. A different kind of challenge arises when partners are well-defined, but also able to clearly decline Northern offers to engage.

One widely publicized crisis in early 2010 was a raid on the Kenya Medical Research Institute (KEMRI) in Mtwapa, a small town along the coast north of Mombasa, Kenya. After a radio station reported unsubstantiated rumors of a same-sex wedding, two religious leaders, Sheikh Ali Hussein and Bishop Lawrence Chai, called for KEMRI to be shut down for providing services to homosexuals. Over the next few days, mobs assembled at KEMRI and attacked individuals in Mtwapa and Mombasa. Victims in many incidents were taken into protective custody to keep them from being injured or killed by the crowds.

The mobs were reported in a number of African and international press outlets. HRW issued a press release and letter to the government of Kenya demanding a stop to the "anti-gay campaign." IGLHRC remained conspicuously silent. For days, a statement on the website, posted on February 12, 2010, simply read:

> There are conflicting media reports of mob violence and arrests at what was alleged to be a "gay wedding" in Kikambala, Kenya on February 12. IGLHRC is consulting closely with partners in Kenya to respond appropriately to any emergency situations.[47]

The next update from Kenya appeared six months later, when a local group, G-Trust, launched a new book on gay rights.

Behind the scenes, the incidents in Kenya sparked a standard response. Johnson, Jones, and Kilonzo communicated about the reported episodes and contacted Kenyan organizations, including GALCK, a coalition with which brokers had worked since its founding in 2006. GALCK functioned as an umbrella group for a host of MSM, WSW, LGBT, and sexual rights organizations in Kenya, and had worked with IGLHRC on various research projects and interventions. In this instance, however, GALCK opted to work primarily on their own, communicating updates to IGLHRC and others while liaising with police to set up response mechanisms when LGBT people were at risk. GALCK and IGLHRC did coauthor a letter to the Kenyan government and a press release, but as other initiatives took priority, these were never publicly released. As events unfolded, IGLHRC was also approached by an organization based in the area of the attack, which requested its assistance through Johnson. In this instance, the different opinions and priorities of a national coalition and a grassroots group complicated whether and how brokers in Cape Town and New York might discourage further violence against the LGBT community in Mtwapa.

From New York, time zones, technology, and conflicting reports made it difficult to distinguish fact from fiction, determine what brokers could say publicly, and establish what, if anything, would be helpful or counterproductive. From the Africa Program, however, GALCK's ability to take the lead and navigate the crisis was an important triumph. According to Kilonzo, who was herself Kenyan:

> The other day, the team from Kenya telling IGLHRC, there's this crisis, everybody acknowledges there's a crisis, but we would like to respond on our own—I think that was my moment of pride. To see a movement that has grown from its formative stages, taking the World Social Forum in 2007 head-on, a lot of hate speeches followed by them registering and standing on their feet, to a point that they are able to stand on their own and tell the world, hey, hold on here [with] your intervention, we're able to respond. And they did respond. And within a week, the crisis had come and gone. That was superb, and for me, that was showing how a well-organized movement can be able to have mechanisms to respond to the worst of the crises. And it's not dependent on outside support. And when you insist on issuing a statement they will either disown you or tell you to your face to stop being imperialistic, because they know they have learned from you—that is good—but let them now practice what they have learned.

For Kilonzo, who, aside from being Kenyan, had always worked in an African context, GALCK's self-sufficiency was a positive development. It showed movements were growing stronger, and were ready to confront daunting challenges. For Johnson, it raised foundational questions about IGLHRC's evolving role in transnational LGBT networks and where it might continue to add value with its limited resources.

As GALCK grew and became increasingly empowered to spearhead responses to incidents happening in Kenya, it also generated important questions about whether IGLHRC could work with other in-country groups. Shortly after this incident, members of GALCK became upset when a broker at IGLHRC with strong ties to the Kenyan LGBT movement reached out to an activist at one of GALCK's constituent organizations, asking to partner on a project. Some activists in the national coalition were reportedly upset that this overture was made without going through them; they felt such a proposal was to be vetted collectively, and the money handled by the coalition. As a result, the project did not proceed. The incident was a valuable lesson for the New York and the Cape Town offices, and seemed to be taken to heart by both. As Johnson pointed out, however, it raised important questions about IGLHRC's role in countries with strong umbrella organizations or networks.

The growth of regional LGBT networks has raised similar questions regarding who can be considered potential partners for which efforts, and which groups or issues are effectively off-limits for one-on-one cooperation with IGLHRC. As Kilonzo described in an interview in 2010:

> With a very strong pan-African lesbian organization in the name of CAL, and now, a very strong gay movement in the name of AMSHeR, they are edging us out and saying, if you want to work on MSM or HIV, we have the network. You can collaborate with us or partner with us, but you cannot go behind our back to start working with the same countries we're working with. We have to be partners in this. You may have the resources in big numbers, but we have the people. So if you need to use your money and big numbers, you need the people who we have. And this has been the challenge. When the pan-African groups don't do much, then how do you check each other? And for us, as an international organization, how do we go above the petty politics of individuals and emerging organizations to still be able to offer the technical assistance? . . . It's that back and forth questioning of our relevance, but also the challenge that there are certain things that maybe we could have done very well five years ago, but now the presence of other actors that are more legitimate, they have the masses. They may not have it physically, but their word is respected within the region.

The limits of partnership were felt acutely when regional networks were ill-equipped or reluctant to work on projects that IGLHRC and potential partners were eager to undertake together. In these instances, a simple dichotomy of North and South was insufficient. There were multiple players with distinctive affinities, priorities, and capacities, and partnering with one could effectively foreclose the possibility of partnering with others. In these instances, IGLHRC's commitment to partnership proved frustrating for brokers who deferred to groups that claimed national or thematic representativeness, but declined to work with Northern NGOs.

CONCLUSION

Within IGLHRC, a high premium was placed on "strong" partnerships, where groups in the South were stable, visible, compatible, credible, and eager to collaborate. Some groups readily embodied this kind of partnership. Others developed partnerships gradually, as they and brokers at IGLHRC found ways to mutually accommodate each other's constituencies, politics, and standards. Both approaches were reinforced by ideological and political affinities and networks of NGOs, donors, and journalists who legitimated activists by looking to them as representatives of or experts on their community.

Challenges to that model triggered a range of responses as brokers sought to uphold partnership's underlying values. After the Senegal fiasco, brokers met with stakeholders to determine whether IGLHRC could be helpful in their work, and began planning a leadership exchange with Cameroonian activists. In the MENA region, brokers had ongoing conversations to identify ways of working on sexual rights that were not predicated on identity politics, visibility, and lobbying. In Uganda, brokers deepened ties with actors besides SMUG, and strengthened alliances through other projects, like Perle visiting Uganda to assist FARUG with a shadow report for CEDAW. These reorientations suggest that stumbling blocks in partnership are not fatal, but inspire their own tactical shifts in transnational LGBT advocacy.

The inadequacy of rigid, formalized models of partnership illustrates the need to think critically about broader notions of political responsibility.[48] While partnership was strongly valued, brokers had little guidance when relationships proved challenging. In many cases, they faced a field of partners with distinct backgrounds, structures, and agendas, whose relationships and intramovement politics were not always immediately apparent. These existed within a wider field of feminist, HIV, and human rights groups in different countries, who occasionally aligned more closely with IGLHRC's ideals of what a good partner might look like. When a group was "the only game in town," brokers had to determine what form their relationship might take, and decide whether to defer to them, to negotiate troubling dynamics, or to work with them minimally or not at all, often at the expense of any advocacy within their country. In cases where IGL-HRC lacked strong, independent partners in a country, brokers faced the dilemma of trying to determine how the partnership principle might be upheld, if at all, and what obligation they had to speak up or remain silent about violations as they came to light. In these instances, a narrow focus on partnership along a North–South axis obscured complex and critical questions of power, responsibility, and accountability that brokers grappled with daily in their work.

5 Knowledge as Power

The Structural and Strategic Complexities of Information Politics

On July 5, 2010, Reverend Erich Kasirye e-mailed activists to report that the disembodied head of a gay activist, Pasikali Kashusbe, had been found in a pit latrine on a farm in rural Uganda. According to the e-mail, Pasikali, a member of the pro-LGBT Anglican group Integrity Uganda, had been missing for nearly a month prior to the gruesome discovery. About five hundred meters away from the latrine, a mutilated torso without genitals had also been found. The story rapidly spread through the blogosphere and was reprinted by publications like the *Advocate,* where it offered a grisly example of the terror and violence LGBT Ugandans faced during the debate over the Anti-Homosexuality Bill.[1]

What ultimately made headlines, however, was the discovery that the incident was a hoax. On July 7, 2010, Mukasa contacted Bishop Ssenyonjo, the head of Integrity Uganda quoted in the story, and confirmed the report was carefully falsified. Authors of the e-mail were said to have used it for their own material gain, and fabricated facts, quotes, and a police report to do so. In an e-mail from SMUG, Ssenyonjo clarified:

> I have never worked with anyone who goes by the name Pasikali in my organization. I also did not make any comments as quoted in earlier statements made by Rev. Erich Kasirye. Rev. Erich Kasirye no longer has any legitimate connection to Integrity Uganda and the e-mail address integrityuganda@yahoo.com is no longer available as a link to the leadership of Integrity Uganda.

When faced with the suspicious claim, Mukasa intervened to verify what had happened. A working relationship with the leader of Integrity Uganda allowed him to detect the hoax and reveal it to the media. After doing so, Mukasa returned to more pressing work.

Even so, several questions remained unanswered. Activists offhandedly mentioned that a head *had* been found in a latrine—and the beheading of one Pascal Kashushu was reported by the *Daily Monitor* on July 4—it just did not belong to an LGBT activist.[2] Whose head was it? Were earlier reports of Reverend Henry Kayizzi Nsubuga disappearing after a pro-LGBT sermon, and the search parties discovering a separated torso and head, themselves true, or also a hoax? More poignantly, without the implication that these grisly incidents were linked to the Anti-Homosexuality Bill, who still cared? How were human rights activists, to say nothing of their ethnographers, to get to the bottom of incidents reported in tense, volatile climates, where the personal and political stakes were high?

As a research fellow, I struggled with the uncertainty that brokers confront on a near-daily basis. In light of incidents like the hoax in Uganda, my hesitation was partly pragmatic; from a desk in New York or Cape Town, it was never possible to know exactly what was happening in crisis situations. Like my informants, however, I also worried whether I was accurately representing groups in the Global South. Ethnographers have convincingly highlighted the limitations of putatively global models in local settings.[3] Brokers at IGLHRC recognized that sexual identities, behaviors, and politics are contingent and dynamic, but faced the challenge of reconciling that understanding with a public insistence on universal standards.

One of IGLHRC's primary, if untouted, activities was generating and disseminating information about SOGI and human rights. Anthropologists examining dissemination have incisively traced how sexual identities and concepts like "Pride" or "coming out" have diffused globally, either through sweeping phenomena like "global queering" or through the advocacy of LGBT networks.[4] As Tom Boellstorff and William Leap observe, these analyses tend to "assume a Western source, and a one-way movement of material and intellectual commodities from that source toward a recipient framed as 'more distant.'"[5] A comprehensive understanding of advocacy requires a more capacious examination of networks and interdependence beyond the global–local dyad.[6]

To this end, anthropologists might consider another side of information politics: how Northern NGOs gather, process, and redeploy information from the South. In this chapter, I explore how pragmatic constraints and the persistence of doubt among Northern brokers practically shape the promotion of LGBT human rights transnationally. Like governments, religious figures, legal and medical professionals, journalists, and other NGOs who shaped discourses about sexuality, brokers trafficked information using the resources and tools available to them. Situating brokers' advocacy in this context is critical for the development of nuanced critiques and solidarity politics alike.

Power/Knowledge in the Human Rights Arena

One of the primary functions of transnational advocacy networks is to transmit information.[7] Within these networks, however, both the information generated and how it circulates are shaped by underlying discursive regimes. In transnational LGBT advocacy, Northern brokers operate through a very specific alignment of legal, sexual, and bureaucratic frames. When asserting human rights claims, legal and moral imperatives shape who is recognized as a "victim," what is recognized as a "violation," and who is deemed blameworthy or responsible for providing redress.[8] Other implicit understandings shape what behaviors, identities, and relationships are recognized as "sexual" in a plural and porous world.[9] Information is also shaped by the bureaucratic setting of an NGO. Concepts like "accountability," "good governance," and "transparency" are not culturally neutral; they have specific meanings and often counsel outsiders to perceive locally acceptable practices, like patronage, in a particular light.[10]

The conjunction of these frames determined where brokers sought information and what they recognized as usable. Brokers' sexual politics and professional ethics encouraged them to turn to their partners, particularly those who embraced inclusivity, accountability, transparency, and rigor in their work. For their legal and political advocacy, brokers typically sought information that related to legal wrongs, was believable and verifiable, and could be shared without serious repercussions.

Many of IGLHRC's tactics depended on the possession of timely, credible information. Crafting action alerts, letters to governments, and reports required collaborative research, documentation, and verification to ensure that campaigning was warranted and politically savvy. Credibility was a core part of IGLHRC's brand, and brokers stressed that they were uniquely positioned to get accurate, timely information from those most proximate to events on the ground.[11]

To funders and policymakers, this was a key source of IGLHRC's utility as a U.S.-based NGO. In the organization's twentieth anniversary video,

Representative Frank made a point of praising IGLHRC for bringing the urgent needs of LGBT populations to the attention of policymakers around the globe. IGLHRC's alerts and publications; convenings, Activist Institutes, and research projects; and advocacy at the UN and regional mechanisms all translated the experiences of partners into political and legal arenas.

Brokers characterized this ability to link the grassroots to policymakers as a unique contribution to transnational networks—something IGLHRC has sought to achieve since Dorf gave her ragtag organization its officious-sounding title. As Perle mused in an interview:

> Because we're U.S.-based, because we have a certain appearance of professionalism, we're really trusted by people in governments, people in international organizations, and they trust our expertise. They don't have the resources or the willingness to go to every single group on the ground, and sort out all the different opinions, and the different in-fighting, and the different ways people are doing work. Nobody is going to have the capacity to do that, whereas that's what we do. And we work really closely with people on the ground, and we can take that information, or take people, or appoint people, or help people get access to these leaders who do actually do things. . . . I really think we're effective in talking to leaders because they trust us. Whether they should or not, I don't know, but they do. And someone has to be in that role. I think now there are a number of organizations that are, but certainly we're the only U.S.-based one doing that, and one of the few at the UN.

As neoliberal globalization shifts the logic of transnational advocacy "away from representation and toward expertise,"[12] trafficking in knowledge has become central to Northern NGO mandates. Amid intensifying attention to LGBT rights globally, brokers felt their long-standing relationships with local movements equipped them to understand unfolding episodes and trends, and to convey these insights to other actors.

Brokers took their connective function seriously, and when I arrived at IGLHRC, a colleague wryly tutored me on how *not* to do it. He recounted how a former employee had received a query from a reporter about conditions facing LGBT persons in Bermuda. To the horror of other brokers, she asked staff to "Google Bermuda" to find out what was happening so they could supply a quote. As the broker animatedly recounted the anecdote, those present in the room sighed and rolled their eyes at the irresponsibility of the response.

Brokers were outwardly skeptical of their ability to speak to conditions in other countries in anything but the broadest of terms; instead, they characterized their role as amplifying and publicizing information from their partners. Having access to timely, firsthand, on-the-ground knowledge about conditions facing LGBT people in a location made IGLHRC a trusted source for policymakers, and IGLHRC's apparent influence with these actors was crucial in convincing Southern partners to supply brokers with information.

That dynamic, in which information and influence were mutually reinforcing, lay at the crux of IGLHRC's advocacy. The concept of power/knowledge has been used by theorists to highlight how both sides of that dyadic construction function in tandem. As Michel Foucault describes the conjunction:

> There can be no possible exercise of power without a certain economy of discourses of truth which operates through and on the basis of this association. We are subjected to the production of truth through power and we cannot exercise power except through the production of truth.[13]

The concept of power/knowledge illustrates why an exclusive preoccupation with the hegemony of Northern or global NGOs is inadequate. Power disparities do shape outcomes when purportedly universal academic, public health, or human rights discourses collide with localized understandings.[14] What power/knowledge adds, however, is a richer understanding of the ways in which the power of Northern or global NGOs fundamentally depends on engagement, input, and affirmation from the South.

Recognizing this mutual imbrication sheds light on the mechanics and limitations of Northern advocacy. As a U.S.-based organization with limited staff capacity in its regional programs, IGLHRC was not logistically or financially able to cover parts of the world in equal measure. Nobody was assigned to Europe or North America, and in IGLHRC's regional programs, between one and four brokers covered whole continents with multiple movements and situations vying for their attention. Furthermore, laws regulating gender and sexuality were fairly opaque. Figures on the number of states that criminalize same-sex sexuality and the number of states where such activity is punishable by death, two perennial indices of LGBT human rights globally, were only approximated by brokers at IGLHRC. Some NGOs did attempt to track and document this data with some regularity; HRW's report on sodomy laws was often cited by activists pressing for law reform, and ILGA put out an annual survey of laws regulating same-sex sexuality.[15] Little was certainly or comprehensively known, however, about laws regarding dress, blasphemy, hooliganism, loitering, solicitation, or other offenses that were (mis)used to persecute people on the basis of SOGI.

During my fieldwork, IGLHRC did not comprehensively compile information about what the laws were in particular countries, what the punishments were in different places, or whether particular areas were better or worse for LGBT people than others. Asking different brokers elicited different responses on each of these questions. When I was preparing to speak to a group of students and asked if IGLHRC had a standardized position on where and how same-sex sexuality was criminalized, I was told to use ILGA's data from that year, with the caveat that there were thought to be some gaps or outdated information in it. As Kilonzo noted, IGLHRC lacked the personnel and resources to gather information firsthand, whether this was regarding laws on the books or the facts of an alleged violation, and relied on partners:

> It's hard, because if you look at other organizations, they've had to send their own person to the field to either do the research or go and confirm particular facts before they can release that to the world. And that is an expensive venture because sending somebody from Country A to Country B in this particular region is quite expensive. [IGLHRC's model is] having a contact person on the ground, and being in constant communication to verify those grounds. First of all, it adds a lot to legitimacy. It also helps to build the capacity of that person and hopefully the group where they work from, on how to do a press release, how to document the issues as they unfold. . . . So going to the field directly, we do it when it's absolutely necessary. We'd rather work with different activists from different countries. That is more empowering.

Brokers' advocacy depended on the insights their partners provided them. Rather than sending a researcher, brokers relied on partnerships, typically mediated through IGLHRC's regional programs, to confirm facts, guide strategy, and authorize any interventions by transnational actors. Partners were supposed to be able to supply up-to-date information about developments on the ground, which often differed markedly from media reports.

For their part, brokers were able to raise the profiles of local partners and link them to opportunities in the North. IGLHRC published research by its partners; supported their travel to summits in New York, Washington, San Francisco, Geneva, and Vienna; helped them obtain passports and visas; connected them to policymakers, funders, and diplomats; amplified their issues; and mobilized public and private pressure when they were under threat. While brokers stressed that IGLHRC was not a funder, they influenced traffic in money, opportunities, and status that could be materially or symbolically important for partners.

In this economy of power/knowledge, brokers provided the benefits of partnership in exchange for information and insights from local groups.[16] The ways this occurred in practice were structured by incentives for both sides, and the different material and symbolic resources they were able to manipulate. As ethnographers of transnational workshops in post-Soviet Russia have emphasized, "When resources are not understood merely as narrowly economic, it is easier to see that the career and organization-building effects of such transnational involvements are typically reciprocal."[17] Brokers were aware of these dynamics, and managed them regularly. Fox, who carried out interviews in Haiti, reflected:

> It's always interesting for me to see the interaction between the leadership of community organizations in-country and the leadership of international organizations, and what the power dynamic is there. What is it that we have that they want, what is it that they have that we want? Obviously, we both want to work together, but there's still questions of resources and authority that play out.

This mutual accommodation was not specific to that trip. As Ettelbrick described it, negotiating these dynamics was a routine aspect of transnational work:

> I mean, there's understandable push and pull, often, with local groups who want to be independent. To be honest, I think a lot of them know that they have to work with the U.S. groups because it means money or whatever. And as long as you're aware of that, you know that that shouldn't be abused, you shouldn't use your ability to make the money thing happen for groups as a quid pro quo. You get embroiled a little bit in the psychology of that kind of almost colonial dynamic.

As both quotes suggest, brokers felt local groups were not unaware of these dynamics, and also used them to their advantage. The remarks speak to the implicit understanding of power/knowledge that structured IGLHRC's relationships. IGLHRC's work simply would not be possible without information from partners in the South, who were called on to verify facts and legitimate any intervention that brokers might undertake. For their part, partners understood that a working relationship with IGLHRC had the potential to deliver material and political benefits.

The relational aspect of information politics was only part of IGLHRC's work, however. As brokers generated and deployed information, they still faced two distinctive sets of concerns. First, brokers operated under *structural* constraints, some self-imposed, in their compilation and dissemination of information. In sifting through what was literally a world of information, brokers utilized particular networks, languages, and technologies that made some voices and accounts more audible and intelligible than others. Second, brokers grappled with *strategic* uncertainty, harboring lingering questions about the validity of information and the likely repercussions it would have in the world. In their transnational work, doubt was never eradicated, but could be minimized and managed. Although these sets of concerns overlap, it is useful to consider each in turn.

IGLHRC's Role in Producing Information

Brokers incorporated information from partners into the various outputs described in chapter 2, including updates, action alerts, letters to governments, press releases, and reports. These outputs were designed both to publicize the struggles of LGBT activists around the globe and to highlight the ways that brokers supported them. They were critical in establishing IGLHRC's credibility as an up-to-date, dynamic source of information on LGBT human rights transnationally. Where this information was circulated and who received it was subtly shaped by the use of particular networks, languages, and technologies that affected how it was collected and disseminated, which in turn influenced the political repercussions of IGLHRC's outputs.

Network Politics and LGBT Human Rights

The fields of human rights and LGBT politics influence the work of transnational brokers in complex ways. These are not static bodies of knowledge, however, and are constantly redefined and reanimated by a range of actors. In addition to human rights defenders, these include activists, legal and medical professionals, policymakers, diplomats, journalists, academics, faith leaders, artists, celebrities, and others who develop, champion, and criticize the bodies of knowledge and agendas with which brokers work.

The diverse actors engaging with LGBT human rights issues are important both because they produce knowledge and because they structure the flows and scapes through which this knowledge circulates globally.[18] Social movement theorists have pinpointed two channels—interpersonal interactions and depersonalized transmission through media—that shape the transnational diffusion of concepts, tactics, and strategies. Doug McAdam and Dieter Rucht helpfully define these as *relational* diffusion, mediated by "direct, interpersonal contact between transmitters and adopters," and *nonrelational* diffusion, or the spread of ideas and artifacts through the media and other impersonal channels.[19] Brokers at IGLHRC facilitated and grappled with both types of diffusion.

In terms of relational diffusion, brokers staged and participated in a number of forums where knowledge was shared among different groups and activists. Some of these were strategy sessions among organizations, including those to prepare for the side event at the UNGA for Human Rights Day on December 10, 2009, the LGBT/SOGI Human Rights Consultation on Ending the Exportation of Homophobia and Global Criminalization of Sexual Orientation and Gender Identity hosted by the UU-UNO on June 14, 2010, and the briefing on LGBT human rights and foreign policy at the U.S. State Department on June 22, 2010. Others were fairly high-level conferences and summits where host organizations and donors invited activists to attend, make presentations, and network with colleagues. In late 2009 and early 2010, these included the CSW in New York; the International Congress on Gender Identity and Human Rights in Barcelona; the International AIDS Conference in Vienna; and a summit to draft a proposal for the Global Fund to Fight AIDS, Tuberculosis, and Malaria in Johannesburg. The relational diffusion of knowledge was furthered through visits by individual activists, particularly from sub-Saharan Africa, to the North during this period. Meetings in the North allowed key figures in African LGBTI movements, including Julius Kaggwa, Val Kalende, and Frank Mugisha of Uganda; Gift Trapence of Malawi; and Sybille Nyeck of Cameroon, to liaise with activists, policymakers, and funders in the United States.

The nonrelational diffusion of information occurred more constantly. A core group of activists, professionals, and donors involved in transnational LGBT advocacy shared information on a listserv where news, calls to action, and job postings were posted on a daily basis. On this and other regional and national listservs, like Euro-Queer in Europe or Queer Talk in Kenya, the diffusion of ideas across borders was strikingly evident. IGLHRC had its own mailing list, website, and presence on Facebook and Twitter, allowing it to host and disseminate its outputs through its own channels.

Brokers at IGLHRC primarily used their website and mailing list to disseminate information, and these channels were accessed by particular segments of their many potential audiences. The heaviest traffic to IGLHRC's website during my fieldwork was not related to issues like Uganda's Anti-Homosexuality Bill or the trial in Malawi—which were simultaneously covered by major media outlets—but to IGLHRC's own landmark bid for consultative status at ECOSOC and the stripping and subsequent restoration of the term "sexual orientation" to a standing resolution in the UNGA on extrajudicial killings. IGLHRC was a unique source for information about its own battles at the UN, and its outputs informed larger discussions of these issues. By contrast, information about other LGBT human rights issues were not only found on IGLHRC's website, but could also be found in the press, from NGOs like AI or HRW, or from regional or domestic groups that were directly involved.

IGLHRC was thus embedded in a wide network of actors, in both the North and South, which shaped its production and circulation of information. Within the culturally and ideologically heterogeneous networks of sexual rights advocacy, IGLHRC relied on personal and virtual relationships to gather knowledge, and set forth that knowledge in a field populated by actors who challenged, corroborated, or drowned out its accounts. The networks through which IGLHRC gathered and set out information were influential, but other structural factors also influenced how knowledge traveled to and from New York, Buenos Aires, Cape Town, and Manila.

The Linguistic Limits of Advocacy at IGLHRC

Brokers' awareness of human rights violations around the globe was most obviously circumscribed by linguistic competencies. For brokers to be privy to breaking news about violations globally, they had to be monitoring local news regularly and able to comprehend the language in which it was disseminated. IGLHRC did not contract with any media-monitoring firms during my fieldwork. In the contexts of Asia and Africa, regions with sizable Anglophone communities, news would typically break and then be relayed to staff by English-language media or an English-speaking activist or journalist. In the LAC and MENA regions, brokers received reports from community members and read independent local media in their language of origin. The linguistic capacity of brokers also affected their work in more subtle ways. The partners that the Asia and Africa staff worked with closely were overwhelmingly Anglophone, or headed by individuals who were at least reasonably fluent in English, whereas the LAC and MENA programs were staffed by brokers who primarily worked in Spanish and Persian.[20]

One factor that consistently shaped how brokers circulated knowledge was the near-exclusive use of English in their published materials.[21] During my fieldwork, limited resources constrained IGLHRC's ability to translate all of its materials, and this was a source of genuine concern for brokers. When IGLHRC produced written outputs, these often were linguistically specific. In trainings, conference calls, e-mails, and other communications, brokers used their own language skills, translators, and other strategies to enable them to work in other languages.[22] The regional offices had distinctive linguistic competencies, although they remained stymied by the full range of linguistic diversity in their regions. In an interview, Kilonzo detailed how this shaped the Africa Program:

> Right now, we're mostly in Anglophone Africa because of the challenge of language, but also outreach in Francophone is quite difficult. And I think we've taken the easier option of not investing in Francophone. There's still need of Lusophone—Angola, Mozambique, Cape Verde—but it's on a small scale as against Francophone. We seriously need a West African Anglophone person to just comb the environment there and just advise us on what exactly needs to be done.

Language served to carve advocacy in the Africa Program into discrete parts, with some regions effectively off-limits to brokers who did not have the requisite linguistic capacity. The multiplicity of languages was even more challenging for brokers in the API Program. The region was rich with languages and dialects, and the finite linguistic capacity of just two brokers from Malaysia and the Philippines had marked effects on their advocacy.

In the MENA Program, Alizadeh saw this not only as a logistical problem, but a political one:

> I have a problem with an organization that only communicates in one language. That simply means that you're not talking to the people. In the Middle

East, illiteracy is a huge problem. In countries [where] you have 70 or 80 percent of people illiterate, the knowledge of English is a luxury, limited to a very, very top elite. . . . They speak the language, they play the game very well, they use the language that is very appealing to the donors and the internationals, so they get all the resources, and they come across as legitimate—the reality is, they have no legitimacy with the people, you know?

Brokers acknowledged that the ubiquity of English in IGLHRC's work was problematic. IGLHRC's written outputs were often inaccessible to non-Anglophone audiences, and potentially confusing to those unfamiliar with the technical concepts and terminology of the human rights system. Information was especially inaccessible to those who were not Anglophone, Hispanophone, or Francophone. At the same time, brokers sought to make local voices intelligible to domestic and supranational bodies that used English as their lingua franca. IGLHRC's investment in translating the shadow reports that local groups produced for the CEDAW Committee, for example, was meant to ensure that linguistic differences did not prevent documentation and analysis from reaching a wider audience.

The challenge of translating materials into other languages was a concern that was frequently raised by brokers, who were often frustrated by the financial, personnel, and logistical pressures that made widespread translation impossible. In many instances, the result was a compromise with the resources available. When *Words of Hate, Climate of Fear* was in the final stages of production, for example, a volunteer translator notified IGLHRC they would no longer be able to help with the project, which had taken longer than originally expected. The cost of hiring a professional to translate the report into French far exceeded the amount that had been budgeted. Upon becoming program director, Jones argued that it was still important to translate as much of the report as possible into French and, ideally, Wolof. Johnson agreed in principle, but was also conscious of the financial constraints on the report. At Johnson's suggestion, the full report in English was accompanied by a four-page executive summary in French that included key findings and recommendations to the government, regional bodies, and NGOs in the region.

This was not an atypical solution. Brokers made a conscious effort to translate materials for the people they concerned; most coverage of Turkey was translated into Turkish, and most coverage of Latin America was translated into Spanish. It was rarely suggested, however, that the same coverage might be translated into Mandarin, Russian, or Thai, both because IGL-HRC did not have projects where these languages were spoken and because brokers were conscious of resource constraints that made this infeasible. While non-Anglophone groups were occasionally able to access materials about their country in their language, particularly when they were involved in compiling or working on them, they were unable to access the full range of IGLHRC's materials to learn about work being carried out elsewhere. The ironic result was that non-Anglophone readers could access information about their own domestic context, but IGLHRC, an international organization, could not tell them much in its published outputs about other LGBT movements internationally.

Under these conditions, IGLHRC's published outputs, trainings, convenings, and regional programs were accessible to different audiences in different ways. This accessibility was not static; depending on who staffed regional programs and what resources were available for translation, linguistic barriers arose and collapsed at various times. In contexts where they lacked linguistic competence and relied on intermediaries, brokers could be forced to grapple with another source of potential misunderstandings and doubt. All of this subtly but decisively steered the flow of particular types of information through those in the North, particularly the United States, and a few key areas of the South in which brokers worked most heavily.

Access and the Technical Constraints of Cyberspace

Even in regions where brokers were linguistically competent, traffic in information was constrained by the particularities of the media they employed. IGLHRC had gradually moved away from the expensive telephone calls, faxes, and mass mailings activists used in the early 1990s, and had come to rely heavily on e-mail, its website, and e-blasts as the main channels through which information was transmitted from New York. Advances in technology made it possible to research widely and to learn about breaking news as it occurred, to engage a global audience of real or imagined supporters, and to collaborate with local, national, and international groups.

At the same time, newer forms of technology and media had their limits. Brokers used a web platform their predecessors had contracted to use years earlier, which significantly limited the website's functionality and the revisions they could affordably make. According to brokers who were on staff at the time, IGLHRC opted to use this platform because it came recommended by a colleague who knew the people who ran it. Years later, the platform was routinely frustrating to those who managed it, particularly Thomas, who found it severely restricted her ability to design pages and arrange content. The constraints made it harder, for example, to make IGLHRC's site navigable and accessible from mobile phones and other devices, which were growing in popularity as a means of accessing information.

The very nature of e-advocacy shaped brokers' work as well. As analysts of civil society and new technologies have argued, e-advocacy "has tended to focus on the activities of individuals who are empowered to point and click, sign petitions, engage as virtual citizens, and register their opinions on millions of blogs, online forums, listservs, and newsgroups, using a variety of devices."[23] Most brokers grasped the limitations of e-advocacy in mobilizing a constituency to make a meaningful impact; with action alerts, for example, it was unclear whether e-mail addresses for key officials were valid, whether a sharp influx of e-mails had the same impact as a flood of physical letters and faxes, who would respond to a call for action, and what messages supporters might send.[24]

Nonetheless, brokers continued to use the Internet as their primary vehicle for transnational engagement. A few sought to use technology in new ways; Perle in particular was interested in social networking and alternative ways of engaging people beyond IGLHRC's limited web interface. Aside from using Twitter, however, there was little emphasis on mobile technology during my fieldwork, even as it outpaced Internet use in huge swatches of the South.[25] The analytics for IGLHRC's website reflected the circumscribed scope of web-based advocacy. Visitors primarily came from the United States, China, the United Kingdom, Canada, the Philippines, Turkey, and India, reflecting issues of accessibility, population, language, and, to a lesser extent, the close relationships that brokers like Cristobal and Alizadeh had with activists in the Philippines and Turkey. Most of IGLHRC's outputs were only available through e-mail and its website, and brokers had no immediate plans to disseminate them through alternative channels.

For partners, IGLHRC's modes of advocacy had benefits as well as limitations. Technological advances made it possible to transmit information and reporting in a way that was unthinkable when IGLHRC conducted the bulk of its campaigning through fax machines, phone trees, and fliers. The Internet allowed brokers to reach large numbers of people quickly, regardless of where they might be located. It also made some activists who sent or received information less susceptible to raids, harassment, or arrest than they might be if they relied on landlines, fax machines, or the post.

Nonetheless, those benefits were not shared equally by activists around the globe. The vast majority of IGLHRC's publications were in PDF format, which limited their utility for those without the technology to open those files. This was not arbitrary; using Microsoft Word or other formats ran the risk of making documents editable by whoever downloaded them, something that could easily be abused by hostile actors. Nonetheless, it affected who could access and read IGLHRC's outputs, and where the knowledge produced by brokers was taken up and deployed. Similarly, the decision to use Skype whenever possible for international calls saved money, but worked best to communicate with partners who had access to a computer with a fast connection. In distant or underresourced areas, it was often considerably choppier and less clear than a landline, and proved frustrating to all involved.

As brokers used the particular networks, linguistic capacities, and technologies at their disposal to learn about and make sense of events occurring around the globe, structural factors partially predetermined how this economy of knowledge operated, influencing what sources were consulted, whose input was considered accurate and repeatable, and who was empowered to pass information along. As I suggest in the following section, IGL-HRC's reliance on partners did not necessarily eradicate doubts about what information to use and how. Quelling doubts was itself a fundamental if unspoken part of daily praxis at IGLHRC, and brokers did this in particular ways to enable or legitimate interventions.

Doubt and the Production of "Good Enough" Knowledge for Advocacy

Even when they acquired information from partners, brokers regularly grappled with decisions about whether, when, and how to use the information they gleaned. From their geographic and epistemological positions at a U.S.-based LGBT human rights NGO with regional offices, brokers had to strategically decide whether and how to use information brought to their attention. One of the persistent factors in those decisions was doubt. The hoax in Uganda is illustrative of the many ways in which doubt complicates LGBT human rights advocacy; in a far cry from 1990, when IGL-HRC was founded, e-mail allowed journalists to contact Kasirye directly, and established groups had no opportunity to question the facts, motives, or repercussions of the story before it spread. With little more than a sensational story and a halfway plausible e-mail address, the perpetrators were able to sow fear through Ugandan and transnational networks and dupe prominent media outlets in a matter of hours. Given this reality, in both New York and Cape Town, a degree of doubt was not the exception, but the rule. Brokers were repeatedly faced with situations where truth was elusive, elaborated, or only partially intelligible. At different times, three types of doubt characterized sexual rights work—about facts, motives, and repercussions—and brokers developed strategies to minimize these uncertainties and produce "good enough" knowledge for advocacy.[26]

Facticity and Ambiguity in Sexual Rights Advocacy

The hoax in Uganda deftly illustrates the most basic problem for activists monitoring LGBT human rights transnationally—the factual uncertainty that often surrounds a situation. Prominent LGBT groups tended to be located in major urban centers, and reports of violations that occurred outside those centers were often relayed secondhand or mediated through the media, police, or other third-party actors.[27] Those who were targeted for engaging in same-sex activity or transgressing gender norms did not always identify as LGBT, and were not affiliated with organizations they might contact. Thus, IGLHRC's partners, which were primarily in urban areas and usually identified as LGBT or MSM NGOs, frequently received information through their networks or accounts in the press, and not initially through firsthand knowledge of the cases in question.

The gulf widened when transnational groups became involved. NGOs like AI and HRW maintained a scattered presence around the globe, and their staff retained a mix of regional and thematic competencies. At IGLHRC, violations were flagged in two ways; they were either noted by regional staff and, if necessary, relayed to New York, or noted by brokers in New York who asked regional staff to get details and determine whether IGLHRC should intervene. On multiple occasions, I learned of major incidents via Twitter, Facebook, or the international press. Accounts of anti-LGBT panics, hostile legislation, and violence were transmitted over global listservs, where brokers learned of them at the same time that bloggers and journalists did. Often, media outlets sought a response from IGLHRC at the same time that brokers were scrambling to verify what had happened with partners in the area.

Establishing what happened in a crisis was complicated for numerous reasons. Incidents were described in terse, short messages or in the most skeletal news stories, often in panicked or polemical terms. It was regularly unclear what had actually transpired. When KEMRI was attacked by a mob, for example, brokers at IGLHRC were under considerable pressure to say something about the incident. Those in New York repeatedly called and e-mailed partners and regional staff for guidance. The details were hazy for a number of days, however, as Kenyan activists worked busily behind the scenes with police to ensure the safety of those involved. As brokers liaised with activists, the incident thus received only the barest mention in IGL-HRC's outputs.

Perhaps the greatest example of factual ambiguity, however, was the case of Chimbalanga and Monjeza in Malawi. For the global attention the saga received, the amount of indeterminacy was striking. Journalists who broke the story called the engagement a gay marriage; this was how it was reported until activists ascertained that Chimbalanga lived full-time as a woman, and that from a Western perspective, the term "transgender" was probably more accurate than "gay." Journalists reported that Chimbalanga menstruated, raising the possibility—which was never really explored by many activists in the North—that Chimbalanga was intersex, and that this was as much a question of biological sex as it was of gender identity. In light of this ambiguity, it was unclear whether Monjeza should continue to be labeled "gay." He was engaged to someone who presented as female, and upon his release from prison, he left Chimbalanga and became engaged to another woman. Brokers alleged he was paid by journalists to do so, but again, the validity of this claim was far from clear.

Depending on their sexual politics and ties to those visiting the couple in prison, some activists referred to Chimbalanga using female pronouns, some continued to use male pronouns and refer to the two as a gay couple, and some, including most brokers at IGLHRC, somewhat awkwardly avoided using any pronouns at all. A broker at IGLHRC informed colleagues that an activist at CEDEP had suggested Chimbalanga preferred to be called "Tionge," a feminine form of her name, rather than "Tiwonge," the masculine construction that journalists were using. The distinction is not entirely self-evident; there is not a gendered difference between "Tiwonge" and "Tionge" in the Tumbuka language, and the variation was more likely a product of mispronunciation by speakers from other regions of Malawi.

Nonetheless, following instructions from partners as they understood them, brokers at IGLHRC began to use "Tionge," and different names for the detainee proliferated. That the pair was in prison with little ability to communicate with the outside world, they had different grasps of sexual identity politics, and they and their defenders had to worry about the repercussions of their self-identification in court made these questions all the more impossible to answer with certainty.

IGLHRC's reluctance to ascribe identity was mirrored to greater or lesser extents by the Malawian and international press, other NGOs, governments, and the judiciary, making the dynamics of the alleged offense profoundly ambiguous to observers. The underlying facts, however, were potentially decisive. If Chimbalanga identified as male, allegations of homosexuality would have to be disputed on the grounds that sexual activity had not taken place, or that criminalizing same-sex activity is unconstitutional or incommensurate with Malawi's obligations under international law. If Chimbalanga identified as female, however, could she be prosecuted under Sections 153 and 156 of the Penal Code, or would those charges be invalidated on the grounds that the engagement was, therefore, heterosexual? Would this invalidation be strengthened if Chimbalanga would be understood by medical practitioners to be intersex?

In the public arena, these issues were never fully resolved, even among the transnational NGOs involved in advocacy around the case. Until the verdict, for example, male pronouns continued to be used publicly by CEDEP, Peter Tatchell, and most local and global media outlets. The female pronoun was used privately by some brokers at CEDEP and IGLHRC. Others, like IGLHRC and the ICJ, remained publicly gender-neutral in their assessments, referring to "the two" or "the couple," despite this making it difficult to specify precisely what laws were at stake. For brokers, Chimbalanga's gender identity was not critically relevant; the arrest for holding an engagement ceremony, the five months of pretrial detention in dismal conditions, and the harsh sentence of fourteen years in prison with hard labor were all human rights violations whether or not Chimbalanga and Monjeza were technically in violation of the law on the books.

Arguably, these kinds of epistemological uncertainties were not the exception, but the rule. Brokers were quite conscious of the dangers of political and sexual misrecognition, and reluctant to impose identities or intervene incorrectly. As suggested in chapter 4, brokers quelled doubt by foregrounding partnership and relying on national or regional groups to tell them what had happened and what might be helpful. Yet this too produced partial or ambiguous answers. Brokers often operated with partial knowledge mediated through the second- or thirdhand accounts of activists with whom they interacted over e-mail, blogs, Facebook, and listservs. Ambiguity was exacerbated by transatlantic time differences; unpredictable telephone, Skype, and Internet connections; and countless demands on activists' time and energy that made them unable to mobilize in a timely way.

As a result, brokers in New York felt pressure to verify information through brokers in the regional offices, who were simultaneously engaged in their own ongoing programmatic work. IGLHRC's organizational structure, reflected in job descriptions and grant contracts, relied on regional staff to document and verify incidents—they were IGLHRC's eyes and ears in the region and a linchpin of its ability to assert a global presence. During my time in Cape Town, the opinion of at least some regional staff was very different. At that time, the Africa Program was under intense pressure to respond to incidents that were seized on internationally as human rights crises at the same time that they continued work on ongoing programmatic priorities. Brokers in that program often found it difficult to juggle these twin imperatives and voiced to me their preference to do more programmatic work; they regarded themselves as a lawyer, a scientist, and an activist and not primarily as journalists. In part, the tension derived from the regional model itself. On one hand, regional offices functioned as *regional* offices, that is, sites that mediated between the transnational NGO and its local partners. On the other, they were regional *offices,* staffed by professionals who regarded their jobs as more complex than simply verifying information and relaying it back and forth from New York to the rest of Africa.

During my fieldwork in Cape Town, I gained a deeper appreciation for those competing demands than I had when I was in New York requesting information and verification from regional staff. Under pressure to respond to cases they themselves had just learned about, brokers in New York urgently sought information from brokers in the regional programs. The regional staff were not always in a position to supply it immediately, and as a broker in the Africa Program explained to me, staff in Cape Town expressed stress or dissatisfaction by taking a step back, not engaging, and remaining silent for a period of time. To them, this signaled that they were upset or did not like how a process was organized. From a vantage point in New York, this response meant that facts on the ground remained ambiguous, and could become even more opaque when the motives of those involved and the potential repercussions of intervention were far from clear.

Motives and Politics in Transnational Advocacy Networks

The factual ambiguity that sowed doubt in brokers' minds was exacerbated by doubt about the motives of those involved. Brokers at IGLHRC, at least, treated many reported incidents with a considerable amount of skepticism. Although they lionized their partners and publicly praised their risky and tireless work on the ground, Kilonzo observed that brokers also had to be wary of self-interested motives and the agendas of newcomers to LGBT advocacy.

The worry was particularly pronounced among brokers in the Africa Program, who worked in a region where the rapid proliferation of groups made it difficult to gauge the legitimacy, stability, and representativeness of their work. Brokers were conscious that those with ulterior motives, like Kasirye, could take advantage of sexual politics for personal gain using little more than a compelling narrative and the bare trappings of a plausible organization. The peddling of false information was a real concern, fueled by the self-interest of individuals holding themselves out as activists in the region.[28] Any dubious claims these individuals made were difficult to verify independently; they advertised themselves as precisely the kinds of local partners who were trusted to guide transnational solidarity work. For this reason, among others, brokers preferred to work with long-standing partners whom they trusted to be honest and not self-serving in their advocacy.

Where brokers lacked long-standing partners to work with, doubt could be difficult to dispel. This became apparent when two brokers heatedly debated whether or not to intervene in a case that had been brought to their attention. The leader of a partner organization had alleged that two transgender women had been arrested and tortured in prison. One broker wanted to intervene, believing that the case fit within the alarming pattern of arrests in the country in question and merited attention. The other complained that the activist who reported the arrests lived in a neighboring country and was unable to verify the incident firsthand, that in-country NGOs had no knowledge of the incident happening, and that the lawyers they had contacted to investigate the claim were unable to come up with any evidence it was valid.

In this case and others, the ways brokers coped with doubts about motives were instructive, as were the terms they used to encapsulate what they sought from partners abroad. Brokers tended to rely heavily on their own character assessments of other activists, particularly whether they were "good" or "smart" in their work. When activists were referred to as "good," it meant they were unselfishly committed to the goals of the movement, effective in their work, and able to responsibly guide transnational NGOs. When they were referred to as "smart," it meant they were savvy in their advocacy and thoughtful about the ways they pursued their goals in contexts that could be quite hostile. In both measures of character, a number of traits were used as proxies to determine whether someone was "good" and "smart"—for example, whether they were financially responsible, whether they were inclusive and built a community in their work, and whether they were strong enough in their convictions to set a course and defend it. These assessments were reinforced by interactions within human rights networks, as brokers publicly and privately shared concerns about the motives of colleagues in the North and South alike. Many of the same dynamics that affected who was identified as a partner also determined who was trusted as a source of information—and indeed, whose knowledge authorized and legitimated transnational interventions.

Truth and Consequences in Transnational Interventions

The politics of doubt were not confined to the South; IGLHRC's interventions had transnational repercussions, and brokers had good reason to doubt how their knowledge would be redeployed. Globalization and the spread of new technologies have made it increasingly difficult for brokers to target messaging at particular audiences; public outputs are typically accessible to supporters, detractors, funders, partners, the media, academics, and hostile governments alike.[29] The implications of this were twofold: first, the production of knowledge was always shaped by considerations of how it might be taken up and used, and second, brokers' awareness of network politics meant that contradictory accounts were sometimes left to uneasily coexist.

Brokers were conscious of the ways their outputs and interventions might be misunderstood, twisted, or even used against them. A lack of firsthand research was not the only or even the primary reason brokers were reluctant to make definitive statements about the state of the world for LGBT people. They were also quite aware of how sloppily that information might be used, or what it might be used to justify. It was not uncommon for brokers to encounter comments via mail, e-mail, or blogs that dismissed whole

regions or populations as "barbaric," "uncivilized," or "inhuman," or suggestions that Northern governments should intervene diplomatically, econom-
ically, or, occasionally, militarily to improve the lives of LGBT people. From
within the organization, I regularly witnessed frustration at the reaction-
ary paternalism, racism, and xenophobia with which allegations of human
rights violations were received.

It was difficult for brokers to remain uninvolved in these discussions.
IGLHRC's work made it a visible source for those interested in these issues,
including journalists. In Communications and Research, I was regularly
contacted by reporters regarding human rights violations. The protocol was
to refer reporters to the regional staff on queries regarding specific countries. The reality of the situation was that with regional staff traveling, facing time differences of up to twelve hours, or simply not having time to
instantly respond to a press inquiry from the United States, many requests
for interviews went unanswered or ended up returning to brokers in New
York. When those of us in New York had been working on a particularly
high-profile issue like Uganda's Anti-Homosexuality Bill, we would occasionally respond directly to reporters.

Concern about how information would be used heavily shaped the way
brokers interacted with journalists. This was certainly something I grappled with, and although I was there as an anthropologist, many of my colleagues complained about it too. In one incident, I was phoned by a producer
who wanted to film a documentary on the ways that the Christian Right in
the United States was exporting homophobia to Africa. He mentioned that
Uganda would be the centerpiece of the documentary, but that the production team needed two other countries to balance the narrative. As the
call went on, it became increasingly clear that the producer knew which
countries he considered homophobic—Malawi and Senegal—and wanted
me to affirm that they should send film crews to both and provide contacts
to make this possible. I was skeptical about Malawi, where the flare-up over
Chimbalanga and Monjeza did not seem immediately or meaningfully trace-
able to evangelicals in the United States. I was adamant, however, that it was
not a good idea to send a crew to Senegal, where the mere mention of homosexuality had set off mob violence and IGLHRC had tactically restricted
its advocacy to working with groups behind the scenes. More prosaically,
Senegal is 95 percent Muslim, with few known links to evangelicals in the
United States; instead, there are strong indications that homophobia has
escalated amid pressure from Saudi Arabia, the politicization of religious

leadership, and a series of publicized, escalating sex panics in 2008 and 2009. My response did not seem to be what the producer was looking for, and the call grew almost hostile as I tried to dissuade him from sending a film crew to ask about homosexuality in Senegal.

These sorts of interactions were not at all uncommon, and placed brokers—and certainly placed me—in the awkward position of having to challenge, ignore, or legitimate narratives that would then be broadcast widely. Perle was frustrated that reporters routinely tried to frame IGLHRC's UN advocacy as a conflict between the West and the rest, despite her insistence that states like Colombia, Nepal, Gabon, and Mauritius either lobbied for or supported LGBT-friendly interventions. With the documentary, I found myself having to operate with the limited knowledge I had about the wishes of groups in Senegal, and under intense pressure to respond on the spot.

At other times, the claims were more innocuous, but still legitimated ways of understanding LGBT human rights that brokers resisted. This was evident during the spate of media coverage in late 2009 and early 2010, when a number of reporters produced pieces on what they dubbed "a wave of homophobia" in sub-Saharan Africa. Journalists frequently called IGLHRC asking whether homophobia was "increasing" in sub-Saharan Africa, and whether it was "the worst place in the world" to be LGBT.[30] Brokers preferred to highlight specific incidents and patterns instead of making sweeping generalizations about increasing or decreasing homophobia, and were reluctant to draw comparisons between different strains of homophobia in different places. (Notably, this was more true of brokers in New York than those in the regions; around the time that I presented a paper criticizing the idea that homophobia was sweeping Africa, Kilonzo matter-of-factly told journalists that reported attacks against LGBT people in Africa had risen by 10 percent in the past year.) Brokers responded to reporters fully conscious of how their words might be used, and were reluctant to act as authorities on the climate for LGBT people facing heightened repression. It was not difficult for reporters to find examples of how bleak the situation for LGBT people might be in areas of the South, and brokers at IGLHRC often found themselves attempting to add as much complexity and nuance to these depictions as possible.

This did not always work, of course. Brokers were under pressure to take some interview requests, particularly from high-profile outlets. It was said in the office that some members of IGLHRC's board wanted to see more of the organization in the *New York Times*—that is, for IGLHRC to be the go-to source for stories about LGBT issues outside the United States. Although brokers felt a desire—or, in some cases, an unwanted duty—to talk to the media, they tended to be approached by journalists and not vice versa, and this meant that what appeared in print often differed considerably from what brokers actually thought or did.

In many instances, quotes were taken out of context or framed in a way that brokers had not necessarily intended, and found alarming when they appeared in print. When Perle used the acronym "LGBT" in an interview with Reuters, for example, the journalist spelled it out in print as "lesbian, gay, bi and transsexual." The sloppy translation would have been merely annoying, except that Perle was engaged in intensive lobbying at the UN, where IGLHRC's terminology was under close scrutiny by hostile states. A similar incident occurred after *Words of Hate, Climate of Fear* was embargoed before its release. When I spoke to a reporter from Voice of America who had planned to run a story on the report, I told him I could only speak about conditions in Senegal in general terms and, given the political sensitivities surrounding the report, asked to see my quotes before they appeared in print. Although he obliged, the piece then ran with the headline "Activists Criticize Senegal for Anti-Gay Persecution," which was precisely the image I was desperately trying to avoid by embargoing the report and downplaying any direct criticism of the government by transnational NGOs.

I may have been especially sensitive to these questions, but my academic background and political leanings were similar to those of many of my informants, who were conscious of the complexity of these issues and expressed frustration about the reductive ways they were discussed. Of course, brokers *did* believe the violations they criticized on a daily basis were unjust, and the mistreatment people faced on the basis of SOGI was unacceptable. At the same time, many had strong feminist, queer, and anti-imperialist politics, and did not want their opinions to be misused to advance arguments they found equally, if differently, objectionable.

The potential repercussions of interventions in the South thus shaped the sentiments that brokers publicly expressed, and produced a fair amount of self-policing and political positioning. Everyone in the office could empathize when one broker came out of her office looking horrified after a radio interview, and ruefully recounted how, in a moment of candor, she had agreed with the host that marriage was a problematically normative institution. Like many of us, she felt there was truth in that assessment, but nonetheless worried that her frank reflections would be taken out of context by anti-gay activists, upset partners or supporters who felt differently, or jeopardize the tireless work being done by so many of her colleagues. Privately, brokers were often skeptical of strategies that counseled assimilation into families, faith communities, and the neoliberal or authoritarian state. At the same time, brokers were understandably reluctant to disrupt these strategies when they were used in places like Uganda and Malawi, and recognized that these served short-term ends that challenged some norms while they reinforced others.

Where disagreements *did* regularly break out was within transnational LGBT human rights networks, which were often intensely combative, territorial, and polarized. A number of schisms have divided the movement, and this aspect of LGBT human rights advocacy has gone largely unremarked in academic discussions. Some divisions result from implicit, low-intensity territorialism among groups like ILGA, IGLHRC, and HRW. Others have gone public in rather spectacular ways, including the open letter from activists in Africa asking Peter Tatchell to cease intervening in their struggles; very vocal critiques in the gay press by Michael Lucas, Michael Petrelis, *Gay City News,* and others who would like to see LGBT NGOs intervening more aggressively; and the allegations of libel Tatchell has levied against critics in the academy. (This has had a particularly chilling effect; Tatchell successfully had the anthology *Out of Place* taken out of circulation because of a chapter that was critical of his work, won a formal apology from Kenneth Roth and Scott Long of HRW for Long's criticism of Tatchell and his advocacy, and received an apology from Routledge for a piece by Long in *Contemporary Politics* criticizing misguided responses to alleged hangings of gay men in Iran.) Incidents like these had a visibly stifling effect; they made brokers reluctant to take a stance on particular issues or to work with activists they considered particularly toxic. As one broker at IGLHRC described these dynamics:

> You have to deal with the politics of the movement—which, by the way, this movement is so *bitchy.* I'm saying that, actually, in all seriousness. Like, really. It's so bitchy. In the women's movement . . . there's a lot of talking about this and that, but not this bitchiness. . . . There's this almost aggressive, like, watching out for people to fuck up to attack them for it that I'm astounded by. I'm astounded by it. Like, just *waiting* to make the critique. . . . This movement is not going to be successful if that dominates.

Of course, brokers did correct each other, especially when they had an opportunity to be critical of somebody they had challenged in the past or when they felt misunderstandings were too egregious to let stand. A few indicative examples emerged in quick succession in early 2010, when a prominent campaigner sent out three press releases that were swiftly challenged by brokers on an open LGBT listserv. The first of these, sent on January 17, relayed the reported arrests of a number of HIV activists in Senegal. This was quickly corrected by a broker at a prominent human rights NGO in the United States, who pointed out that the arrests had actually occurred a year earlier and had been resolved after considerable legal and media advocacy. On February 16, the campaigner sent another press release with the sensational headline "Execute Gay Scouts, Says Chief Scout of Uganda." The logic of the claim was that David Bahati, a major proponent of the Anti-Homosexuality Bill, was also the chief of the Scout Board of Uganda. The release asserted, "The leader of the scout movement in Uganda is demanding the execution of all scouts and scout leaders who commit repeated homosexual acts," which was perhaps deductively true, but was still a fairly tortured argument for opposing the bill. A number of activists voiced discomfort with the strategy, objecting that there were enough damaging aspects of the bill that inventive approaches were unnecessary, distracting, and counterproductive. On March 9, the campaigner sent another press release calling for AI to adopt Chimbalanga and Monjeza as prisoners of conscience. This was quickly followed by a reply from a broker at AI noting that the couple had, in fact, been adopted, and that she had already told him as much. In these instances, policing was done within networks to correct obvious inaccuracies and discourage counterproductive strategies before they spread any further into LGBT and mainstream media, in both the North and the South.

At other times, however, the facts were not particularly clear, and contradictory narratives proliferated without being countered and settled. In the case of Chimbalanga and Monjeza, the same campaigner repeatedly and publicly insisted that Monjeza had contracted malaria and was deathly ill in prison. By contrast, partners at CEDEP who were doing prison visits told brokers at IGLHRC that Monjeza had contracted malaria, was quickly treated and recovered, and was doing fine. They complained that claims that Monjeza was on his deathbed were generating criticism in Malawi that activists were spreading lies and blowing the incident out of proportion, which they did not need as they prepared to defend Monjeza in court. While brokers at IGLHRC made a point of explicitly stating in their outputs that Monjeza was well, and privately wrote to the campaigner who was spreading misinformation, they opted not to publicly correct him for spreading a different view.

In this situation, brokers were placed in a difficult position. On one hand, they did not want to appear to scold their counterparts around the globe. They were aware that feuds would bruise egos and make it difficult to work together, but were also concerned that the press—particularly the LGBT press—would seize on any public disagreements as a sign of infighting among different activists and groups. On the other hand, partners at CEDEP were being inundated with questions and worried that sensationalized reports would damage their credibility and hamper their efforts to free the couple from prison. Rather than escalating this to a matter of dispute within the network—which, judging by historical precedent, would very quickly have made headlines and possibly triggered legal action—IGLHRC maintained its own organizational line, and reached out privately to try to reconcile the contradictory narratives.

Brokers did not publicize every piece of information that came to their attention. They regularly grappled with doubts about facts, motives, and repercussions, and used various techniques to minimize these doubts and produce "good enough" knowledge for advocacy. Their assessments about what actually transpired in a given incident, whether those involved were trustworthy, and what they could do with that information all shaped the advocacy that they actually carried out on behalf of LGBT persons. To some extent, these doubts are inevitable in transnational work—what varies is how seriously they are taken and what import they are given by brokers and NGOs, and it is this aspect of transnational advocacy that demands close and sustained attention.

CONCLUSION

In transnational LGBT advocacy, asymmetrical patterns of collecting and disseminating information, multiple and persistent forms of doubt, and the politics of those who animate advocacy networks all shape whose voices are heard, who hears them, and what message they send. As this knowledge is institutionalized in regional mechanisms, the UN, and other arenas of norm creation and reglementation, too, it takes on a particular significance, with funding and policy changes resting on its authority. Although they relied on partners for the information needed to do their work, brokers at

IGLHRC nonetheless struggled both with structural limitations and with persistent sources of doubt, and acknowledging these gaps and fissures in global projects is critical if alternative ways of conducting them are to be conceived. What might it mean to acknowledge not only that Northern brokers depend on Southern counterparts for information and legitimacy but also that practical limitations and doubt make this enterprise a somewhat uncertain project?

On one hand, it is easy to invoke the partiality and ambiguity of brokers' information to argue that transnational NGOs cannot or should not interfere in local struggles. On the other hand, brokers who think self-reflexively about these limitations can not only cultivate relationships and strengthen transnational campaigns, but also offer important counterpoints to Northern activists who blindly or self-righteously intervene without holding themselves accountable to a wider community. As political and technological changes facilitate fraudulent reports of violence from the South as well as racist or neocolonial interventions from the North, there may be good reason to cultivate thoughtful, self-critical networks rather than repudiating transnational work wholesale.

Many brokers, in both the North and South, are acutely aware of their limitations in speaking authoritatively about LGBT human rights globally. This is not unfailingly true in every situation; personal and institutional pressures have occasionally goaded brokers into speaking out even when information was recognizably imperfect. Nonetheless, brokers have developed tactics for sifting through information to find the facts that allow them to call something a violation of a human right, assign some responsibility to the state, and issue a demand for redress. When they recognized that their networks, linguistic capacity, and technological reach were partial or limited, brokers sought and welcomed opportunities to render them more complete and robust. Rather than forging blindly ahead, they treated doubt as something that was to be eradicated as much as possible, usually by relying heavily on partners and regional programs to supply credible information. For both activists and ethnographers, it is important not only to understand how economies of knowledge shape transnational human rights advocacy but also to develop a body of work that explores better or worse ways of navigating them.

The impetus to eradicate doubt and the acknowledgment of ineradicable imperfection are not mutually exclusive. To the contrary, both are critical if solidarity work is to be done effectively and responsibly. Recognizing that all knowledge is partial is necessary but not sufficient to develop a robust transnational politics; what is also needed is a critical exploration of what the partiality of that knowledge means for political action. It is important to identify how uncertainty arises in transnational work, but also important to identify strategies that responsibly cabin or control that ambiguity, and call to task those activists and groups who do not hold themselves accountable.

In both endeavors, ethnographic analysis of the diverse ideological and tactical approaches brokers take to this work is an indispensible tool. In processes of knowledge production and diffusion, brokers played a fundamental role, and their circulation of knowledge was shaped by the political and structural conditions under which they operated. Although it is important to recognize these conditions, it is also important to recognize the ways in which the politics of those who animate transnational advocacy networks, the partnerships they actively forge, and the opportunities they seize to advance their agenda all also shape whose voices are heard, who hears them, and what they say. This is perhaps particularly true insofar as this knowledge is institutionalized in the UN system and other arenas of norm creation and reglementation, a phenomenon I explore in chapter 6.

6 Demanding Rights, Compelling Recognition

LGBT Advocacy in the Global Human Rights Arena

Institutionalization, or the codification of viewpoints in laws, policies, and practices, has been part of IGLHRC's mission since Dorf sought to secure a place for LGBT persons in AI's mandate in 1990. Institutionalizing processes meaningfully shape how global norms are produced.[1] The targets of these processes and the ways they unfold, however, are shaped by situational, fast-changing calculations that brokers make, which are often obscured in bird's-eye views of human rights norms and their development.

Any analysis of human rights norms is enriched by attentiveness to human rights practice. In this chapter, I consider IGLHRC's history as an institutionalizing force, the ways brokers navigated and lobbied human rights mechanisms, and the lasting impacts of their interventions. As previous chapters suggest, institutionalization was shaped by a variety of factors. IGLHRC's history and the backgrounds of brokers were relevant, as were the ways brokers constructed the category of "LGBT human rights" and promoted it through partnerships and the diffusion of knowledge. Under the unique pressures of the UN and regional mechanisms, brokers' work was further shaped by particularistic and often competing objectives—for example, to be recognized by officials, to secure maximally inclusive protections, to build consensus among states, or to press for sweeping change. How they maneuvered within these opportunities and constraints had important effects on the growing recognition of LGBT rights globally.

IGLHRC's HISTORICAL ROLE AS AN INSTITUTIONALIZING FORCE

Whether in their campaign for AI to address sexuality or their intensive lobbying to get the phrase "sexual orientation" into the Platform of Action in

Beijing, brokers at IGLHRC have consistently sought to enshrine the view that LGBT people have human rights worth protecting and promoting. While the venues and tactics brokers employed to institutionalize their views have shifted somewhat over time, this general aim has remained central to their advocacy.

As the lobbying in Beijing illustrates, however, LGBT NGOs have made sporadic and uneven progress in international and regional mechanisms.[2] Brokers faced a number of initial setbacks; the most high profile occurred after ILGA, a confederation of nearly three hundred groups in fifty countries, secured special consultative status to ECOSOC. U.S. Senator Jesse Helms learned that NAMBLA, a pederastic group, was a member of ILGA, and threatened to cut off U.S. funding for the UN unless ILGA's accreditation was revoked.[3] At the time, Dorf was a senior officer of ILGA as well as IGLHRC's executive director, embroiling IGLHRC in the wider conflict.

Amid a firestorm of controversy, ECOSOC passed Resolution 1994/50, suspending ILGA's status and authorizing the Committee on NGOs to explore whether ILGA members condoned pedophilia. The committee demanded ILGA circulate a questionnaire to member organizations asking their name, address, aims and purposes, activities, publications, position on pedophilia, and any subsidiaries' position on pedophilia.[4] When responses had been collected from every member organization, the Committee on NGOs required that ILGA forward them along with a list of ILGA's members, copies of ILGA and its members' publications, and a statement certifying that ILGA and its members rejected pedophilia.[5] The committee would then render a decision on ILGA's accreditation.

ILGA responded that the demands were impossible. The confederation had hundreds of members; many would put themselves at risk by sending their address to an intergovernmental forum, were not easily reachable by mail, or simply would not respond. As a result, ILGA's consultative status was suspended, and other LGBT groups were dismissed or rejected for over a decade until three NGOs—ILGA-Europe, LSVD, and the Danish National Association for Gays and Lesbians (Landsforeningen for Bøsser og Lesbiske, or LBL)—finally secured consultative status in December 2006.[6]

Subsequent disputes shaped early struggles to be formally recognized by intergovernmental bodies. As described in chapter 1, one of the most memorable battles was in 2001, when IGLHRC successfully lobbied states to restore then–HIV Program officer Karyn Kaplan to a UNGA panel on the impact of the HIV/AIDS pandemic. In venues like this, IGLHRC established a more regular presence at the UN, offering technical advice and engaging in discussions with agencies and member states.

In the years that followed, LGBT NGOs did advance initiatives to formally enshrine recognition of LGBT rights at the UN. The first of these, known as the Brazil Resolution, was a draft resolution introduced to the CHR in 2003. Like the Yogyakarta Principles that were drafted by human rights experts just three years later, the Brazil Resolution "[did] not in any manner create any new rights, but merely affirm[ed] that the existing rights framework should apply regardless of sexual orientation."[7] More than nineteen countries voiced support, but Pakistan, Egypt, Libya, Saudi Arabia, and Malaysia, backed by the Holy See, threatened to amend the resolution to the point of irrelevance by removing all references to sexual orientation.[8] Ultimately, the CHR voted twenty-four to seventeen, with ten abstentions, to defer consideration of the draft resolution until 2004.[9] Brazil vowed to reintroduce the resolution in the next session, but it never moved past this stage. Unflagging political opposition led one human rights scholar to conclude during this period that "in the short and medium run, there is no chance of anything even close to an international consensus on even a working text for a draft declaration on the rights of homosexuals."[10]

The dire outlook improved somewhat in 2005, when New Zealand delivered a joint statement on SOGI before the CHR on behalf of thirty-two states, and again in 2006, when Norway delivered a joint statement on SOGI before the HRC on behalf of fifty-four states. In 2008, another statement, known colloquially among activists as the French Resolution, was introduced at the UNGA.[11] The statement was delivered by Argentina; signatories affirmed "that human rights apply equally to every human being regardless of sexual orientation or gender identity" and that they were "deeply concerned by violations of human rights and fundamental freedoms based on sexual orientation or gender identity."[12] Overall, sixty-six countries signed the statement, with the number increasing to sixty-eight after the Obama administration signed on behalf of the United States in 2009 and Costa Rica added its signature in 2010. While brokers saw the statement as a turning point for LGBT human rights, it was not without controversy. In response to the statement, Abdullah al-Hallaq of Syria read a counterstatement signed by fifty-seven states. The remaining states, constituting roughly a third of the UNGA, abstained from taking a position.[13]

While the Bush administration was agnostic or hostile toward efforts to promote LGBT human rights at the UN, and abstained from the French

Resolution, the Obama administration quickly demonstrated willingness to engage NGOs on these issues. From a White House briefing on Uganda's Anti-Homosexuality Bill to a Pride Month forum at the State Department to support for IGLHRC's bid for ECOSOC status, the Obama administration worked especially closely with IGLHRC, CGE, and other U.S.-based NGOs promoting LGBT human rights. Cooperation between the Obama administration and LGBT NGOs accompanied a far stronger commitment to LGBT human rights in U.S. foreign policy.[14]

Shortly after I left IGLHRC, this was evident in the strong support the United States showed in advocacy around a standing resolution on extrajudicial, summary, or arbitrary executions. The resolution affirmed the importance of state intervention to respect and protect the right to life, and included a nonexhaustive list of grounds on which discriminatory killings might be based. For ten years, sexual orientation had been among the specified grounds. In November 2010, when the resolution was brought before the Third Committee for renewal, representatives from Mali and Morocco introduced an amendment on behalf of the African Group, the Arab Group, and the Organization of the Islamic Conference to strip "sexual orientation" from the text of the resolution.[15] The amendment passed with 79 votes in favor, 70 opposed, 17 abstentions, and 26 states absent.[16]

As the amended resolution advanced to the full UNGA, the United States and other delegations mobilized to reinsert "sexual orientation" into the resolution. The lobbying succeeded, and the U.S. amendment passed with 93 votes in favor, 55 opposed, and 27 abstentions. From there, the full resolution was passed with 122 votes in favor, 1 opposed, and 62 abstentions. The vote was notable for many reasons; the United States aggressively courted states to support or abstain from the amendment, Rwanda broke from the African Group and spoke convincingly about the importance of nondiscrimination, and South Africa offered support after a long period of inaction on LGBT issues at the UN.[17]

These efforts have been among the most high-profile attempts to institutionalize LGBT human rights, but they represent a fraction of the work brokers do with human rights mechanisms. Many efforts do not depend on the votes of a majority of sovereign states or widespread agreement on sexual rights language. Indeed, if the UN's inability to agree on a definition of "gender" is any indication, any consensus on these issues is a long way off. Instead, brokers have made piecemeal advances in various corners of the human rights arena, slowly building a framework in which the human rights of LGBT people are explicitly recognized by those who interpret and apply international law.

IGLHRC and Rights Protections in the Human Rights Arena

When they highlighted incidents, brokers were conscious of two factors that, held in tension, shaped their approaches. The first was whether particular rights could be persuasively read into a situation, and the second was which mechanisms might be receptive to such a reading. In the following section, I consider how rights were invoked and how brokers targeted bodies and officials who might be most receptive to their claims.

Situating LGBT Issues within the Human Rights Framework

With a vast human rights apparatus to draw on, brokers could respond to the persecution of LGBT people in countless registers. With only three law graduates on the staff—Kilonzo in the Africa Program and Cook and Perle in the Communications and Research Department—IGLHRC's responses to human rights violations were only rarely grounded in the binding precedents of domestic or regional courts. More often, brokers linked a perceived violation with a perceived standard under the ICCPR, ICESCR, regional mechanisms, or a domestic constitution, regardless of how these texts had been interpreted in practice. Where a student was ejected from a school in Chile for being a lesbian, or Argentina for being transgender, or Belize for being effeminate, for example, brokers pointed to the right to education. In one of the more comprehensive compilations, an action alert for a student named Jose Garcia in Belize stated:

> All people have the right to education under international human rights law without discrimination based on, and taking into account sexual orientation and gender identity (Yogyakarta Principle 16). Article 26 of the Universal Declaration of Human Rights (UDHR), Article 13 of the International Covenant on Economic, Social, and Cultural Rights (ICESCR), Article 28 of the Convention on the Rights of the Child (CRC) and the Convention against Discrimination in Education, all of which Belize is party to, ensure the right to education of all. Additionally, the International Covenant on Civil and Political Rights (ICCPR), the Convention Against Torture (CAT), and the ICESCR are explicitly interpreted to include protection from discrimination on the basis of sexual orientation and/or gender identity (Human

Rights Committee: Toonen v. Australia; Committee on Economic, Social and Cultural Rights General Comment 20; Committee Against Torture General Comment 2).

Furthermore, the right to education without discrimination exists in Belize law as well. The preamble to the Belize Constitution states that "a just system should be ensured to provide for education and health on the basis of equality," and the Education Act dictates that "[s]chools shall be free of gender, racial and other biases (Art. 25 (2))." Jose Garcia's rights to education and non-discrimination under international and Belize law are being violated by his expulsion, threatening all other rights underpinned by equal access to education, including his right to work, to housing, and to health.[18]

The statement is representative in many ways. Brokers deliberately foregrounded the Yogyakarta Principles, which they were trying to entrench as a soft-law instrument, but also invoked firmly established rights in the UDHR, ICCPR, ICESCR, and CRC. They pointedly highlighted domestic guarantees; in Jose Garcia's case, they cited the preamble to the Belize Constitution, the country's Education Act, and the binding and nonbinding instruments the government had signed and ratified. The approach stressed breadth rather than depth. Brokers did not scrutinize the precedential weight of the right or the degree to which it was meaningfully justiciable in the country in question. Instead, they sought to demonstrate the demanded right was recognized and affirmed by a range of actors and instruments, giving rhetorical force to their demand for governmental action.

These invocations of human rights were more carefully developed in institutional appeals to governments, regional mechanisms, and UN treaty bodies and Special Rapporteurs. Nonetheless, brokers understood that a critical component of these interventions was the decisiveness with which they reified violations against LGBT people as human rights violations. As Ettelbrick noted, this was not inconsequential:

At heart, it's about the old-fashioned word "consciousness-raising." That's what it is. Once you're conscious of something, once you're aware of a problem, once you're aware of a situation, you begin to start seeing things. Have you ever had that situation where you read something and it's like, oh, I never knew that, and then all of a sudden, everywhere you look, it seems like you're seeing things in a different way? . . . I think that's very much the human rights process. In the end, implementation, yeah—would it be great to have some magical wand somewhere that could call on governments and say, you have to do this? Yes. But it's about building a new norm, that's the thing. It's not about daddy or mommy coming in and saying you're wrong. It's about building a new norm, a normative way, normative approaches in society, and that doesn't just happen.

As Ettelbrick's comments suggest, tangible triumphs were not brokers' only measure of success. Brokers understood that they were engaging in norm creation, and were productively disrupting taken-for-granted understandings of the violability of LGBT persons. With that conviction in mind, virtually any body at the UN could be potentially important to their project, and this gave brokers wide latitude in framing and targeting their claims.

Formal Reporting and Recognition in the Charter- and Treaty-Based Bodies

The strategic use of sympathetic points of entry into the human rights system constitutes a type of "forum shopping," where claimants selectively seek venues where they are most likely to succeed.[19] Brokers considered which human rights mechanisms were most likely to respond favorably to their appeals, and this shaped how they framed and targeted advocacy.

The UN has two types of human rights bodies: charter-based bodies, which originate from the UN Charter, and treaty-based bodies, which originate from legal instruments ratified by states. The former includes the HRC, including the UPR Working Group and Advisory Committee and Special Procedures with thematic or country-specific mandates. The latter includes mechanisms that interpret and monitor compliance with agreements ratified by states since the founding of the UN.

Brokers targeted both types of human rights bodies based largely on assessments of where their appeals might have the greatest impact. Within the charter-based bodies, some of IGLHRC's most regular and private engagement has been with Special Procedures, many of whom have signaled willingness or even eagerness to work on SOGI under their mandate. Brokers occasionally submitted reports to Special Procedures alerting them to violations committed against LGBT persons. These were not typically advertised, because they were meant to encourage private and diplomatic investigations, without politicizing the mandate of the Special Procedure being approached. Brokers have, however, publicly stated that IGLHRC submitted reports to the Working Group on Arbitrary Detention, which subsequently condemned violations in Cameroon and Egypt, and to the Special Rapporteur on Human Rights Defenders, which subsequently voiced concern about violations in Iran. They similarly appealed to the Special Rapporteur on Extrajudicial, Summary, or Arbitrary Executions; the Special Rapporteur on Torture and Other Cruel, Inhuman, or Degrading Treatment or Punishment; and the Working Group on Enforced or Involuntary Disappearances in the case of a series of vigilante murders of men in Iraq. Brokers also reported submissions to the Special Rapporteur on Violence Against Women, the Special Rapporteur on the Right to Health, and the Special Rapporteur for Freedom of Expression.

As Perle observed, advocacy was not only about identifying which rights had been violated, but which Special Rapporteur was likely to act on a particular complaint. Officials like Anand Grover, the Special Rapporteur on the Right to Health, were outspoken proponents of LGBT human rights, and brokers noticed when these officials wrote on SOGI issues, spoke at LGBT rallies, or privately conveyed commitment and support. The perception that certain Special Procedures were more amenable to claims by LGBT groups—or to broader interpretations of their mandates—encouraged brokers to frame their complaints under particular rights or themes.

The strategy involved in this advocacy was evident when five activists from Pembe Hayat, a transgender rights organization in Turkey, were detained and beaten by police. On the night of May 17, 2010, four officers stopped the car in which the activists were riding and accused them of planning to engage in sex work. When the five phoned for help, they were pulled from the car, sprayed with tear gas, and beaten with batons. They were then taken to the police station, held in custody overnight, and released, and were charged with resisting arrest over a month later.[20]

In addition to working with Pembe Hayat and transnational NGOs, including HRW, Global Advocates for Trans Equality (GATE), ILGA-Europe, and COC Netherlands, brokers stressed the importance of conveying the incident to somebody who might investigate it further or, at the very least, record it as part of a pattern of persecution of transgender women in Turkey. Who they might approach however, was an open question. Various themes covered by Special Procedures were potentially relevant, including those addressing violence against women, minority issues, or arbitrary detention. As one broker suggested, however, the most likely avenues were the Special Rapporteurs dealing with arbitrary detention, torture, health, and possibly human rights defenders. These were not necessarily the most thematically relevant—the women were targeted for appearing to be sex workers, and women's rights and the freedom of expression may have been more intuitive—but these Special Rapporteurs were thought to be most likely to note the abuses and raise concerns about them.[21]

Special Rapporteurs' willingness to regard such incidents as part of their mandate affected where and when LGBT issues were raised at the UN, which was vividly demonstrated when Martin Scheinin, the Special Rapporteur on the Promotion and Protection of Human Rights and Fundamental Freedoms while Countering Terrorism, submitted a controversial report in 2009. Scheinin sought "to explore the complex relationship between gender equality and countering terrorism," including "the gendered impact of counter-terrorism measures both on women and men, as well as the rights of persons of diverse sexual orientations and gender identities."[22] The response from states, NGOs, and the press was swift. Critics seized on particularly controversial aspects of the report, including the assertion that "gender is not static; it is changeable over time and across contexts," and Scheinin's use of the Yogyakarta Principles to insist that identity papers should reflect a person's self-defined gender identity.[23] Although the Scheinin Report's analyses were relatively common in feminist and queer circles, they were far more aggressive than the positions brokers sought to institutionalize in efforts like the Brazil Resolution, the French Resolution, or bids for ECOSOC status. Many activists believed they had not been consulted sufficiently, if at all; the report was written with the help of professors and students at NYU, and some LGBT NGOs felt they were included in the conversation only after it was finalized. Although many approved of the report's findings, they found themselves on the defensive to contain its fallout and minimize its impact on other hard-won gains.

Brokers targeted treaty-based bodies in a more systematic way. At the time of my fieldwork, there were nine bodies charged with monitoring UN human rights treaties: the Human Rights Committee; Committee on Economic, Social and Cultural Rights; Committee on the Elimination of Racial Discrimination; CEDAW Committee; Committee against Torture; Committee on the Rights of the Child; Committee on Migrant Workers; Committee on the Rights of Persons with Disabilities; and Committee on Enforced Disappearances.[24] These bodies are often opaque and difficult to approach, and NGOs with UN access have facilitated their work by helping activists write and submit shadow reports.[25]

IGLHRC did not work routinely with most of these treaty bodies, with the notable exception of the CEDAW Committee. Just prior to my arrival, IGLHRC published *Equal and Indivisible: Crafting Inclusive Shadow Reports for CEDAW.* The publication provided a guide for activists interested in shadow reporting, a process in which NGOs were invited to submit reports on the status of women, or particular groups of women, in a country under review.[26] Brokers actively commissioned, edited, translated, and ensured the completion of shadow reports, and had a standing item in their budget to bring activists to testify or answer questions at CEDAW sessions in Geneva and New York.

In many ways, the CEDAW Committee was a prime target for intervention. Spaces opened by women's movements provided opportunities to articulate inclusive understandings of rights, and encouraged brokers to connect claims under the sexual rights rubric. Brokers highlighted state policing of particular bodies and practices, abuse or violence in the so-called private sphere, and the ways patriarchy and heteronormativity prevented persons from meaningfully exercising their rights. Beyond these general connections, interventions at the CEDAW Committee drew on a theme in lesbian organizing globally—namely, that it often grew from feminist movements rather than gay men's movements, and that sex and gender roles were as relevant as SOGI in the multiple marginalizations that LBT women faced. As the women's rights activist Charlotte Bunch stressed at the launch of *Equal and Indivisible,* "Universality is not the opposite of diversity . . . intersectionality is the only road to universality."[27] The focus on LBT women and subgroups of LBT women, like elderly women, highlighted complex intersections of different forms of vulnerability.

At the same time, interventions using CEDAW pressured activists to adopt a form of identity politics that did not necessarily align with the personal or organizational ideologies of many brokers at IGLHRC. The CEDAW Committee was specifically interested in the conditions facing women in a particular country. Brokers who hesitated to use gendered labels unless they were certain of their accuracy found the category of "women" was not necessarily self-evident, and could obscure a range of gender identities and expressions that were relevant to these discussions.

The difficulty was apparent when brokers attempted to incorporate trans populations into shadow reports. Often, brokers included both male-to-female and female-to-male populations in their work, but still retained the term "LBT women," or, more awkwardly, "lesbian and bisexual women and transgender people," when discussing the violations they faced. Brokers were conscious that debates about the definition of "gender" had proved deeply divisive at the UN, and that their interpretations would likely be co-opted by forces seeking to undermine efforts to create a unified gender entity. Here, as elsewhere, the desire to be maximally inclusive was balanced against political calculations of which framings would generate widespread, meaningful support.

Brokers' work with the CEDAW Committee appeared to have an impact. Since 1999, the committee has periodically highlighted SOGI in its reviews of states, criticizing those that criminalized same-sex activity and praising those that incorporated SOGI into nondiscrimination laws.[28] In October 2010, however, the committee further codified its stance amid lobbying by IGLHRC and other groups. References to SOGI and lesbian women appeared in two of the committee's General Recommendations, which it issued periodically to guide state implementation of CEDAW. In the first, focused on older women, the committee noted:

> The discrimination experienced by older women is often multidimensional, with the age factor compounding other forms of discrimination based on gender, ethnic origin, disability, poverty levels, sexual orientation and gender identity, migrant status, marital and family status, literacy and other grounds.[29]

In the second, which focused on CEDAW's broader mandate, the committee explicitly reached a conclusion LBT activists had been advocating for years:

> Intersectionality is a basic concept for understanding the scope of the general obligations of States parties contained in article 2. The discrimination of women based on sex and gender is inextricably linked with other factors that affect women, such as race, ethnicity, religion or belief, health, status, age, class, caste, and sexual orientation and gender identity.[30]

And, more forcefully:

> States parties have an obligation to take steps to modify or abolish existing laws, regulations, customs and practices which constitute discrimination against women. Certain groups of women, including women deprived of their

liberty, refugees, asylum-seeking and migrant women, stateless women, lesbian women, disabled women, women victims of trafficking, widows and elderly women, are particularly vulnerable to discrimination through civil and penal laws, regulations and customary law and practices.[31]

These public articulations of LGBT human rights were precisely what IGL-HRC and other NGOs sought to secure at the UN. By institutionalizing them in General Recommendations, reviews of states, and public statements by members of the CEDAW Committee, brokers hoped to send a strong signal that the rights of LGBT people were human rights, and should be respected as such.

Of course, the immediate implications of the committee's references to SOGI and lesbian women remained to be seen. General Recommendations are not binding, and only provide guidance to states implementing CEDAW. What was virtually certain, however, was that brokers would invoke these references to demand that states respond to discrimination against LBT people. By 2009, 186 states were party to CEDAW.[32] Some were supportive of brokers' interventions, some were agnostic, and some refused to recognize the term "SOGI" at all, insisting it was not official UN language. The attention to SOGI and lesbian women in the General Recommendations aided work with all these states. It provided a credible point of reference for supporters, offered cover to states that were open to reforms but had to justify them to a skeptical domestic constituency, and undermined the increasingly dubious assertion that SOGI is not officially recognized by the UN.

As their advocacy struck a chord with the CEDAW Committee, brokers considered turning to other treaty bodies. Perle, who was heavily involved in UN work, commented:

We're doing really well with CEDAW and women's movements, but getting us tied into the antiracist movements, getting us tied into environmental, children's, youth movements—I think we'll be the most effective that way.

One thing I found so surprising in the last session of the NGO Committee was, there was this antiracist organization, doing antiracist work. In their constitution, they had a nondiscrimination clause, or in their mission, they had something about nondiscrimination on the basis of sexual orientation. And they got tons of questions; almost all their questions were about that. You've got antiracism groups getting held back based on sexual orientation, and a lot of groups that do LGBT work are held back by racism, and a lot of the progressive movements are involved in these antiracist movements.

There's a treaty about nondiscrimination on the basis of race. There's a treaty about disability. We already have a foot in the door with the treaty about women. I think that we can get a lot of work done that way. I'm always so surprised that there's so little, not even like a pinky toe, in the world of the Millennium Development Goals. . . . I'm sure we could find common ground in any of that.

Brokers at IGLHRC, who came to LGBT advocacy from many different movements, intuitively understood that human rights are indivisible and interconnected. Embracing those connections created tactical opportunities to vocalize LGBT concerns in all their complexity.

As Perle's reflections suggest, the practice of advocacy itself reinforced this catholic approach to LGBT human rights. Opponents made SOGI a source of conflict virtually every time it appeared at the UN, even when it surfaced in something as tangential as a group's nondiscrimination policy. The politicization of passing references invited countermobilization by an LGBT movement emboldened by growing support and a string of victories at the UN. The result was that activists built new alliances and emphasized LGBT human rights in spheres they might not have prioritized otherwise, expanding the scope of their advocacy.

The incorporation of SOGI by various treaty bodies served two functions. First, it affirmed that states should protect the human rights of LGBT people under treaties to which they had already acceded. Forging consensus in the technical language of UN documents is painstakingly difficult,[33] and recognition by treaty bodies allows brokers to bypass much of this process. When brokers struggled to get 67 states to sign a nonbinding statement condemning gross human rights violations on the basis of SOGI, it was remarkable for the CEDAW Committee to instruct the 186 states that were party to CEDAW to address discrimination on the basis of SOGI in a comprehensive, intersectional way.

Second, and more basically, the formal incorporation of SOGI affirmed that LGBT human rights were worth addressing. As Cook, who had extensive experience at the UN, noted:

It basically aids what I call "fake it 'til you make it" advocacy. You keep saying something until everyone really does believe it's true. If I tell people enough times that a Security Council resolution is undoubtedly, no questions asked, international law that is binding, eventually it will be, by all the other means that international law becomes binding [*laughs*].

Since adjudicatory bodies often balk at initial attempts to expand their mandates, it was crucial for brokers to engage officials and build legitimacy in the corridors of the UN.[34] Recognition by treaty bodies was an especially strong affirmation of the relevance of LGBT human rights, but in other interventions, brokers achieved similar ends without institutionalizing any official position.[35] Instead, they simply maintained a presence in the orbit of the UN and worked with various officials and agencies on projects with particular relevance to LGBT populations. The inroads brokers made through informal engagement were subtle, but reinforced a foundational understanding that LGBT populations were relevant to the UN system and its work. When it came to demanding a place at the table or seeking formal recognition, this preliminary engagement was tremendously helpful, and merits closer attention as a key tactic for LGBT advocates.

A Seat at the Table:
Visibility and Legitimation in the Human Rights Arena

From Beijing onward, brokers engaged venues where formal protections under binding international law were not their immediate goal. Instead, they sought to claim a place as stakeholders in debates that occurred at the UN and elsewhere. In this legitimating work, brokers ultimately sought legalistic ends, but did so through decidedly performative means. By acting like a stakeholder in the human rights arena—meeting with authorities, obtaining consultative status, speaking in official venues, crafting statements, using legal language, and partnering with UN agencies—brokers made IGLHRC an active participant in the human rights arena, a crucial prerequisite to the formal work with which they were often associated.

Brokers worked closely with staff from the United Nations Development Programme (UNDP), which was especially supportive of their work at regional mechanisms. UNDP staff helped coordinate IGLHRC's meeting and panel of LGBT activists at the NGO Forum before the Forty-Fifth Session of the ACHPR in May 2009, for example, and collaborated to bring Caribbean activists to speak to IACHR commissioners about LGBT rights in October 2010. At times, the UNDP provided public legitimation; during IGLHRC's contentious bid for consultative status at ECOSOC, a U.S.

representative read a message from the UNDP arguing that IGLHRC's work on HIV and human rights "opened up conversations, communication and cooperation in communities that are key to achieving crucial public health, human rights and development goals."[36]

Brokers also worked with the Joint United Nations Programme on HIV/ AIDS (UNAIDS). In April 2010, IGLHRC honored UNAIDS executive director Michel Sidibé with its Outspoken Award, given to allies who had been vocal advocates for LGBT human rights—and who brokers wanted to encourage in that role. On the day of the event, Sidibé spoke at a UN Foundation luncheon where he condemned Uganda's Anti-Homosexuality Bill, called it unacceptable for countries to criminalize same-sex relations, and blamed criminalization for the spread of HIV.[37]

At human rights summits, brokers made an especially conscious effort to be visible and vocal. One example was the CSW, where IGLHRC coordinated with LGBT and women's rights NGOs to ensure LGBT issues were kept on the agenda. During my fieldwork, LGBT activists at the CSW organized a panel on homophobia in schools sponsored by ILGA and a panel on U.S. evangelicals exporting homophobia sponsored by ARC International, CGE, HRW, and IGLHRC. More subtly, they collectively ensured activists would be present at virtually every forum at the CSW, asking questions about LBT women at panels, highlighting LBT women's issues in group discussions, and regularly engaging with colleagues from around the globe.

With the growth of IGLHRC's regional programs, similar interventions were made within regional human rights mechanisms. The influence of these bodies varied widely; some exercised quasi-judicial power, while others monitored and advised governments but lacked any robust mechanism to hold offending states accountable. In either case, brokers actively encouraged regional mechanisms to incorporate the human rights of LGBT people into their mandate.

IGLHRC was given especially substantial credit for putting LGBT human rights on the agenda of the ACHPR. Ettelbrick remembered the Africa Program's engagement:

> It gave us a presence there among human rights people. Like, they're supposed to be the human rights people, they're supposed to be the ones who are responding. . . . If it's become so accepted that you're simply rounding up these guys and throwing them in jail or whatever, with no challenge, that's kind of what happens. The interference with that expectation is part of what we do.

Of course, brokers also sought formal gains; IGLHRC, through its LAC Program, cofounded and co-coordinated what became a body of twenty-four NGOs that worked for three years to get a resolution on SOGI and human rights passed by the OAS. Overall, however, IGLHRC's primary role has been to introduce LGBT issues to various mechanisms and persistently mainstream those issues into discussions of human rights. To facilitate this work, brokers conducted trainings for advocates and policymakers and provided financial and logistical support for activists to make presentations, participate in NGO forums, or secure consultative status for their organizations.

As part of their efforts to mainstream LGBT issues, brokers looked beyond human rights bodies for opportunities. The LAC Program worked within Mercosur, the Africa Program engaged with the EAC, and brokers explored the possibility of pressuring the Commonwealth to take a firmer stance on human rights. Although many of these bodies were reticent to actively trumpet human rights reforms, brokers were prepared to engage with any that were willing to incorporate LGBT issues into their mandate in a systematic way. With these efforts, brokers sought a seat at any table where relevant issues were being discussed.

During my fieldwork, IGLHRC was less involved—virtually not at all—with advocacy in Europe, something that was a consequence of both its political outlook and its material realities. Since IGLHRC's founding, there have been sensitivities around work in Europe, where ILGA already had a strong presence and worked with governments. ILGA's privileged role was institutionalized when ILGA-Europe, a regional group, began receiving funding from the European Commission to lobby for LGBT persons in the region. With a base in Brussels and a specific focus on the region, ILGA-Europe has been the primary leader on European advocacy and programming.

IGLHRC's focus on the South was further shaped by the theory of change espoused by brokers and the limited resources available for transnational LGBT work. In the mid-2000s, brokers had debated whether IGLHRC should take the lead on U.S. foreign policy advocacy, but ultimately declined to adopt that focus. When the CGE was created—with IGLHRC as a founding member—it filled this role, and there was less of an impetus for IGLHRC to focus its attention on U.S. foreign policy. Staff at IGLHRC were also conscious of critiques of "pinkwashing," and tactically avoided initiatives that might be perceived as broadly legitimating U.S. foreign policy.

Although Johnson and Jones indicated they would ideally like to do more to highlight violations in the United States, they doubted this was the best use of finite resources. Instead, there was a strong sense that IGLHRC's resources were best spent strengthening capacity and offering technical assistance to Southern partners.

In these efforts to establish a visible presence in the human rights arena, the likely impact of an intervention did not decisively determine whether or not to speak out. Even when redress was unlikely, brokers identified human rights violations and brought complaints before bodies nominally charged with preventing or remedying them. For much of their work, brokers simply stressed, repeatedly and forcefully, that the human rights of LGBT persons were inviolable.

In some instances, brokers appealed to governments or bodies that were almost certainly not going to act on their appeal. One example was IGLHRC's letter to the government of Iraq, which expressed concern about militias targeting gay men in Baghdad's Sadr City.[38] The post-invasion government had criminalized homosexuality, lacked affirmative protections for LGBT persons, and consistently voted against any recognition of LGBT rights at the UN. Nevertheless, the public letter, signed by Johnson, cited the Charter of the Ministry of Human Rights (CMHR) to request that the ministry do the following:

1. Actively and thoroughly document cases of human rights abuses against LGBT people and include this information in [its] annual report on the status of human rights in Iraq for submission to parliament and the cabinet (Article 3, Section 2, CMHR).

2. Prepare a comprehensive report on state, community and family violence based on sexual orientation with concrete recommendations on how to stop such human rights violations (Article 3, Section 3, CMHR).

3. Launch an investigation into the Iraqi legal system—including police, judiciary, and penal systems—to assure the full enjoyment of human rights principles by all people, regardless of their real or perceived sexual orientation or gender identity.

4. Promote a culture of tolerance and respect for the rights of LGBT people at the tribal level and within the larger Iraqi society (Article 3, Section 11, CMHR).

Judged by the likelihood that such a letter would succeed in any of its stated objectives or secure redress for Iraqi victims, it was arguably not a valuable use of time and energy. Judged by its impact in raising the visibility of human rights abuses, maintaining internal consistency in IGLHRC's concern with the worst abuses wherever they occur, and galvanizing those who could download PDFs and read English to pressure their governments, it may have been a useful tool.

As they simultaneously sought recognition and redress, brokers were not *always* looking for resolution of their claims. Instead, they also seized opportunities to reiterate the unacceptability of human rights violations against LGBT persons. Public letters to intransigent governments were part of a strategy to decry the most egregious violations and to affirm long-term inclusion in the human rights framework, rather than to secure immediate redress. To *not* act, and to tacitly acknowledge it was a waste of time to insist on LGBT rights in some contexts, would actively undermine those goals.

At times, even engagements with treaty bodies were less about institutionalization than they were about conveying a normative message. In IGLHRC's collaboration on shadow reports for the UPR, a likely impact was not always evident. The UPR had no enforcement mechanism, and merely suggested to states where they might change laws, policies, and practices to more closely align with the letter and spirit of the ICCPR. When states complied, they rarely did so in any immediate way. Even when brokers convinced states to make SOGI-related recommendations to a state under review, they made few efforts to ensure these were actually implemented, although they often cited them when governments were obviously intransigent. In this process, like so many others, what was important was being a vocal participant in discussions about whom and what the human rights framework protected, with the hope that this would solidify and advance a much larger project.

THE POLITICS OF INSTITUTIONALIZATION: STATE AND NGO ENGAGEMENT WITH IGLHRC

Of course, efforts to be a visible, recognized participant in the transnational human rights arena were not without controversy, and brokers frequently clashed with allies, opponents, and NGOs that had different ideas about SOGI and the scope of the human rights framework. Brokers' interventions were almost always politically contentious, and the positions their advocates and detractors took were as important as eventual outcomes.

One effort that proved controversial was IGLHRC's high-profile fight to win special consultative status at ECOSOC. Over a decade after the ILGA debacle, LGBT NGOs still had an inordinately difficult time getting accredited by ECOSOC's Committee on NGOs. A guide for LGBT groups seeking the status highlighted its practical advantages: "The accreditation allows NGOs to circulate statements at ECOSOC meetings at a maximum of 500 words, and circulate statements at ECOSOC's subsidiary bodies' meetings at a maximum of 1500 words. Besides this the NGOs can, if they get permission, speak at ECOSOC subsidiary bodies' meetings."[39] Accreditation also enabled brokers to obtain passes to the UN to be present for deliberations, giving them a voice and lessening dependence on the goodwill of allies who had a limited number of passes themselves.

The social meaning of accreditation was arguably more important than these nominal privileges. Since the revocation of ILGA's status, ECOSOC has been a deeply symbolic venue for LGBT NGOs seeking recognition in the human rights arena. IGLHRC's decision to seek consultative status was a momentous one; no U.S.-based LGBT organization had been accredited by the body, and the only transnational LGBT NGO that was successfully accredited was ILGA-Europe, which primarily worked in the North.

The prolonged battle illustrated what was at stake for various players as LGBT issues advanced in the human rights arena. It revealed a great deal about the stances NGOs and governments had taken on SOGI, the political repercussions of their positions, and how engagement among different actors shaped understandings of LGBT human rights.

Even prior to the debate, the push for consultative status required a conscious framing of IGLHRC's work within the bounds of international law. In the initial application, the aims and purposes of the organization were summarized in the following way:

> [IGLHRC] is an international human rights nonprofit nongovernmental organization whose mission is to secure the full enjoyment of the human rights of all people and communities subject to discrimination or abuse on the basis of sexual orientation or expression, gender identity or expression, and/or HIV status. IGLHRC implements its mission responsibly, in the spirit of the UN Charter, in a measured fashion, upon request from local human rights advocates, and within local norms.[40]

The final sentence did not typically appear in IGLHRC's materials, and was specifically appended for the purposes of accreditation. The reference to IGLHRC acting "responsibly" was likely a preemptive response to suggestions of pedophilia that brokers expected to face after the ILGA controversy. The emphasis on local human rights advocates served to minimize the charge that IGLHRC was a Northern organization seeking to spread a Northern agenda, just as the reference to local norms sought to reassure skeptical states that LGBT human rights would not ride roughshod over other rights, norms, and values.

The rest of the application was similarly framed, highlighting IGLHRC's engagement with the UN and regional mechanisms. It did not reformulate IGLHRC's aims, but simply reproduced the six strategic goals identified in the organization's three-year plan from 2006: to "decriminalize sexual and gender expression and behavior; establish free speech, assembly, association and expression for LGBT people and organizations; challenge workplace and other forms of discrimination; promote HIV/AIDS policies that destigmatize same-sex sexual practices; develop human rights principles to address violations related to gender identity and expression; and build and strengthen alliances with other social justice colleagues."[41]

IGLHRC formally applied for accreditation in May 2007, then spent over three years answering questions from governments, submitting supplementary materials, and attending ECOSOC meetings before the final votes were taken on the application in mid-2010. The first set of questions was sent from the NGO Section on May 9, 2008, requesting clarification regarding IGLHRC's finances and registration in the United States. IGLHRC sent a response on December 9, 2008. The NGO Section responded with another list of questions on February 24, 2009, requesting another financial statement; clarification about the exact dates, countries, and cities in which IGLHRC's human rights activities had taken place; a summary of how decisions were made at the organization; a list of members by country and continent; and an explanation of how IGLHRC used the surplus from its budget. IGLHRC quickly responded and sent these clarifications on March 5, 2009.

IGLHRC finally received questions from the states on the Committee on NGOs on May 11, 2009. The questions were predictable to those engaged in work at the UN. They inquired into "the basis for using in [IGLHRC's] application form the terms 'sexual minorities,' 'sexual orientation,' and 'gender identity,' which are not UN terminology"; whether IGLHRC pressured governments to adhere to established human rights or sought to develop or reinterpret those rights; how IGLHRC was qualified to convey the concerns of Africans as a U.S.-based organization; the nationalities of IGLHRC's IAB members; and what IGLHRC's role was in developing the controversial Yogyakarta Principles. IGLHRC responded on May 12, 2009.[42]

On May 19, 2009, IGLHRC received oral questions from states. Most questions were friendly; the United Kingdom and Romania asked how IGLHRC would advance the work of ECOSOC and requested to hear more about its work in Romania and on HIV/AIDS. Others were more equivocal; Sudan asked how IGLHRC ensured that its work on lesbian issues did not impose on the internal affairs of a country. IGLHRC swiftly responded to these requests.[43] The Committee on NGOs then decided to defer the application, delaying it until early 2010.

Another round of questions followed on February 1, 2010, which were answered by IGLHRC the following day. In this round, the queries became more pointed. Qatar asked whether the organization "believe[d] that individual nations do not have the right to make laws and govern their societies as their people see fit," and took issue with IGLHRC's use of the Yogyakarta Principles and recognition of "homosexuality as a human right." Egypt again objected to IGLHRC's use of the terms "sexual minorities," "sexual orientation," and "gender identity"; questioned its stance on the Vienna Declaration and Programme of Action; asked about its role in interpreting treaties and human rights instruments; and objected to the Yogyakarta Principles, asking if they would infringe on the First Amendment of the U.S. Constitution. Pakistan concluded by asking whether IGLHRC believed the Yogyakarta Principles were internationally agreed upon. Perle, Jones, Johnson, and a board member worked together to craft responses, stressing that IGLHRC recognized the Yogyakarta Principles were not a binding legal instrument, re-enclosing over three hundred pages of references to "sexual orientation" and "gender identity" in UN documents, and clarifying that IGLHRC "works to promote respect for international human rights obligations under relevant UN instruments and national laws."[44]

As Perle noted, this emphasis on the UN Charter and binding international law required stepping back from the Yogyakarta Principles, which other LGBT NGOs were actively foregrounding in their UN advocacy:

> It used to be some sexual rights groups got questions about the Yogyakarta Principles, now it's just all of them. Maybe it's because they're all referencing them, and that's the response. But we have to talk about them, at least to the committee, very, very carefully.... I mean, there's definitely a difference

between saying the Yogyakarta Principles is law, and the Yogyakarta Principles is a statement on the application of law, and emphasizing one or the other. And I think at least until we have status, we have to be careful, or at least, to the committee, we have to be careful in how we conceive of these things.

The questions also confounded understandings of terms like "LGBT," "sexual orientation," and "gender identity," which some states simply refused to use. As Perle recalled:

> One of Egypt's number one complaints—I'm saying Egypt as a representative of a bloc that opposes sexual rights at the UN—one of their number one ways of framing their opposition to sexual orientation is not that gays are icky or immoral, it's that sexual orientation as a concept doesn't exist, and it certainly doesn't exist in law. So they always say "so-called sexual orientation." Egypt, Qatar, and Pakistan, they have the same way of talking about sexual orientation and gender identity, where they don't want to use those terms. And they don't want to use the terms lesbian, gay, bisexual, transgender, because then it affirms those things' existence. So they have verbal tics around them, on purpose.

The adamant refusal to recognize the populations and terminology with which IGLHRC worked presaged the opposition that followed. When IGLHRC's application was finally considered on June 3, 2010, it was blocked by the Committee on NGOs. Although the United States brought the application to a vote, Egypt successfully moved to not consider the U.S. motion. The result was that IGLHRC's application was not rejected, but also would not proceed.

The vote garnered a tremendous amount of media attention, and triggered months of intensive networking by staff in New York, regional program coordinators, and a member of IGLHRC's board of directors. By working with governments and circulating a petition signed by over two hundred NGOs from fifty-nine countries, brokers prepared to push for consideration of IGLHRC's application when the full ECOSOC convened. When the matter was brought to the body on July 19, 2010, the United States had a final opportunity to bring the disputed motion for reconsideration. Amid heavy lobbying, the U.S. motion prevailed, and IGLHRC's application was approved.

The repercussions of the victory, however, remained to be seen. Prior to the vote, there was concern that Egypt's growing frustration with IGLHRC at the UN would be realized in backlash elsewhere in the world. Brokers received word that Egypt planned to introduce a resolution at the ACHPR clarifying Africa's opposition to recognizing LGBT rights, which, if introduced, would almost certainly pass. As Perle noted in an interview just prior to the ECOSOC vote:

> It's two days before we're supposed to get ECOSOC, or before ECOSOC, possibly on the same day. And I think that's going to affect our work at the UN. Because right now, we have a chance to get some African states to abstain—and they have in the past abstained on votes, at least on organizations getting status. We've got a couple African countries who signed the declaration on sexual orientation and gender identity in the UNGA, and making, very small, but some inroads, and I worry that this would just wipe that out like that. I'm really, really worried about it.

Perle added, however, that advocacy with regional mechanisms had also bolstered IGLHRC's efforts at the UN:

> In the NGO Committee, Colombia cited the Declaration in the OAS . . . and was like, no, we've signed this and we've endorsed it, and we can't in good conscience allow discrimination on these bases. So they're feeding into each other.

Interestingly, domestic laws did not necessarily indicate how states would engage with LGBT human rights in supranational forums. The most notorious example was South Africa, which constitutionally prohibited discrimination on the basis of sexual orientation but offered minimal support for supranational LGBT initiatives in the early 2000s. By contrast, Brazil, which had more to achieve in its domestic law, was extraordinarily proactive in early efforts at the UN.

The lines drawn in the ECOSOC battle were similarly evident when IGLHRC co-sponsored a side event at the UNGA for Human Rights Day on December 10, 2009. The panel discussion, "Opposing Grave Human Rights Violations on the Basis of Sexual Orientation and Gender Identity," was hosted by the Permanent Mission of Sweden to the UN and the missions of Argentina, Brazil, Croatia, France, the Netherlands, and Norway, in coordination with ARC International, COC Netherlands, GATE, HRW, IGLHRC, and ILGA. The panel was moderated by Hans Ytterberg of the

Swedish Ministry of Integration and Gender Equality, and brought together five panelists: Victor Mukasa from IGLHRC; Vivek Divan, a consultant with UNDP and former member of the Lawyer's Collective in India; Reverend Kapya Kaoma, a project director at PRA and the author of *Globalizing the Culture Wars: U.S. Conservatives, African Churches, and Homophobia;* Sass Sasot, a founder of the Society of Transsexual Women of the Philippines (STRAP) and member of ILGA's communications team in Asia; and Indyra Mendoza, the coordinator of Red Lésbica Cattrachas in Honduras. The panel itself was a challenge to coordinate, with multiple LGBT NGOs proposing, vetting, and signing off on potential speakers; ensuring there was representation of different regions, identities, and perspectives; and suggesting alternatives when scheduling conflicts, visas, and other logistical issues got in the way. Settling on a final lineup was a complex process.

The side event provided a platform for a number of strategic interventions. The most obvious was to assert a visible presence at the UN on Human Rights Day, something activists replicated in other years. In 2010, a side event featured Secretary General Ban Ki-moon, U.S. Ambassador to the UN Susan Rice, Assistant Secretary-General Ivan Šimonović of the Office of the High Commissioner for Human Rights (OHCHR), Linda Baumann of Out-Right Namibia, and Vidyaratha Kissoon of the Society Against Sexual Orientation Discrimination (SASOD) in Guyana, with another statement from Buse Kilickaya of Pembe Hayat in Turkey read aloud. The panel's theme affirmed a long-standing emphasis on egregious, uncontroversial human rights violations, cultivating the broadest support possible from states. At the time, this approach had a special resonance as activists decried Uganda's Anti-Homosexuality Bill, warning it would eviscerate basic human rights.

Brokers also leveraged the event to secure commitments from UN members. Prior to the discussion, one human rights activist intensively lobbied the Holy See, which was rumored to be planning a statement opposing grave human rights violations on the basis of SOGI. The opportunity to have this statement made publicly at the UN, where the Holy See had taken the lead in galvanizing opposition and blocking efforts to recognize LGBT rights, was considered momentous.

The perceived import of the statement became especially clear when Mendoza voiced concerns before the panel that Opus Dei, a notoriously conservative prelature in the Catholic Church, was implicated in some of the killings of LGBT persons in Honduras that had happened in late 2009.

When Mendoza stressed the importance of raising this at the UNGA, brokers seemed visibly conflicted. On one hand, they recognized Mendoza's concerns were critically important to her constituency in Honduras and important if the injustice was to be brought to light. On the other hand, they worried that singling out the Catholic Church for criticism would deter its spokesperson from making a precedent-setting statement. Although brokers voiced both concerns, they left it to Mendoza to say what she felt she needed to say in light of these considerations.

On the afternoon of the session, Ytterberg opened by noting that grave violations of the human rights of LGBT persons happened in all six UN regions, and that all states present had a stake in these issues. The panelists then addressed different issues in their regions, alternately using terms like "homosexuals," "homosexual persons," "LGBT," "LGBTI," and "sexual minorities" in their presentations.

The statements that followed were fairly predictable; the governments that delivered them were among the most vocal supporters and opponents of recognizing SOGI at the UN. France stressed the principle of universality, reiterated the broad support for the French Resolution, and announced the creation of a fund for LGBT human rights defenders. A representative of the Holy See then made the much-anticipated statement clarifying that the Vatican opposed grave violations against "homosexual persons." Nicaragua emphasized the importance of solidarity with "LGTTBI," and noted it had recently decriminalized same-sex activity and appointed a special prosecutor to deal with violations of the human rights of LGBT people.

At this point, Egypt, a vocal opponent of recognizing SOGI, interjected. Although the representative stressed that the government opposed discrimination, he asserted that the speakers were advancing controversial concepts that were not recognized by the UN. He asked Divan to explain his role at the UNDP and what mandate he had to defend sexual rights. He asked which of the twenty-eight sexual orientations the speakers were referring to, presumably referencing the argument that "sexual orientation" might refer to any desire or fetish (for example, pedophilia, zoophilia, or scopophilia) and not only the gender of one's partners. He then asked panelists what they thought about religious expression and freedom of expression, and whether these would be endangered by the privileging of other rights. The three questions reflected three objections that Egypt consistently voiced in these debates—contesting the affirmation of LGBT rights by NGOs and UN agencies, objecting to the adoption of concepts like "sexual orientation" and "gender identity" without these being defined by UN member states, and expressing concern that LGBT rights might infringe on the rights of others.

After Egypt, supportive states took the floor once more, with the Netherlands and the United States recalling the language of the UDHR and noting the momentousness of holding the panel on the sixty-first anniversary of the document's adoption. The final statement from the floor came from St. Lucia, however, and poignantly reflected the ambivalence of states that were still developing a position on the recognition of SOGI and LGBT persons in the human rights arena. While the representative stressed that all persons are "born with inherent dignity," she was equivocal about what this meant for states, and whether SOGI could be subject to any legal or social sanction. As vocal governments sparred with each other, her inconclusive remarks spoke to the knot of concerns that quieter states were attempting to untangle.

Public engagements with states illuminated points of disagreement and assisted brokers in recalibrating their strategy and framing of human rights issues. After the panel, brokers considered its implications for their advocacy. They had focused on grave violations of human rights to maximize state support, but increasingly wondered whether this strategy stifled a broader conversation about the full range of human rights at stake. A narrow focus was likely to build support among hesitant states like St. Lucia, but did not speak to the range of discriminatory practices mentioned by speakers on the panel, nor to the panoply of human rights that activists and supportive states thought LGBT people should enjoy. Brokers had also focused on SOGI to accommodate a wide range of people, behaviors, and identities that did not comfortably fit within an LGBT framework, but Egypt's critique of the ambiguity of "SOGI" called this seemingly forward-thinking move into question. Some friendly governments suggested that NGOs specify that they were talking about LGBT people, foreclosing objections that "sexual orientation" and "gender identity" could include an excessively vast array of sexual desires and practices.

Disputes at the UN illuminate the complex terrain on which brokers operate. After years of advocacy, brokers still confront basic epistemological and strategic questions, for example, whether to promote "nondiscrimination" but avoid enumerating specific categories, to adopt categories like "sexual orientation" or "gender identity" to make guarantees unequivocal but expansive, or to defend a narrower population of self-identified "LGBT" people. Beyond these choices lay decisions about which rights to demand and the extent to which discussions about relativism, balancing, and responsibilities should be downplayed to insist on the indivisible, inviolable human rights of LGBT persons. All of these strategic calculations were further complicated when brokers held positions that were not necessarily commensurate with the tactical stances of governmental and intergovernmental allies. These dilemmas have no easy answers, but they do suggest that a considerable array of agendas, options, and possibilities remain in play as norms are institutionalized.

CONCLUSION

Brokers spent substantial time, energy, and political capital attempting to institutionalize LGBT rights in the human rights arena. Why did they consider this important, and what did they achieve?

First, brokers recognized that a simple act of institutionalization could have important legal and symbolic consequences, both immediately and in the long term. As women's rights activists have recognized, a treaty "may also be interpreted in a way that advances its goals in contemporaneous circumstances, even if they were not imaginable when the treaty was drafted."[45] The Human Rights Committee's 1994 opinion in *Toonen v. Australia* provides an instructive example. *Toonen* found that Tasmania's sodomy law violated the ICCPR, but did so by broadly concluding that the right to privacy encompassed consensual sex between adults in private, and that the term "sex" in the ICCPR's nondiscrimination clause should be read to include "sexual orientation." Fifteen years later, brokers still reliably invoked *Toonen* as an authority in their transnational advocacy. The opinion not only invalidated a law, but established a powerful standard for states parties to the ICCPR that extended far beyond Tasmania—one that would have been difficult to reach by consensus.

Regional advocacy sought to establish similarly far-reaching standards. The long-term repercussions of efforts at the ACHPR remain to be seen, but commissioners have already begun to raise the criminalization of same-sex activity in their reviews of states.[46] They have left the door open for more robust protections in the future; in *Zimbabwe Human Rights NGO Forum v. Zimbabwe*, the ACHPR suggested that nondiscrimination principles encompassed "nationality, sex, racial or ethnic origin, political opinion, religion or belief, disability, age or sexual orientation."[47] As Kilonzo pointed out, these small victories often escaped notice. If popular support grew in the future, however, brokers could draw attention to these milestones to argue that LGBT human rights had been recognized by the ACHPR.

Second, IGLHRC's work has been deeply symbolic, securing places for LGBT people at literal and figurative tables where human rights are discussed. When asked about the import of various statements before treaty bodies and the UNGA, Perle observed:

> I think they've been helpful, if nothing else, in that the states that signed them, for the most part, seem to take it very seriously. And the states that didn't could care less. . . . They talk about it a lot, they cite it, it's something you can hold against people, you can hold it up to them. And it sounds official, even though it's not. I think it's symbolic. . . . It's a great symbol. And sometimes, I think the symbols are more important than actually getting stuff into the comments.

IGLHRC's efforts to institutionalize LGBT human rights have publicly signaled that LGBT people have asserted a place in the human rights arena. As Perle pointed out, IGLHRC's website got its highest number of hits when the phrase "sexual orientation" was removed from the standing resolution on extrajudicial, summary, and arbitrary executions. IGLHRC's update on the vote was viewed 30,000 times, with 5,000 views on a single day. Other days of especially high traffic were also linked to UN advocacy; when "sexual orientation" was restored to the resolution, it generated 1,700 hits, and when IGLHRC received ECOSOC status, it generated 1,600 hits.

Finally, and less tangibly, brokers' work at the UN and regional bodies generated and strengthened relationships among grassroots groups, IGL-HRC, and policymakers around the globe. As Perle noted, this alone was reason for optimism:

> I mean, the UN, you can argue about whether it's useful, productive, does anything, ever, quickly. But if you believe that it is a useful institution, and it does some good in the world, [then it's about] being a connector [for] people on the ground, whether you're speaking for them or helping them speak to people. Which, sometimes you can do one, sometimes you can do the other, sometimes you can do both.

Brokers actively sought to bring grassroots groups into the international arena, commissioning shadow reports, hosting side events, and sponsoring activist travel. The aim was what Cook called "the snackwich approach," in which transnational NGOs coordinated pressure from domestic and international actors simultaneously.[48] The snackwich approach was far more common for IGLHRC than the classic boomerang model, where domestic actors solicit external allies to pressure their governments.[49] IGLHRC's emphasis on partnership and its informational model meant brokers rarely condemned foreign governments in supranational forums. Instead, IGLHRC brought activists themselves to these spaces, providing support so they could voice concerns internationally as well as domestically. When governments sympathized with IGLHRC's goals, collaboration generated lasting dialogues and relationships, such that working together on issues like grave violations of human rights could gradually build support for interventions that are more proactively protective of LGBT populations.

It remains to be seen whether IGLHRC's recent victories at the UN will create lasting precedents or whether political forces will eventually neutralize or reverse them. Through their work in supranational spaces, however, brokers have bolstered the legitimacy of LGBT issues, entrenched understandings that LGBT rights are human rights, and galvanized NGOs and governments to make LGBT human rights a meaningful priority. Although its efforts remain controversial, the growing visibility and legitimacy of IGLHRC as a participant in these debates has helped place LGBT issues squarely within the ambit of human rights institutions in a lasting and meaningful way.

Conclusion:
For Everyone, Everywhere

Universality, Relativism, and the Anthropology of Human Rights

> We are not born equal; we become equal as members of a group on the strength of our decision to guarantee ourselves mutually equal rights.
>
> —HANNAH ARENDT, *The Origins of Totalitarianism*

In divisive debates about gender, sexuality, and law, proponents and opponents of LGBT human rights have vested interests in reifying claims in particular ways. Proponents frame LGBT rights as straightforward issues of dignity and fairness, insisting universal human rights must be extended to and enjoyed by all. Opponents construct these rights—and, typically, LGBT populations—as foreign, contrary to local morality and custom, and inexorably shaped by global power disparities. In highly politicized environments, there has been precious little space to acknowledge the nuances and partial truths of these positions.

Contests over SOGI thereby reanimate familiar epistemological and political disputes about the universality or relativity of human rights. For legal anthropologists, setting aside these intractable debates about the ontology of human rights in order to explore the *practice* of human rights has been a deeply productive move.[1] As sexual rights advocacy demonstrates, however, asserting universality and decrying relativism can be powerful *tactical* maneuvers, and are foundational to efforts to construct, promote, and institutionalize human rights for marginalized groups.

Even before 1948, advocates sought to extend the promise of universal human rights to vulnerable populations. As Olivia Harris observes, "Certain categories of people . . . are almost *ipso facto* outside the law, and to a certain extent therefore deprived of the status of legal subject."[2] In various places and times, unpropertied males, slaves, laborers, colonized peoples, women, and national, ethnic, linguistic, and religious minorities have been denied recognition as rights-bearing subjects.[3] In recent years, efforts to specify the rights of children, people with disabilities, indigenous peoples, and LGBT people have proven deeply controversial in domestic and supranational forums.[4]

Although advocates stress the universality of human rights, they inject specificity into their campaigns by constructing, promoting, and institutionalizing particular understandings of those rights that reflect the needs of the group they represent. Brokers at IGLHRC actively specified a mission and constituency; forged partnerships; produced and transmitted knowledge; and navigated the politics of law and norm creation. Instead of setting aside debates about the ontology of rights, their advocacy demonstrates why it is productive to look at universalism and relativism processually, and to understand how ever-widening circles of humanity are absorbed into the masses protected by human rights.

In this conclusion, I argue that IGLHRC's advocacy illustrates the importance of ethnographic engagement with brokers who are contesting and developing the boundaries of the human rights project. In doing so, I trace three aspects of brokers' work that recur throughout the preceding chapters. First, I examine how brokers simultaneously construct, promote, and institutionalize a particular corpus of rights, and how these dimensions of their work are mutually constitutive. Second, I return to the idea of contestability, and explore how insistence on the universality of human rights nonetheless involves disagreement, compromise, and political decisions about who and what should be foregrounded in the human rights arena. Third, I look at the concept of opacity, arguing that ethnographic exploration of brokerage is crucial in understanding how the specific origins of rights might be acknowledged without undermining their legitimacy as political claims. Ultimately, IGLHRC's advocacy sheds light on the ways defenders of marginalized groups—and perhaps all human rights defenders—balance universality and specificity to make human rights more responsive to human experience.

FOREGROUNDING CONSTRUCTION, PROMOTION, AND INSTITUTIONALIZATION IN THE ANTHROPOLOGY OF HUMAN RIGHTS

Throughout its history, IGLHRC has alternately foregrounded formal advocacy and movement building, a dualism that arises in part from the hybridity of the organization's mandate. IGLHRC is a human rights commission, invested in using a rights-based framework as the organizing principle for its work. It also has a putative constituency of LGBT persons and foregrounds mistreatment on the basis of SOGI, using human rights as a strategic tool for LGBT movements to seek recognition and redress.[5]

While the preceding chapters have focused on LGBT rights, this is not the only area of law where universal protections are invoked to address the needs of specific populations.[6] A similar balance between demanding entry into the human rights framework and seeking to transform the framework itself is struck by contemporary movements for children's rights,[7] disability rights,[8] and indigenous rights,[9] and has been particularly apparent in women's rights advocacy.[10] All of these movements seek human rights protections, but also seek to make those protections cognizant of the unique issues their constituencies face as a result of their social position.

The dialectical relationship between universality and specificity in these campaigns has been profoundly generative. In their work, women's rights activists have not only insisted on the legal recognition of women, but have challenged hegemonic understandings of so-called public and private spheres, the culpability of nonstate actors, and the centrality of civil and political rights.[11] They have institutionalized their perspectives with instruments like CEDAW and rulings like *Jessica Gonzales v. U.S.A.*, in which the IACHR faulted the United States for failing to protect women and girls from domestic violence.[12] In the process, they have not only secured women's rights, but have broadly redefined what a *human* rights framework considers cognizable and justiciable.

These types of efforts are not merely symbolic, but are about creatively forging *legal* instruments. Brokers attempt to design and refine tools that a wider range of populations can use to make claims and obtain meaningful justice. One obvious example is indigenous rights advocacy, which has developed robust theories of group rights and actively asserted these collective rights within the UN system.[13] The proposed creation of legal instruments to recognize and protect group rights—whether they are framed as a "right to culture" or not—has sparked controversy in both domestic and supranational contexts. Nonetheless, promoting group rights has meaningfully shaped systems of political participation; laws regarding dress, education, and language; and the scope of rights to association, belief, expression, and property. In the process, group rights have taken the experiences of indigenous or minority groups and transformed them into legal frameworks to which individuals as well as groups can appeal for recourse.

Like other movements, brokers at IGLHRC engaged in formal advocacy to affirm the human rights of LGBT people under regional and international law. They spelled out precisely why and how LGBT people should enjoy the human rights guaranteed by supranational bodies. They urged governments and intergovernmental bodies, particularly the United States and various officials and agencies at the UN, to speak out or pressure countries where there were clear and immediate threats to LGBT rights. They engaged in naming and shaming, using partnerships and their role in knowledge production to generate action alerts, letters to governments, and shadow reports in conjunction with in-country groups. In all of these efforts, they stressed how stigmatization and marginalization meaningfully deprive LGBT people and others not only of human rights but of dignity, well-being, autonomy, and intimate relationships.

By engaging in this advocacy, brokers also operated in a decidedly *normative* register. As global networks develop, "one of the main ways these efforts at transnational collective action work is by creating and enforcing international norms."[14] Brokers at IGLHRC not only developed and advanced *particular* LGBT human rights, *but the normative concept of LGBT human rights itself.*

The normative aspect of IGLHRC's work went largely unremarked, but asserting the humanity of LGBT people has been foundational to brokers' legal and political work. As Ellen Messer argues, "Human rights are less a problem of the correct legal formulations of rights and more a problem of human classification, of who is not counted as a complete human being and social member deserving of rights."[15] In *The Origins of Totalitarianism*, Hannah Arendt underscores the importance of "the right to have rights," which was routinely denied to refugees, stateless people, displaced people, and minorities amid the wars of the twentieth century.[16] The ability to be recognized as a human person, judged by the character of one's thoughts and actions rather than one's identity or affiliation, is central to the contemporary efforts of countless marginalized groups.[17]

What Arendt's formulation makes clear is that the legal and normative aspects of rights-based claims are inextricably intertwined. As Seyla Benhabib argues, the first use of the term "right" in Arendt's phrase articulates "a moral imperative" addressed to all of humanity, while the second use of the term is a "juridico-civil" demand for actionable rights, duties by others, and protection by the state.[18] By making legal and normative claims, brokers in human rights movements not only engage in advocacy but also seek to enshrine particular understandings about rights and the populations that deserve them.[19] The disability rights movement is one of many examples in which activists have not only sought formal legal protections, but have insisted on the humanity of a population and advanced ontological arguments through rights-based advocacy.[20]

Ontological arguments can be made in various registers. Yet rights have become a hegemonic frame through which groups discursively assert their humanity, such that claiming rights has practically become a necessary component of any political claim-making by marginalized groups. Sonia Corrêa, Rosalind Petchesky, and Richard Parker allude to this when they emphasize a "paradox of indispensability and insufficiency" in human rights advocacy—that is, that engaging with rights is imperative, even if rights alone fail to deliver meaningful justice.[21]

The normative dimension of brokers' work generated efforts that fell outside the boundaries of formal advocacy in a traditional human rights framework—for example, promoting the inclusion of MSM in NSPs to combat HIV/AIDS in sub-Saharan Africa, or exploring how religious fundamentalism shaped homophobia in LAC. The emphasis on norms also exceeded the strictures of movement building. Although brokers worked diligently to boost the capacity of activists, NGOs, and networks, they also articulated their own views about the rights and recognition owed to LGBT persons in exchanges with supranational bodies, governments, funders, journalists, and other NGOs and movements.

In pursuit of these legal and normative ends, brokers have constructed, promoted, and institutionalized particular understandings of LGBT human rights as part of their work. This trifecta of practices is especially pronounced in sexual rights advocacy, where brokers' tactical maneuvers are aggressively politicized, but it is arguably common to all movements seeking to expand the enjoyment of human rights.

What is not always clear to those who witness frontstage advocacy is how these processes of construction, promotion, and institutionalization are both simultaneous and mutually constitutive. Each of the previous chapters shows that these processes are never wholly distinct, and are inextricably intertwined in transnational human rights advocacy. Precisely because their work was simultaneously legal and normative, brokers at IGLHRC sought to advance the idea of LGBT human rights in a variety of ways. Their operative understandings of human rights; the dynamics of the partnerships and wider networks through which they promoted those rights; and their attempts to enshrine those rights in laws, policies, and practices all inevitably fed into each other in a series of feedback loops.

The complexities are not always obvious, but they have implications for brokers and ethnographers alike. During my fieldwork, brokers at IGLHRC never described their work as constructing ideas about human rights and sexual subjectivity. Most framed their advocacy as holding states account-able to an obligation to respect the human rights of all persons, regardless of SOGI, under domestic, regional, and international law. Brokers tended to see the promotion of human rights as their primary mission and, in their discourse and praxis, foregrounded the partnerships and outputs through which they pursued that goal. While some brokers were keen to see IGL-HRC develop international law at the UN, others were skeptical of its cen-trality to their mission, seeing it as a massive expenditure of time, energy, and resources with little immediate payoff.

Often, scholarly analyses have focused on discrete strands of human rights advocacy without exploring how they wind together into a complex whole. Studies that only look at the discursive or ideological construction of rights neglect the meaningful ways these understandings are inflected by brokers' experiences as they simultaneously promote and institutional-ize those rights in practice. Analyses of the ways that brokers promote rights through partnerships, coalitions, and networks are most compelling when they acknowledge the distinctive, historical understandings of rights and long-term objectives that motivate various actors in those constellations.[22] Examinations of formal human rights jurisprudence and the activity of inter-governmental bodies too often fail to consider the lengthy struggles in which brokers develop and politicize concepts that finally become codi-fied in law and policy. Even ethnographers, whose assessments tend to be far more holistic and conscious of the many dimensions of human rights, often take one or another of these dimensions as their primary object of analysis, looking at the construction, promotion, or institutionalization of human rights as a project in itself.

Focusing on discrete aspects of human rights work can be extraordinarily insightful. What the preceding ethnography suggests, however, is that there is also good reason to highlight the holism of issue-specific human rights movements, and to acknowledge the ways in which their work is never simply about constructing, promoting, or institutionalizing rights. It is nec-essarily about all of these aspects of advocacy. What is understood by bro-kers as an LGBT human right, foregrounded in a partnership, or tactically advanced at the UN all feed into each other, and all give the term "LGBT human rights" its legal and normative content.

In brokers' praxis, there were innumerable instances where these feedback loops were critical. What was discursively constructed as a human right for LGBT people, for instance, was meaningfully shaped by the actual praxis of brokers. Robust discussions about fundamentalisms were largely inspired by the fact that Ferreyra, Alizadeh, Poore, and Kilonzo recognized—and heard from partners in their regions—that religious leaders were playing an outsize role in spreading animus on the basis of SOGI. The recognition of violations by those leaders, families, and others in the so-called private sphere affected the way that brokers conceptualized human rights and thought about the responsibility of state actors for nonstate persecution. The resulting views were not confined to IGLHRC, but shaped how brokers engaged with the UN and other intergovernmental bodies. Brokers highlighted nonstate violence and the importance of proactively promoting LGBT human rights in submissions to the CEDAW Committee, the UPR, and Special Procedures. They brought speakers, including Kaoma and Mendoza, to highlight these issues before supranational forums. Alongside other transnational NGOs, they encouraged institutions like the Holy See to condemn the criminalization of same-sex activity, recognizing its influence as a moral and religious actor as well as a political actor within the UN.

Relatedly, how brokers perceived LGBT human rights, and human rights more generally, influenced what they chose to promote or advance transnationally. The hate crimes discussion is a telling example of this. While many partners were enthusiastic about hate crimes legislation and considered it a legal and symbolic asset for at-risk constituencies, brokers remained skeptical that a human rights organization should ever advocate sending anyone to a South African prison, and were uncomfortable making that a priority. Despite the wishes of many partners, IGLHRC did not incorporate a robust position for or against hate crimes or hate speech legislation into its understanding of LGBT human rights, nor did it actively advance the issue with governments or intergovernmental bodies.

Finally, institutionalization meaningfully shaped what was and was not conceptualized as an LGBT human right and promoted publicly. Brokers were quite conscious of global sensitivities surrounding everything from sex work and public sex to same-sex marriage and adoption rights. It was no accident that brokers tended to speak out most forcefully and unequivocally about criminalization of same-sex activity and discrimination on the basis of SOGI, emphasizing how these practices deprived LGBT persons of basic, widely agreed-on human rights. While brokers and their partners may have shared richer understandings of LGBT lives and the rights needed to live them fully, they grasped the urgent need to establish and codify the most fundamental protections. What would and would not be politic at the UN and other intergovernmental or governmental forums has always shaped how brokers discuss topics like sex work; public sex; bondage, domination, and sadomasochism; marriage; adoption; and the prospect of balancing sexual rights with rights to assembly, association, expression, and belief, among other issues. Notably, the pressures of institutionalization have also affected how other movements talk about SOGI; lesbian-baiting has historically made LGBT advocacy a liability for groups defending women's rights, for example, and complicated cross-movement work domestically and transnationally.[23] In these ways, institutionalization and its imperatives subtly shape how LGBT human rights are constructed and promoted even by committed defenders.

The contentiousness of LGBT human rights owed a great deal to the inseparability of these different aspects of transnational LGBT advocacy. Although a large part of brokers' work is simply extending and applying existing law to marginalized populations, brokers *are* simultaneously engaged in defining, advancing, and codifying rights in their advocacy. Critics often point this out to delegitimize these rights as historically or culturally specific, but it is, at bottom, characteristic of advocacy that has shaped any number of targeted applications of universal human rights since 1948. Every advocacy network in the human rights arena is composed of brokers simultaneously engaging in the construction, promotion, and institutionalization of human rights. While this ethnography stresses the utility of exploring how these aspects are mutually constitutive within an NGO, it is also useful to consider how these competing prerogatives play out in practice.

CONTESTABILITY AND THE UNIVERSALITY OF LGBT HUMAN RIGHTS

If appropriating and adapting human rights discourse is not a new phenomenon, what makes LGBT rights so fiercely contested? LGBT human rights defenders insist they are merely ensuring existing human rights are equally protected and respected for everybody regardless of SOGI—a strategy exemplified by the Yogyakarta Principles.[24] Yet if the preceding chapters have a primary message, it is that articulating and advancing LGBT human rights involves no small degree of agency and creativity. It was that agentive engagement, in all its complexity, that often triggered opposition.

Consider the construction of LGBT human rights. It was not always evident to brokers at IGLHRC who should be included under the LGBT umbrella, or how they should be identified. Throughout IGLHRC's history, "LGBT human rights" were variously construed to include people living with HIV/AIDS, trans and intersex persons, MSM and WSW, and indigenous queer subjectivities like the *bakla, gor jigen,* or *hijra,* often subsumed under the categorical protection of SOGI. Other movements have struggled with analogous questions. The strategic use of terms like "minority," "indigenous," or "First Nation"; or "youth," "young people," or "children" can convey subtly different things and have distinctive political repercussions.[25]

In the sexual rights context, as in others, the contingency of these framings sparked fierce contestation.[26] Opponents seized on variations to argue that LGBT rights were indeterminate, and touted the relatively recent emergence of these forms of self-identification as evidence that these were "new" rights.[27] Brokers responded that universal human rights should apply to all the populations with which they worked, even as they recognized that particular framings and strategies—for example, foregrounding MSM or trans women—brought unique concerns to light as human rights issues.

Brokers also shaped which rights were considered foundational to the concept of "LGBT human rights." A focus on particular kinds of rights is evident in various movements seeking to expand enjoyment of the human rights framework to marginalized groups. As Michael Ashley Stein deftly shows in his analysis of the disability rights movement, different paradigms of disability have been promulgated by activists and governments at different times, which have each generated distinctive understandings of attendant rights.[28] At IGLHRC, the emphasis on decriminalization and nondiscrimination influenced the advocacy brokers undertook.

Disputes became particularly intense when movements clashed over competing rights. The relatively recent construction of "fetal rights," for example, has not only sought to define the fetus as a human, legal, and rights-bearing entity, but has sparked innumerable contests over the rights the fetus might enjoy relative to women, genitors and extended kin, and the state.[29] Opposition to LGBT rights on the basis of sovereignty, freedom of expression, and freedom of conscience was regularly voiced in supranational forums, which shaped how brokers articulated their demands.

The promotion of LGBT human rights produced similarly fierce conflicts. In nation-states where support for LGBT rights is low, politicians have gained considerable political capital at little cost by vehemently opposing LGBT rights. In these contexts, mobilizing external pressure through the boomerang model, or any naming and shaming, can trigger violent backlash. These classic approaches presume that external pressure or shame provides leverage for activists to press governments to recognize rights. When leaders instead use that pressure as evidence of neocolonialism and mock attempts at shaming as the frivolous hand-wringing of a decadent West, transnational advocacy fails—and indeed, plays directly into the rhetoric of its opponents.

Many critiques of transnational LGBT advocacy focus at least in part on this dynamic. Joseph Massad's analysis of IGLHRC's response to the Queen Boat case in Egypt in 2001, under Long's leadership as program director, argues that transnational NGOs construct "gay" subjects around the globe who can then be regulated and repressed.[30] Long's own exploration of activist responses to arrests in Iran similarly highlights the potentially fatal consequences of misrecognition and poorly planned interventions from the North.[31] Brokers at IGLHRC were quite aware of these dangers. Even if they did not always manage to avoid them, their caution reinforced the centrality of partnership, the insistence on verifying facts with trusted activists and NGOs in a region, and the nondirective nature of much of IGLHRC's work.

Finally, brokers sparked contestation by seeking to institutionalize LGBT human rights. At the UN and other supranational forums, brokers sought rights and recognition for LGBT populations under intense political pressure. These contests forced brokers to make a number of tactical choices. Brokers debated the relative merits of focusing on identities, behaviors, or categories—that is, whether to demand rights for LGBT people, same-sex practicing people, or those marginalized on the basis of SOGI. They also had to decide which rights to foreground to whom, and when. They regularly forum-shopped, focusing on officials, agencies, and venues—for example, Special Rapporteurs, the UNDP and UNAIDS, and the HRC—that were likely to be sympathetic to their claims. They also timed their interventions carefully, waiting when possible to build support among states before reintroducing statements that might tactically consolidate support for LGBT human rights.

All of these interventions took place under the auspices of universal human rights, and indeed, relied heavily on the rights enshrined in the ICCPR and ICESCR. These had been explicitly extended to all people regardless of SOGI in *Toonen v. Australia* and in the Committee on Economic, Social and Cultural Rights' General Comment 20, and affirmed by treaty bodies monitoring implementation of the CRC, CAT, CEDAW, and other instruments.[32] Brokers consciously focused on human rights that were well established under international law, which was understandable from a tactical standpoint, but tended to divert attention from discussions about socioeconomic rights and preclude difficult debates about group rights, self-determination, and sovereignty.

The structures in which brokers operated and the decisions they made illustrate how LGBT human rights, however universal in scope and application, are nonetheless given concrete form and practically advanced by actual people in particular ways. The contests that erupted over LGBT human rights often surfaced precisely when brokers exercised agency and creativity to give them content and meaning. While sexual rights may seem especially polemical, they illuminate dynamics that are common to human rights advocacy more generally. In various movements, from those focusing on *jus cogens* norms to those insisting on the full enjoyment of human rights by marginalized populations, the rhetoric of universality masks tactical decisions about how to construct, promote, and institutionalize rights—and, indeed, the controversial recognition of the human role in animating the promises of human rights.

OPACITY AND THE SPECIFICITY OF LGBT HUMAN RIGHTS

In large part, the human rights of LGBT persons are controversial because LGBT identities are a highly contingent development, which emerged from a very specific time, place, and set of conditions. Within the academy, analyses of transnational LGBT NGOs that couch their advocacy in terms of white Western maleness have been deeply insightful in understanding the historical and political specificity of LGBT rights, and why they might spark contestation. Nonetheless, these analyses are ill-equipped to grasp why brokers operate as they do, and how brokers navigate pressures they experience from a range of actors, including—not inconsequentially—themselves and their coworkers. Understanding who engages in human rights advocacy and what motivates their action is critical if analyses are to go deeper than imputing motivations based on race, nationality, and gender.

This not only holds true for LGBT rights, women's rights, and other movements in which Northerners' roles have been productively interrogated, but for human rights advocacy more broadly. Context has always shaped how human rights have been articulated and realized, and deter-mined where the boundaries of universality lie.[33] IGLHRC's advocacy illus-trates that questions of universality and specificity are not solely ontological. They are also political, and in contentious debates about human rights, it is possible to trace the universalizing and relativizing tactics actors use to strengthen and undermine rights-based claims.

A major obstacle to frank and open discussion about sexual rights advo-cacy, however, is that any recognition of the historical specificity of LGBT human rights tends to be appropriated to undermine their legitimacy. While LGBT human rights and their defenders have often been maligned by out-siders as inherently white, Western, and male, it is important to consider what these descriptions do and do not tell us about the ways these rights are developed and advanced in practice. By doing so, one can begin to grasp how these rights *are* resolutely specific yet remain viable and compelling as political claims.

To some extent, LGBT people are unique in human rights law, and can be productively counterpoised against other populations that have claimed these rights. Women, for example, are presumed to exist in every country, are usually recognizable as women to outsiders, and are almost universally understood to bear a greater risk of subordination, discrimination, and mis-treatment than nonwomen.[34] Analogous claims are often made for racial, ethnic, or religious minorities; refugees; children; and other groups, albeit to a lesser extent. By contrast, leaders do deny that queer people exist in their country; it is not always clear who is queer or how that is defined; and if queer people *are* recognized as targets of ill-treatment, this is routinely regarded as the consequence of their being criminal, sick, immoral, or oth-erwise corrosive to the social fabric. If anything, then, human rights viola-tions are often regarded as a useful deterrent to aberrant sexual behavior. As Sibongile Ndashe argues:

> The big distinction between discrimination against sexual minorities and the discrimination that other groups are subjected to is that the law serves to authorise, normalise and legitimise the discrimination by criminalising the sexual conduct of sexual minorities. In almost all cases, governments will gladly own up to the laws and justify their existence. The other forms of dis-crimination are often issues that the governments themselves feel that they do not have a solution to and have taken steps to prohibit discrimination on that basis.[35]

Although virtually every marginalized group has had to fight for entry into the human rights arena, epistemological questions about what it means to be queer or LGBT, combined with active hostility from political leadership, make claims to universality especially difficult.

Yet the sociocultural specificity that haunts LGBT human rights advocacy is perhaps not an exception, but a rule. Ideas like childhood, indigeneity, and disability are profoundly specific, and painstaking negotiations to construct transnational agreements around such categories belie the fact that states still argue that their own understanding of these categories is exceptional. Even for women, racial or ethnic minorities, and religious sects, it is not self-evident who counts as "deserving" of human rights protection. While governments may endorse the protection of a wide number of numerical or social minorities, they regularly take exception when populations within their own territories are classified as such and demand protection. States routinely assert what they consider overriding sovereign prerogatives—for example, national security, public health, or migration controls—in order to justify convenient exceptions to universal human rights. A focus on LGBT rights highlights the wide range of tactics states employ to signal inclusion and exclusion of various populations, and underscores that supranational agreements do not resolve these contests over universality with any finality.

Disputes over sexual rights are good to think with politically, then, but they also offer fresh perspectives on familiar questions about the biases of the human rights framework: its focus on state actors, its demarcation of public and private spheres, and its penchant for juridical processes that make robust discussions of balancing or qualifying rights difficult. As a form of law, human rights require categorization for their very operation, and sexuality is a field that, to put it mildly, resists easy categorization.[36] Brokers have resisted identity politics and embraced a more categorical approach by seeking to protect "sexual orientation" rather than homosexual acts or gay, lesbian, and bisexual persons. Nonetheless, this seemingly inclusive category itself presumes that "sexual orientation" is a discrete, stable, and intrinsically important part of selfhood.[37] As critics query these underlying assumptions, they might also question categories like race, sex, religion, language, nationality, childhood, indigeneity, and ability, which similarly aspire to crosscultural intelligibility and importance.

Activists are not necessarily oblivious to these complexities; indeed, many struggle with them on a daily basis. What they conclude, however, is that the specificity of identities and categories does not preclude a robust political project. One aspect of activist praxis that emerges in ethnographies of human rights NGOs is that a tremendous amount of energy is devoted to universalizing human rights. The goal is not only to construct universal categories that can be used to claim protections and entitlements for the populations in question but also to endow their rights with the normative force of international law: to demand them at the UN, to enshrine them in declarations, and to not only require state compliance, but have states take these rights seriously enough to police themselves and offer their own guarantees.

Too often, these universalizing practices—and the relativizing practices undertaken by opponents—are obscured in critical analyses that fail to look at which actors are promoting a human rights framework, which other politics they hold dear as they do so, and how the rights and priorities of different groups are worked out processually. The studies that do exist have been enormously insightful insofar as they track debates about the language, content, and justiciability of different rights at the UN and other bodies. These often focus on the stage, however, when states are negotiating these rights as a matter of policy, and not the prior stages when brokers themselves are developing rights-based projects and defining who and what they might protect. Virtually every human rights movement has been shaped by these processes to different extents. They spawn questions about who counts as "indigenous," what rights are considered important for children to exercise in vastly different sociocultural contexts, and how women's rights might require distinctive theories of culpability. They also draw attention to who answers such questions in human rights movements, how, and why.

The tension between universalizing and relativizing practices gives human rights their dynamism, and disputes over sexual rights are a particularly good place to examine how these practices are deployed politically.[38] LGBT rights are among the most controversial assertions of human rights at the UN and other intergovernmental forums and, like the rights of children, indigenous peoples, or disabled persons, helpfully illuminate the hierarchies, geopolitics, and power dynamics of international law. They are also indubitably part of the construction of new forms of sexual subjectivity, and globalize particular understandings of SOGI as meaningful parts of selfhood that must be respected and protected in all their diversity. Disputes about how this kind of sexual subjectivity is codified domestically, regionally, and internationally can reveal a great deal about how the state, the nation, the family, and other social units are conceptualized and politicized in comparative perspective.

In these myriad ways, the anthropology of human rights can benefit from the questions raised by brokerage at IGLHRC. Although human rights as a concept are the product of a very specific history, they are too often treated as an ideological monolith. The work that brokers do on a day-to-day basis to define, advance, and codify human rights offers one snapshot of the ways that human rights are perpetually being reconfigured and redeployed, and draws much-needed attention to the role that activists play in these processes.

On the Anthropology of Transnational Human Rights Advocacy

The underlying concept that has persisted throughout this text and definitively shaped every chapter is the centrality of brokerage. It is difficult to overestimate how important brokerage is at IGLHRC itself, where individuals exert considerable influence over which projects are undertaken, how they are implemented, and what effect they ultimately have. These individuals are not only activists agitating for justice, but brokers, who actively work through wider networks of legitimacy, information, influence, and resources to affect global change.

The centrality of brokerage is the primary reason that I have discussed IGLHRC's work in the past tense. IGLHRC is a dynamic organization, and it would be disingenuous for me to discuss its advocacy in any sort of timeless present. The ethnography describes the year of my fieldwork from September 2009 to September 2010—it offers a snapshot of a particular moment in IGLHRC's history, not a guide to what brokers currently do or believe. In the name of exploring dilemmas and themes in LGBT advocacy and human rights advocacy more broadly, it necessarily ossifies something that derives its energy and power from entropy. To give a hint of that dynamism, a few subsequent changes merit discussion as a kind of coda.

Just months after I left the organization, IGLHRC closed its office in Cape Town. With the lease about to expire on the physical space, brokers in the Africa Program questioned whether it made sense to have a highly mobile, multinational staff based in South Africa. As staff departed, it was a prescient time to review the future of the office, and it was closed. Shortly after I left, Cook decided to return to graduate school and Perle left for another job doing online advocacy and fundraising for progressive nonprofits, leaving Thomas as the sole person on the Communications and Research staff in New York. Ampatuan left, too, and a new director of development was brought onto the staff to take IGLHRC in a different direction. The LAC Program was then reorganized to have only one staffer, such that D'Elio left and Ferreyra remained. By this point, just months after my departure, only half of the brokers from my fieldwork remained on staff, and many more developments have taken place in the three years since.

During this period, IGLHRC revisited its mission and adopted a new strategic plan. After lengthy discussions, brokers decided that IGLHRC would focus on the two key areas of human rights documentation and global advocacy. The former would involve multicountry convenings, in-country trainings, learning exchanges, and collaborative projects with partners, while the latter would involve work with UN agencies in New York, with CEDAW and the ICCPR, and with the ACHPR, Asia-Pacific Forum, and IACHR. Brokers would also focus their attention at the regional level, and work intensively with a maximum of three to five countries in each of the four regions. Given those priorities, brokers also reorganized the structure of the organization itself. The position of program director was to be split in two, with Jones focusing on formal human rights advocacy and a second broker located outside the United States focusing on work with grassroots groups. A South African activist was hired to work as the Africa Program coordinator from Johannesburg, while Ferreyra, Poore, and Alizadeh all stayed on in their roles to oversee their regions.

Shortly thereafter, Johnson himself left IGLHRC. The new coordinator of the Africa Program left and was replaced. After a decade at IGLHRC, Ferreyra left shortly thereafter. The LAC Program was then staffed by Andres Rivera Duarte, a leading trans activist from Chile, as a part-time consultant until Maria Gomez, a Colombian activist and academic, could begin as regional program coordinator. With new funding, the MENA Program expanded its work, and Poore and Cristobal continued their efforts in the API region. By 2013, IGLHRC had changed in myriad ways. The organization hired a full-time digital communications manager, expanded the Africa Program in Johannesburg, and revamped its strategy.

It is too early to know how these structural changes will affect IGLHRC's advocacy. What they do decisively illustrate, however, is that human rights NGOs are profoundly dynamic, and grounded ethnography is critical if we are to understand how and why the human rights project takes shape and the important roles individual brokers can play at critical moments. Without grasping what advocates do, it is difficult to understand the subtleties of the strategies brokers employ, or to identify alternative ways movements might pursue their vision of a more just and humane order. If anthropologists are to participate fully and constructively in these discussions—and to understand what is at stake for those involved—taking seriously the complexities of constructing, promoting, and institutionalizing rights in practice is an indispensable first step.

Acknowledgments

Even more than other kinds of work, ethnography depends on the trust, generosity, and thoughtfulness of those who put faith in the researcher and project. When the researcher is young and the actors involved are doing demanding work of their own, that faith is truly extraordinary.

Transnational LGBT Activism began as my doctoral dissertation in anthropology at Oxford University. It took shape under the supervision of David Pratten and Fernanda Pirie, whose thoughtful, engaged supervision of the project enriched it in innumerable ways. Prescient insights from Jane Cowan, David Gellner, and Elizabeth Ewart are peppered throughout the book. At Oxford, Khumisho Moguerane, Michelle Osborn, and the participants in the Mbembe/Nuttall Reading Group were wonderful interlocutors on this project and larger questions of anthropology and postcolonialism.

During my fieldwork, my thoughts about the issues at the core of the book were enriched by exchanges with Sally Engle Merry, Jean Comaroff, Zackie Achmat, Keletso Makofane, Sami Zeidan, William Leap, Steven Robins, Codou Bop, and Kapya Kaoma. I benefited a great deal from feedback from participants at the LGBT/Queer Studies: Toward Trans/national Scholarly and Activist Kinships Conference in Madrid, the American Anthropological Association's Annual Meeting in San Francisco, the Yale Law School Doctoral Conference in New Haven, and the Homonationalism and Pinkwashing Conference at the City University of New York. As I wrote and rewrote, Marc Epprecht, Marcel LaFlamme, Soo-Ryun Kwon, Brian Johnsrud, and an anonymous reviewer all offered feedback on the manuscript, giving generously of their scarce time and abundant expertise.

The project would not have been possible without the generosity of the Rhodes Trust, which funded my study at Oxford, or the R. Scott Hitt

Foundation, which supported my position at IGLHRC. Don Markwell, Mary Eaton, and James Vellequette put human faces on that support. Kent Brintnall and Patrick Cheng were wonderful mentors as I embarked on the book project, and at the University of Minnesota Press, Jason Weidemann and Danielle Kasprzak provided expert editorial guidance.

The writing of this manuscript spanned four years, and I was sustained in no small way by friends and family who encouraged, supported, and put up with me throughout. In Oxford, Erika Hanna, Mark McGranaghan, Maria Cecire, Leana Wen, Aaron Mertz, Casey Cep, Chase Mendenhall, and Brian Johnsrud were the best interdisciplinary support system I could have asked for. Brady Littlefield and Emma Beavers made New York feel like home, and were exceedingly patient with me as I puzzled through the challenges of activism and ethnography. During my time in Cape Town, Anna and Daleen Retief opened their home to me and were generous, lovely hosts. My ability to engage the topics in this book owes a lot to my family, who have been supportive of my work for as long as I can remember, and to Marcel LaFlamme, Lee Strock, and David Norton, who have profoundly shaped the ways that I think about anthropology, law, and activism. And last but certainly not least, I'm forever grateful to Matthew, who gave me space to write, constant encouragement, and gentle reminders to take breaks from writing about human interactions and actually have them.

Most of all, I thank the staff at IGLHRC, who bravely opened themselves to this project and thoughtfully engaged with my assessments, and to all the activists, donors, and academics who shared their time and thoughts with me. I learned an incredible amount over the course of this project, and owe that in particular to all of them.

Notes

1. The Matthew Shepard and James Byrd Jr. Hate Crimes Prevention Act added disability, gender, sexual orientation, and gender identity to federal legislation in the United States that dealt with hate crimes committed on the basis of race, color, national origin, and religion. Among its provisions, the act gave state and local authorities an extra $5 million per year to investigate and prosecute these crimes, authorized federal authorities to investigate when state or local authorities were unwilling or unable to do so, and required the FBI to collect data on crimes committed on the basis of gender and gender identity. The act did not contain any penalty enhancements for hate crimes, though such enhancements do exist under the Hate Crimes Sentencing Enhancement Act, passed as part of the Violent Crime Control and Law Enforcement Act of 1994.

2. Joseph A. Massad, *Desiring Arabs* (Chicago: University of Chicago Press, 2007), 160–90; Neville Hoad, *African Intimacies: Race, Homosexuality, and Globalization* (Minneapolis: University of Minnesota Press, 2007); Jin Haritaworn, Tamsila Tauqir, and Esra Erdem, "Gay Imperialism: Gender and Sexuality Discourse in the 'War on Terror,'" in *Out of Place: Interrogating Silences in Queerness/Raciality*, ed. Adi Kuntsman and Esperanza Miyake (York: Raw Nerve Books, 2008), 71–95; Scott Long, "Unbearable Witness: How Western Activists (Mis)recognize Sexuality in Iran," *Contemporary Politics* 15, no. 1 (2009): 119–36.

3. The heads of IGLHRC's programs were hired at different times and thus had slightly different titles, for example, the Middle East and North Africa program coordinator, the regional coordinator for Asia and the Pacific Islands, the program coordinator for Latin America and the Caribbean, and the Africa program coordinator.

4. Within the United Nations, Special Rapporteurs are experts tasked with researching, analyzing, and reporting on a particular country or thematic area.

5. Juan A. Nel and Melanie Judge, "Exploring Homophobic Victimisation in Gauteng, South Africa: Issues, Impacts and Responses," *Acta Criminologica* 21, no. 3 (2008): 19–36; Rainbow Rights Project (R-Rights) and Philippine LGBT Hate Crime Watch,

"The Status of Lesbian, Gay, Bisexual, and Transgender Rights in the Philippines," submission to the UN Human Rights Council for the Universal Periodic Review, 13th Sess., 2011.

6. Joke Swiebel and Dennis van der Veur, "Hate Crimes against Lesbian, Gay, Bisexual and Transgender Persons and the Policy Response of International Governmental Organisations," *Netherlands Quarterly of Human Rights* 27, no. 4 (2009): 485–524.

7. The terms "North" and "South" plot global inequalities in the wake of the East–West divide that predominated during the Cold War. Rafael X. Reuveny and William R. Thompson, "The North–South Divide and International Studies: A Symposium," *International Studies Review* 9, no. 4 (2007): 557. They originated as economic terms, but are widely used by human rights advocates, including my informants, whose advocacy largely focused on transnational institutions and the Global South.

8. International Commission of Jurists (ICJ), "International Human Rights Law and the Criminalization of Same-Sex Sexual Conduct," ICJ Briefing Paper (Geneva: ICJ, 2010); ICJ, *Sexual Orientation and Gender Identity in Human Rights Law: References to Jurisprudence and Doctrine of the United Nations Human Rights System,* 3rd ed. (Geneva: ICJ, 2006).

9. Andrea Cornwall, Sonia Corrêa, and Susie Jolly, "Development with a Body: Making the Connections between Sexuality, Human Rights and Development," in *Development with a Body: Sexuality, Human Rights, and Development,* ed. Andrea Cornwall, Sonia Corrêa, and Susie Jolly (London: Zed Books, 2008), 2; Pinar Ilkkaracan and Karin Ronge, "Integrating Sexuality into Gender and Human Rights Frameworks: A Case Study from Turkey," in Cornwall, Corrêa, and Jolly, *Development with a Body,* 225.

10. Neil MacFarquhar, "In a First, Gay Rights Are Pressed at the U.N.," *New York Times,* December 18, 2008, http://www.nytimes.com/2008/12/19/world/19nations.html.

11. Human Rights Watch (HRW), "UN Human Rights Council: A Stunning Development against Violence," March 22, 2011, http://www.hrw.org/news/2011/03/22/un-human-rights-council-stunning-development-against-violence.

12. UN Human Rights Council, "Human Rights, Sexual Orientation and Gender Identity," UN Doc. A/HRC/17/L.9/Rev.1 (June 15, 2011).

13. Martha C. Nussbaum, *Sex and Social Justice* (New York: Oxford University Press, 1999), 15–16. See also Sangeeta Budhiraja, Susana T. Fried, and Alexandra Teixeira, "Spelling It Out: From Alphabet Soup to Sexual Rights and Gender Justice," in *Development, Sexual Rights and Global Governance,* ed. Amy Lind (London: Routledge, 2010), 132.

14. Helene Cooper, "Ahmadinejad, at Columbia, Parries and Puzzles," *New York Times,* September 25, 2007, http://www.nytimes.com/2007/09/25/world/middle east/25iran.html.

15. Hoad, *African Intimacies,* xii; Matthew Engelke, "'We Wondered What Human Rights He Was Talking About': Human Rights, Homosexuality, and the Zimbabwe International Book Fair," *Critique of Anthropology* 19, no. 3 (1999): 295.

16. Baden Offord, "Singaporean Queering of the Internet: Toward a New Form of Cultural Transmission of Rights Discourse," in *Mobile Cultures: New Media in Queer*

Asia, ed. Chris Berry, Fran Martin, and Audrey Yue (Durham, N.C.: Duke University Press, 2003), 133–37.

17. Shauna Fisher, "It Takes (at Least) Two to Tango: Fighting with Words in the Conflict over Same-Sex Marriage," in *Queer Mobilizations: LGBT Activists Confront the Law*, ed. Scott Barclay, Mary Bernstein, and Anna-Maria Marshall (New York: New York University Press, 2009), 207–30; Jonathan Goldberg-Hiller, "Do Civil Rights Have a Face? Reading the Iconography of Special Rights," in Barclay, Bernstein, and Marshall, *Queer Mobilizations*, 231–56.

18. Carl F. Stychin, *A Nation by Rights: National Cultures, Sexual Identity Politics, and the Discourse of Rights* (Philadelphia, Pa.: Temple University Press, 1998); Jasbir K. Puar, *Terrorist Assemblages: Homonationalism in Queer Times* (Durham, N.C.: Duke University Press, 2007); Judith Butler, *Frames of War: When Is Life Grievable?* (London: Verso, 2009), 104–11.

19. John D'Emilio, "Capitalism and Gay Identity," in *Powers of Desire: The Politics of Sexuality*, ed. Ann Snitow, Christine Stansell, and Sharon Thompson (New York: Monthly Review Press, 1983), 100–113; David M. Halperin, *One Hundred Years of Homosexuality, and Other Essays on Greek Love* (New York: Routledge, 1990); Jonathan Ned Katz, *The Invention of Heterosexuality* (New York: Dutton, 1995).

20. Marc Epprecht, *Hungochani: The History of a Dissident Sexuality in Southern Africa* (Montreal: McGill-Queen's University Press, 2004), 7.

21. Antonia Chao, "Global Metaphors and Local Strategies in the Construction of Taiwan's Lesbian Identities," *Culture, Health and Sexuality* 2, no. 4 (2000): 377–90; Timothy Wright, "Gay Organizations, NGOs, and the Globalization of Sexual Identity: The Case of Bolivia," *Journal of Latin American Anthropology* 5, no. 2 (2000): 89–111; Alyssa Cymene Howe, "Undressing the Universal Queer Subject: Nicaraguan Activism and Transnational Identity," *City and Society* 14, no. 2 (2002): 237–79; Cindy Patton, "Stealth Bombers of Desire: The Globalization of 'Alterity' in Emerging Democracies," in *Queer Globalizations: Citizenship and the Afterlife of Colonialism*, ed. Arnaldo Cruz-Malavé and Martin F. Manalansan IV (New York: New York University Press, 2002), 195–218; Epprecht, *Hungochani*; Robert Lorway, "Defiant Desire in Namibia: Female Sexual-Gender Transgression and the Making of Political Being," *American Ethnologist* 35, no. 1 (2008): 20–33; Ashley Currier, "Deferral of Legal Tactics: A Global LGBT Social Movement Organization's Perspective," in Barclay, Bernstein, and Marshall, *Queer Mobilizations*, 21–37; Rafael de la Dehesa, *Queering the Public Sphere in Mexico and Brazil: Sexual Rights Movements in Emerging Democracies* (Durham, N.C.: Duke University Press, 2010); Ashley Currier, *Out in Africa: LGBT Organizing in Namibia and South Africa* (Minneapolis: University of Minnesota Press, 2012); Kaitlin Dearham, "NGOs and Queer Women's Activism in Nairobi," in *Queer African Reader*, ed. Sokari Ekine and Hakima Abbas (Oxford: Pambazuka Press, 2013), 186–202.

22. Peter Drucker, ed., *Different Rainbows* (London: Gay Men's Press, 2000); Peter Drucker, "'In the Tropics There Is No Sin': Sexuality and Gay-Lesbian Movements in the Third World," *New Left Review* 218 (1996): 75–101; Martin F. Manalansan IV, "In

the Shadows of Stonewall: Examining Gay Transnational Politics and the Diasporic Dilemma," *GLQ* 2, no. 4 (1995): 425–38; David A. B. Murray, "Between a Rock and a Hard Place: The Power and Powerlessness of Transnational Narratives among Gay Martinican Men," *American Anthropologist* 102, no. 2 (2000): 261–70; Howe, "Undressing the Universal Queer Subject."

23. Donald L. Donham, "Freeing South Africa: The 'Modernization' of Male-Male Sexuality in Soweto," in *The Anthropology of Globalization: A Reader,* ed. Jonathan Xavier Inda and Renato Rosaldo (Oxford: Blackwell, 2002), 410–27.

24. Dennis Altman, "On Global Queering," *Australian Humanities Review* 2 (1996), http://www.australianhumanitiesreview.org/archive/Issue-July-1996/altman.html; Drucker, "In the Tropics"; Tom Boellstorff and William L. Leap, "Globalization and 'New' Articulations of Same-Sex Desire," in *Speaking in Queer Tongues: Globalization and Gay Language,* ed. William L. Leap and Tom Boellstorff (Chicago: University of Illinois Press, 2004), 2–3, 5–7.

25. Bettina Heinz et al., "Under the Rainbow Flag: Webbing Global Gay Identities," *International Journal of Sexuality and Gender Studies* 7, nos. 2/3 (2002): 107–24; Chris Berry, Fran Martin, and Audrey Yue, "Introduction: Beep-Click-Link," in Berry, Martin, and Yue, *Mobile Cultures,* 1–18.

26. Tom Boellstorff, "Dubbing Culture: Indonesian *Gay* and *Lesbi* Subjectivities and Ethnography in an Already Globalized World," *American Ethnologist* 30, no. 2 (2003): 225–42.

27. Hoad, *African Intimacies;* Massad, *Desiring Arabs,* 160–90.

28. Kate Bedford, "Loving to Straighten Out Development: Sexuality and 'Ethnodevelopment' in the World Bank's Ecuadorian Lending," *Feminist Legal Studies* 13 (2005): 295–322; Kate Bedford, "The Imperative of Male Inclusion: How Institutional Context Influences World Bank Gender Policy," *International Feminist Journal of Politics* 9, no. 3 (2007): 289–311; Stacy Leigh Pigg, "Globalizing the Facts of Life," in *Sex in Development: Science, Sexuality, and Morality in Global Perspective,* ed. Vincanne Adams and Stacy Leigh Pigg (Durham, N.C.: Duke University Press, 2005), 39–65.

29. Some analysts have persuasively argued that sweeping changes in ideas about sex and society, and not LGBT movements per se, have in fact been the primary engines of sodomy law reform globally. David John Frank, Steven A. Boutcher, and Bayliss Camp, "The Reform of Sodomy Laws from a World Society Perspective," in Barclay, Bernstein, and Marshall, *Queer Mobilizations,* 123–41.

30. John L. Comaroff and Jean Comaroff, "Law and Disorder in the Postcolony: An Introduction," in *Law and Disorder in the Postcolony,* ed. Jean Comaroff and John L. Comaroff (Chicago: University of Chicago Press, 2006), 22.

31. Gerald N. Rosenberg, *The Hollow Hope: Can Courts Bring About Social Change?,* 2nd ed. (Chicago: University of Chicago Press, 2008), 339–429. U.S. activists tend to appeal to the human rights framework in particular when civil rights regimes appear to be closed. Sally Engle Merry et al., "Law from Below: Women's Human Rights and Social Movements in New York City," *Law and Society Review* 44, no. 1 (2010): 122–23.

32. Gerald L. Neuman, "Human Rights and Constitutional Rights: Harmony and Dissonance," *Stanford Law Review* 55 (2003): 1863–1900.

33. Sally Engle Merry, "Legal Pluralism and Transnational Culture: The *Ka Ho'oko-lokolonui Kanaka Maoli* Tribunal, Hawaii, 1993," in *Human Rights, Culture and Context: Anthropological Perspectives*, ed. Richard A. Wilson (London: Pluto Press, 1997), 28–48; Sally Engle Merry, "Transnational Human Rights and Local Activism: Mapping the Middle," *American Anthropologist* 108, no. 1 (2006): 38–51; Daniel M. Goldstein, "Human Rights as Culprit, Human Rights as Victim: Rights and Security in the State of Exception," in *The Practice of Human Rights: Tracking Law between the Global and the Local*, ed. Mark Goodale and Sally Engle Merry (Cambridge: Cambridge University Press, 2007); Lauren Leve, "'Secularism Is a Human Right!': Double-Binds of Buddhism, Democracy, and Identity in Nepal," in Goodale and Merry, *Practice of Human Rights*, 78–113; Shannon Speed, "Exercising Rights and Reconfiguring Resistance in the Zapatista Juntas de Buen Gobierno," in Goodale and Merry, *Practice of Human Rights*, 163–92; Jean E. Jackson, "Rights to Indigenous Culture in Colombia," in Goodale and Merry, *Practice of Human Rights*, 204–41.

34. Kay Warren, "The 2000 UN Human Trafficking Protocol: Rights, Enforcement, Vulnerabilities," in Goodale and Merry, *Practice of Human Rights*, 242–69.

35. Sally Engle Merry, *Human Rights and Gender Violence: Translating International Law into Local Justice* (Chicago: University of Chicago Press, 2006).

36. Stephen Hopgood, *Keepers of the Flame: Understanding Amnesty International* (Ithaca, N.Y.: Cornell University Press, 2006).

37. Naz K. Modirzadeh, "Taking Islamic Law Seriously: INGOs and the Battle for Muslim Hearts and Minds," *Harvard Human Rights Journal* 19 (2006): 191–233.

38. Mark Goodale, "Locating Rights, Envisioning Law between the Global and the Local," in Goodale and Merry, *Practice of Human Rights*, 24.

39. Richard A. Wilson, "Human Rights, Culture and Context: An Introduction," in Wilson, *Human Rights, Culture, and Context*, 10–14; Goodale, "Locating Rights, Envisioning Law"; Jo Becker, *Campaigning for Justice: Human Rights Advocacy in Practice* (Stanford, Calif.: Stanford University Press, 2013).

40. Richard A. Wilson, "Tyrannosaurus Lex: The Anthropology of Human Rights and Transnational Law," in Goodale and Merry, *Practice of Human Rights*, 351.

41. Matthew Waites, "Critique of 'Sexual Orientation' and 'Gender Identity' in Human Rights Discourse: Global Queer Politics beyond the Yogyakarta Principles," *Contemporary Politics* 15, no. 1 (2009): 137–56; Neville Hoad, "Between the White Man's Burden and the White Man's Disease: Tracking Lesbian and Gay Human Rights in Southern Africa," *GLQ* 5, no. 4 (1999): 559–84.

42. Hoad, "White Man's Burden"; Massad, *Desiring Arabs*, 160–90.

43. Jane K. Cowan, "Culture and Rights after *Culture and Rights*," *American Anthropologist* 108, no. 1 (2006): 9–24; Jane K. Cowan, "The Uncertain Political Limits of Cultural Claims," in *Human Rights in Global Perspective: Anthropological Studies of Rights, Claims and Entitlements*, ed. Richard Ashby Wilson and Jon P. Mitchell (London:

Routledge, 2003), 140–62; Valerie Sperling, Myra Marx Ferree, and Barbara Risman, "Constructing Global Feminism: Transnational Advocacy Networks and Russian Women's Activism," *Signs* 26, no. 4 (2001): 1179–82; Shivaji Bhattacharya, "Contradictions and Transgressions: Exploring Implementation of HIV/AIDS Policy at a United Nations Office," *Outliers: A Collection of Essays and Creative Writing on Sexuality in Africa* 3 (2010): 51–67.

44. Hopgood, *Keepers of the Flame*, vii–viii.

45. For notable exceptions, see Dearham, "NGOs and Queer Women's Activism"; Currier, *Out in Africa*; Lorway, "Defiant Desire in Namibia"; Vincent Doyle, "'But Joan! You're My Daughter!' The Gay and Lesbian Alliance against Defamation and the Politics of Amnesia," *Radical History Review* 100 (2008): 209–21.

46. Erving Goffman, *The Presentation of Self in Everyday Life* (Garden City, N.Y.: Doubleday, 1959).

47. Lisa Markowitz, "Finding the Field: Notes on the Ethnography of NGOs," *Human Organization* 60, no. 1 (2001): 42. See also Sharon Macdonald, "Ethnography in the Science Museum, London," in *Inside Organizations: Anthropologists at Work*, ed. David N. Gellner and Eric Hirsch (Oxford: Berg, 2001), 77–96.

48. Eric Hirsch and David N. Gellner, "Introduction: Ethnography of Organizations and Organizations of Ethnography," in Gellner and Hirsch, *Inside Organizations*, 4.

49. Bruno Latour and Steve Woolgar, *Laboratory Life: The Construction of Scientific Facts* (Princeton, N.J.: Princeton University Press, 1986).

50. Richard A. Wilson, "Representing Human Rights Violations: Social Contexts and Subjectivities," in Wilson, *Human Rights, Culture, and Context*, 134–60; Kirsten Hastrup, "Representing the Common Good: The Limits of Legal Language," in Wilson and Mitchell, *Human Rights in Global Perspective*, 16–32; Sally Engle Merry, "Introduction: Conditions of Vulnerability," in Goodale and Merry, *Practice of Human Rights*, 195–203; Alice M. Miller and Carole S. Vance, "Sexuality, Human Rights, and Health," *Health and Human Rights* 7, no. 2 (2004): 5–15; Oliver Phillips, "Blackmail in Zimbabwe: Troubling Narratives of Sexuality and Human Rights," *International Journal of Human Rights* 13, no. 2 (2009): 357–59.

51. Hirsch and Gellner, "Introduction," 12.

52. Arturo Escobar, "Culture, Economics, and Politics in Latin American Social Movements Theory and Research," in *The Making of Social Movements in Latin America: Identity, Strategy, and Democracy*, ed. Arturo Escobar and Sonia E. Alvarez (Boulder, Colo.: Westview Press, 1992), 70–71.

53. Norman Long, "Introduction," in *Battlefields of Knowledge: The Interlocking of Theory and Practice in Social Research and Development*, ed. Norman Long and Ann Long (London: Routledge, 1992), 3–15.

54. David Mosse and David Lewis, "Theoretical Approaches to Brokerage and Translation in Development," in *Development Brokers and Translators: The Ethnography of Aid and Agencies*, ed. David Lewis and David Mosse (Bloomfield, Conn.: Kumarian Press, 2006), 10.

55. Norman Long, *Development Sociology: Actor Perspectives* (London: Routledge, 2001), 24.

56. Jeffrey W. Rubin, "Meanings and Mobilizations: A Cultural Politics Approach to Social Movements and States," *Latin American Research Review* 39, no. 3 (2004): 109. See also Marc Edelman, "Social Movements: Changing Paradigms and Forms of Politics," *Annual Review of Anthropology* 30 (2001): 309–11.

57. In 2008, ILGA members voted to change the confederation's name to the International Lesbian, Gay, Bisexual, Trans, and Intersex Association, but retained the acronym "ILGA."

58. Annelise Riles, *The Network Inside Out* (Ann Arbor: University of Michigan Press, 2000).

59. Ryan Richard Thoreson, "Somewhere over the Rainbow Nation: Gay, Lesbian and Bisexual Activism in South Africa," *Journal of Southern African Studies* 34, no. 3 (2008): 679–97; Ryan Thoreson, "Capably Queer: Exploring the Intersections of Queerness and Poverty in the Urban Philippines," *Journal of Human Development and Capabilities* 12, no. 4 (2011): 493–510; Ryan Richard Thoreson, "Realizing Rights in Manila: Brokers and the Mediation of Sexual Politics in the Philippines," *GLQ* 18, no. 4 (2012): 529–63; Ryan Thoreson, "Beyond Equality: The Post-Apartheid Counternarrative of Trans and Intersex Movements in South Africa," *African Affairs* 112, no. 449 (2013): 646–65.

60. Akhil Gupta and James Ferguson, "Discipline and Practice: 'The Field' as Site, Method, and Location in Anthropology," in *Anthropological Locations: Boundaries and Grounds of a Field Science,* ed. Akhil Gupta and James Ferguson (Berkeley: University of California Press, 1997), 1–46.

61. Laura Nader, "Up the Anthropologist—Perspectives Gained from Studying Up," in *Reinventing Anthropology,* ed. Dell Hymes (New York: Pantheon, 1969), 290.

62. James Clifford, "Introduction: Partial Truths," in *Writing Culture: The Poetics and Politics of Ethnography,* ed. James Clifford and George E. Marcus (Berkeley: University of California Press, 1986), 1–26.

63. Hugh Gusterson, "Studying Up Revisited," *Political and Legal Anthropology Review* 20, no. 1 (1997): 116.

64. Gavin Brown, "Mutinous Eruptions: Autonomous Spaces of Radical Queer Activism," *Environment and Planning A* 39 (2007): 2686. See also David Mosse, "Social Research in Rural Development Projects," in Gellner and Hirsch, *Inside Organizations,* 160–61; Brian Moeran, "From Participant Observation to Observant Participation," in *Organizational Ethnography: Studying the Complexities of Everyday Life,* ed. Sierk Ybema et al. (London: Sage, 2009), 139–55.

65. Brown, "Mutinous Eruptions," 2686.

66. Mosse, "Social Research in Rural Development," 160–61.

67. Susan Wright, "'Culture' in Anthropology and Organizational Studies," in *Anthropology of Organizations,* ed. Susan Wright (London: Routledge, 1994), 1–31; Isabel

Emmett and D. H. J. Morgan, "Max Gluckman and the Manchester Shop-Floor Ethnographies," in *Custom and Conflict in British Society,* ed. Ronald Frankenberg (Manchester: Manchester University Press, 1982), 140–65.

68. Orlando Fals-Borda, *Knowledge and People's Power: Lessons with Peasants in Nicaragua, Mexico and Colombia* (New Delhi: Indian Social Institute, 1988), 94–95.

69. I describe these reports in chapters 3, 4, and 5.

70. Hirsch and Gellner, "Introduction," 10.

71. Macdonald, "Ethnography in the Science Museum."

72. Nader, "Up the Anthropologist," 285.

73. Nancy Scheper-Hughes, "The Primacy of the Ethical: Propositions for a Militant Anthropology," *Current Anthropology* 36, no. 3 (1995): 414.

74. Ibid., 419. But see also Jonathan Spencer, "Anthropological Order and Political Disorder," in *Order and Disorder: Anthropological Perspectives,* ed. Keebet von Benda-Beckmann and Fernanda Pirie (Oxford: Berghahn, 2007), 150–65.

75. The project and the politics it involved are discussed at length in chapter 4.

76. At the time of my fieldwork, there were no staff members specifically dedicated to work in North America and Europe.

77. Malcolm Chapman, "Social Anthropology and Business Studies: Some Considerations of Method," in Gellner and Hirsch, *Inside Organizations,* 26.

78. I secured a grant from the R. Scott Hitt Foundation that enabled IGLHRC to hire me as an independent contractor while I was in New York. When I was in Cape Town, IGLHRC paid me $2,200 per month to work full-time on their report on blackmail and extortion, which I discuss in chapter 3.

79. Macdonald, "Ethnography in the Science Museum," 88–90.

80. Of course, no activist or ethnographer is omnipotent. It perhaps goes without saying that this ethnography reflects my own perspective, and others would characterize events from the period of my fieldwork differently than I would.

81. Judith Okely, "Anthropology and Autobiography: Participatory Experience and Embodied Knowledge," in *Anthropology and Autobiography,* ed. Judith Okely and Helen Callaway (Oxford: Routledge, 1992), 1–27.

82. Nadz, "Export 'Hope?' No, Thanks, America," *Bekhsoos,* March 21, 2010, http://www.bekhsoos.com/web/2010/03/export-hope-no-thanks-america.

83. Markowitz, "Finding the Field," 43.

84. IGLHRC's size may have facilitated this amity and understanding. At a larger NGO, this may have been different; Stephen Hopgood's ethnography of AI, *Keepers of the Flame,* reportedly raised some hackles within the organization.

85. Jonathan Spencer, "Anthropology as a Kind of Writing," *Man* 24, no. 1 (1989): 150–52.

86. Hirsch and Gellner, "Introduction," 10; David Mosse, "Anti-Social Anthropology? Objectivity, Objection, and the Ethnography of Public Policy and Professional Communities," *Journal of the Royal Anthropological Institute* 12 (2006): 935–56.

87. Faye Ginsburg, "The Body Politic: The Defense of Sexual Restriction by Anti-Abortion Activists," in *Pleasure and Danger: Exploring Female Sexuality*, ed. Carole S. Vance (London: Routledge and Kegan Paul, 1984), 173–88.

88. Macdonald, "Ethnography in the Science Museum," 77; Simon Pulman-Jones, "Observing Other Observers: Anthropological Fieldwork in a Unit for Children with Chronic Emotional and Behavioural Problems," in Gellner and Hirsch, *Inside Organizations*, 117–35.

89. "Queer" can also signal a particular political stance. Sokari Ekine and Hakima Abbas, "Introduction," in Ekine and Abbas, *Queer African Reader*, 3–4.

90. Deborah Elliston, "Anthropology's Queer Future: Feminist Lessons from Tahiti and Her Islands," in *Out in Theory: The Emergence of Lesbian and Gay Anthropology*, ed. Ellen Lewin and William L. Leap (Chicago: University of Illinois Press, 2002), 290.

91. Hannah Arendt, *The Origins of Totalitarianism* (New York: Harcourt, 1968), 296–97.

1. FROM THE CASTRO TO THE UN

1. Micheline R. Ishay, *The History of Human Rights: From Ancient Times to the Globalization Era* (Berkeley: University of California Press, 2008), 6–7.

2. Judith Resnik, "Law's Migration: American Exceptionalism, Silent Dialogues, and Federalism's Multiple Ports of Entry," *Yale Law Journal* 115 (2006): 1591–93.

3. Makau Mutua, "Sexual Orientation and Human Rights: Putting Homophobia on Trial," in *African Sexualities: A Reader*, ed. Sylvia Tamale (Oxford: Pambazuka Press, 2011), 452, 454.

4. Craig J. Konnoth, "Created in Its Image: The Race Analogy, Gay Identity, and Gay Litigation in the 1950s–1970s," *Yale Law Journal* 119 (2009): 316–72.

5. Dorf found herself torn between Japanese and Soviet studies, but joked that she opted for the latter because of her political sympathies, her love for Russian literature, and the fact that the department served vodka during Wesleyan's shop-around period.

6. Sidney Tarrow, *Power in Movement* (Cambridge: Cambridge University Press, 1998), 25. See also David A. Snow and Robert D. Benford, "Master Frames and Cycles of Protest," in *Frontiers in Social Movement Theory*, ed. Aldon D. Morris and Carol McClurg Mueller (New Haven, Conn.: Yale University Press, 1992), 133.

7. Françoise Girard, "Negotiating Sexual Rights and Sexual Orientation at the UN," in *SexPolitics: Reports from the Frontlines*, ed. Richard Parker, Rosalind Petchesky, and Robert Sember (Rio de Janeiro: Sexuality Policy Watch, 2007), 317–18.

8. UN Human Rights Committee, *Toonen v. Australia*, UN Doc. CCPR/C/50/D/488/1992 (1994).

9. Rachel Rosenbloom, ed., *Unspoken Rules: Sexual Orientation and Women's Human Rights* (New York: Cassell, 1996); Rachel Rosenbloom, "Putting Sexual Orientation on the Agenda," *Journal of the International Institute* 3, no. 2 (1996): 17, 23.

10. Girard, "Negotiating Sexual Rights," 331. References to sexual orientation were deleted on the last day of the conference, but references to sexuality were retained in Paragraph 96.

11. IGLHRC used similar tactics to demand gay and lesbian rights whenever opportunities presented themselves. At Beijing, Dorf recalls riding an escalator with activists in lesbian rights tee-shirts and realizing that then–first lady Hillary Clinton, flanked by Secret Service agents, was coming toward them on the opposite escalator. As they crossed paths, the lesbian activists yelled, "Hillary, are lesbian rights human rights?" As Dorf recalls, Clinton turned her head toward them and simply smiled.

12. Julie Dorf and Gloria Careaga Pérez, "Discrimination and the Tolerance of Difference: International Lesbian Human Rights," in *Women's Rights, Human Rights: International Feminist Perspectives,* ed. Julie Peters and Andrea Wolper (New York: Routledge, 1995), 324–34; Rosenbloom, "Putting Sexual Orientation on the Agenda"; Ara Wilson, "Lesbian Visibility and Sexual Rights at Beijing," *Signs* 22 (1996): 214–18.

13. Scholinski used the name "Daphne" during this period; Dylan Scholinski is now an artist and author.

14. For accounts of this period, see Kagendo Murungi, "Small Axe at the Crossroads: A Reflection on African Sexualities and Human Rights—Life Story," in Ekine and Abbas, *Queer African Reader,* 229–43; Zandile Makahamadze and Kagendo Murungi, "*Nhorondo—Mawazo Yetu:* Tracing Life Back: Our Reflections—Life Story," in Ekine and Abbas, *Queer African Reader,* 290–304.

15. Long later became IGLHRC's program and research director, then program director.

16. The Argentine financial crisis prompted the LAC Program to relocate to Mexico City for over a year, but the program returned to Buenos Aires in 2003.

17. Judith Butler, *Gender Trouble: Feminism and the Subversion of Identity* (New York: Routledge, 2006), xviii.

18. The possibility of merging with HRW was floated to the board again in the early 2000s, but was never pursued.

19. David Mosse has warned of the "discursive determinism" that places too much emphasis on published outputs as representative of actual NGO practice. See David Mosse, *Cultivating Development: An Ethnography of Aid Policy and Practice* (Ann Arbor, Mich.: Pluto Press, 2005), 15.

20. In this chapter, I pay particular attention to the different executive directors that have managed IGLHRC throughout its history. First, informants themselves focused on the role that various executive directors played in defining IGLHRC's advocacy and working environment. Second, IGLHRC has always been a small NGO, and executive directors have been primarily responsible for hiring staff, liaising with major donors and the board, and setting the organization's priorities.

21. Beth Berlo, "Religious Fundamentalists Refuse to Allow Gays on AIDS Panel," *Bay Windows,* July 5, 2001, http//www.baywindows.com/religious-fundamentalists -refuse-to-allow-gays-on-aids-panel-64685.

22. UN Working Group on Arbitrary Detention, *Yasser Mohamed Salah et al. v. Egypt*, UN Doc. E/CN.4/2003/8/Add.1 (2002), 68–74.

23. For an account of this convening, see Currier, *Out in Africa*, 140–46.

24. Celina Romany, "State Responsibility Goes Private: A Feminist Critique of the Public/Private Distinction in International Human Rights Law," in *Human Rights of Women: National and International Perspectives*, ed. Rebecca J. Cook (Philadelphia: University of Pennsylvania Press, 1994), 85–115.

25. For an explicit discussion of IGLHRC's emphasis on sexual rights and SOGI during this period, see Budhiraja, Fried, and Teixeira, "Spelling It Out."

26. For a description of this report's production, see Alejandra Sardá, "Discrimination against Lesbians in the Workplace," in Cornwall, Corrêa, and Jolly, *Development with a Body*, 107–20.

27. Of course, HIV/AIDS was still relevant to IGLHRC's work on SOGI. As I mention in chapter 2, IGLHRC hired a health and human rights officer in its Cape Town office in 2010, whose focus during my fieldwork was largely related to HIV/AIDS.

28. IGLHRC consistently used the acronym "LGBTI" in the 2007 Annual Report, but reverted back to "LGBT" the following year.

29. The concept of partnership, which was expressly highlighted in numerous places in this annual report, became a core part of IGLHRC's approach to advocacy and is explored in depth in chapter 4.

30. Many of IGLHRC's files were put online so they could continue to be used by asylum seekers, refugees, and their advocates, and the ADP was integrated into the Heartland Alliance's immigration and asylum work.

31. In our interview, Araujo explained, "I recognize, in working within a human rights framework, that the organization was working to support activists in their countries—and I kept saying to them, jokingly, 'If you do your job right, I don't have a job,' because then people won't be leaving their countries." Perhaps a larger tension was that activists in some countries were not supportive of those seeking asylum abroad, arguing that they should stay and fight for change. Araujo recognized that tension, but believed that a human rights organization could do both: "Certainly we didn't want to jeopardize our relationships to activists for the sake of the asylum seeker. . . . Our interest ultimately was to the activists in the country, and the individual we could help in other ways. There was sort of a contradiction there, but I think we managed that very well."

32. Movement Advancement Project (MAP), *International LGBT Advocacy Organizations and Programs: An Overview* (Denver, Colo.: MAP, 2008), 11.

33. Debates about the UN helped clarify IGLHRC's eventual role; as I discuss in chapter 6, brokers brought partners to the UN and regional bodies and assisted them with documentation and advocacy.

34. David Lewis, *The Management of Non-Governmental Development Organizations*, 2nd ed. (London: Routledge, 2007), 22, 77–78.

35. The Lawyers Committee for Human Rights, founded in 1978, later became Human Rights First.

36. AMSHeR's first executive director was Joel Nana, a former IGLHRC employee. See Marc Epprecht, *Sexuality and Social Justice in Africa: Rethinking Homophobia and Forging Resistance* (London: Zed, 2013), 170.

37. MAP, *International LGBT Advocacy Organizations*, 9.

38. Ibid.

39. Of course, HRW, AI, and other large NGOs have resources that IGLHRC lacks. Staff in their LGBT programs not only draw on in-house legal, media, and publishing resources, but possess reputational capital that allows them to more easily disseminate and publicize their work.

40. Ettelbrick's assessment remained accurate during my fieldwork. The Africa Program had the largest budget—approximately $400,000 annually—with funding from SIDA, Atlantic Philanthropies, and other major donors. The LAC Program received $25,000 from Overbrook for their Activist Institute, the MENA Program was funded by general operating funds, and the API Program passed funding from the Global Fund for Women directly to its partners.

41. Warren F. Ilchman et al., eds., *Philanthropy in the World's Traditions* (Bloomington: Indiana University Press, 1998).

42. Sperling, Ferree, and Risman, "Constructing Global Feminism," 1159. Ashley Currier offers one account of this phenomenon when she describes how working together on a crisis in Uganda allowed Behind the Mask to build ties with IGLHRC: "These ties raise Behind the Mask's international profile, in turn, allowing the organization to mention these accomplishments when they request future funding from foreign donors." Ashley Currier, "Behind the Mask: Developing LGBTI Visibility in Africa," in Lind, *Development, Sexual Rights and Global Governance*, 164.

43. The U.S. State Department routinely integrates rights violations based on SOGI into their reporting as a result of a presidential memorandum on December 6, 2011. Prior to the memorandum, IGLHRC and other groups submitted information on country conditions when they considered it appropriate to do so, but the information was integrated into the reports on an ad hoc basis.

44. Epprecht, *Sexuality and Social Justice in Africa*, 159.

2. Bodies of Law

1. Massad, *Desiring Arabs*, 161. See also Sokari Ekine, "Contesting Narratives of Queer Africa," in Ekine and Abbas, *Queer African Reader*, 87–88.

2. Ulf Hannerz, *Transnational Connections: Culture, People, Places* (London: Routledge, 1996), 67; David Lewis, "Revealing, Widening, Deepening? A Review of the Existing and Potential Contribution of Anthropological Approaches to 'Third-Sector' Research," *Human Organization* 58, no. 1 (1999): 79; Stella Mascarenhas-Keyes, "Understanding the Working Environment: Notes towards a Rapid Organizational Analysis," in Gellner and Hirsch, *Inside Organizations*, 215.

3. Lewis, "Revealing, Widening, Deepening?," 75.

4. Andil Gosine, "The World Bank's GLOBE: Queers In/Queering Development," in Lind, *Development, Sexual Rights and Global Governance,* 67–85; Kate Bedford, *Developing Partnerships: Gender, Sexuality, and the Reformed World Bank* (Minneapolis: University of Minnesota Press, 2009).

5. The financial staffer was then hired by the firm to continue working part time at IGLHRC.

6. After our interview, some of Jones's quotes were edited for clarity.

7. Although high turnover is not uncommon among small NGOs, it was something that brokers at IGLHRC highlighted in interviews. The characteristics I describe here shaped how advocacy occurred at IGLHRC, but that should not be taken to mean that they were unique to the organization.

8. Massad, "Re-orienting Desire: The Gay International and the Arab World," *Public Culture* 14, no. 2 (2002): 361–62. See also Murungi, "Small Axe at the Crossroads," 236.

9. At times, this gave brokers a fresh and unique perspective on human rights. One manager was frustrated by references to "arbitrary detention," and complained that there was nothing "arbitrary" about targeting people on the basis of SOGI. This in turn exasperated those in the office with legal training, who explained that arbitrary detention was a legal term of art. The exchanges suggest how dominant frames might be disrupted when advocates for specific populations encounter the rhetoric of human rights in their advocacy. I discuss this further in chapter 3 and the conclusion.

10. Hossein Alizadeh and Grace Poore, "Iran: Iran's Sodomy Law—Reading between the Lines," July 20, 2007, http://www.iglhrc.org/content/iran-iran%E2%80%99s-sodomy-law-reading-between-lines.

11. Ettelbrick was also a prominent, long-standing critic of the focus on marriage. See Paula L. Ettelbrick, "Since When Is Marriage a Path to Liberation?," *Out/Look* (Autumn 1989): 8–12; Paula L. Ettelbrick and Julie Shapiro, "Are We on the Path to Liberation Now? Same-Sex Marriage at Home and Abroad," *Seattle Journal for Social Justice* 2, no. 2 (2004): 475–93.

12. Melissa Parker, "Stuck in GUM: Life in a Clap Clinic," in Gellner and Hirsch, *Inside Organizations,* 143.

13. The deep familiarity that brokers had with particular movements and activists could at times complicate their work as well. As Ukwimi explained, it could be difficult to explain to activists with whom one had worked closely that IGLHRC did not have the resources or expertise to assist with certain projects: "If I was maybe somebody just hired from Bombay, it would be easier, much easier, because I could be like, I'm so sorry, we'd love to help you, but it's just not our mandate." Brokers navigated this in a number of ways—incorporating new issues into IGLHRC's work, linking groups with other organizations, and working on projects in their personal capacity, among others.

14. Of course, this does not always work. One example, which IGLHRC was not involved with, was a transgender conference held in Barcelona in the spring of 2010.

Despite backing from groups like HRW, the conference did not result in any kind of declaration. As one attendee described it, many activists were unimpressed by the declaration that was presented, and insisted they had not been given sufficient opportunities to participate in the drafting and solicit feedback from the constituencies they represented.

15. Gabrielle Le Roux, "'Proudly African & Transgender'—Collaborative Portraits and Stories with Trans and Intersex Activists," in Ekine and Abbas, *Queer African Reader,* 55.

16. About a year before my fieldwork began, Clarke had developed a communications manual detailing a process for action alerts, press releases, and other outputs, which Ettelbrick had approved. When Johnson arrived, he wanted to rethink how action alerts were restructured. Here, as elsewhere, staff turnover had programmatic repercussions.

17. The steps were as follows: the author drafts the letter, her supervisor edits it, the author incorporates the edits, a draft goes to the director of programs and director of communications and research simultaneously, and those directors or Communications and Research staff work collaboratively with the author until a final draft is produced. In practice, one or more of these parties was often absent, other parties would be brought into the process, or the executive director would ask to see and approve the output, usually requiring further edits.

18. Wilson, "Representing Human Rights Violations." Clifford Geertz similarly writes about the "skeletonization" of facts in legal argumentation. Clifford Geertz, "Local Knowledge: Fact and Law in Comparative Perspective," in *Local Knowledge: Further Essays in Interpretive Anthropology* (New York: Basic, 1983), 170–74.

19. Modirzadeh, "Taking Islamic Law Seriously."

20. The difficulties of translation—specifically, the difficulty of translating the phrase "cross-dressing males," used by a group in Nepal, into Spanish—are vividly highlighted in an essay by former IGLHRC staff. See Budhiraja, Fried, and Teixeira, "Spelling It Out," 131.

21. HRW, Alternatives-Cameroun, L'Association pour la Défense des Droits des Homosexuels (ADEFHO), and IGLHRC, *Criminalizing Identities: Rights Abuses in Cameroon Based on Sexual Orientation and Gender Identity* (New York: HRW, 2010).

3. Fusing Human Rights and Sexual Politics

1. Rosalind Pollack Petchesky, "Sexual Rights: Inventing a Concept, Mapping an International Practice," in *Sexual Identities, Queer Politics,* ed. Mark Blasius (Princeton, N.J.: Princeton University Press, 2001), 118–39; Henry Armas, "A Democracy of Sexuality: Linkages and Strategies for Sexual Rights, Participation and Development," in Cornwall, Corrêa, and Jolly, *Development with a Body,* 210–24; Epprecht, *Sexuality and Social Justice in Africa,* 26, 150.

2. Wendy H. Wong, *Internal Affairs: How the Structure of NGOs Transforms Human Rights* (Ithaca, N.Y.: Cornell University Press, 2012), 3.

3. Executive Board of the American Anthropological Association, "Statement on Human Rights," *American Anthropologist* 49, no. 4 (1947): 542–43.

4. Lisette Josephides, "The Rights of Being Human," in Wilson and Mitchell, *Human Rights in Global Perspective,* 229–34.

5. Alison Dundes Renteln, *International Human Rights: Universalism versus Relativism* (London: Sage, 1990); Abdullahi Ahmed An-Na'im, ed., *Human Rights in Cross-Cultural Perspectives: A Quest for Consensus* (Philadelphia: University of Pennsylvania Press, 1992).

6. Martin Chanock, "Human Rights and Cultural Branding: Who Speaks and How," in *Cultural Transformation and Human Rights in Africa,* ed. Abdullahi A. An-Na'im (London: Zed, 2002), 60–61.

7. Chris Dunton and Mai Palmberg, *Human Rights and Homosexuality in Southern Africa* (Uppsala: Nordiska Afrikainstituet, 1996), 9–10.

8. Jack Donnelly, *Universal Human Rights in Theory and Practice,* 2nd ed. (Ithaca, N.Y.: Cornell University Press, 2003), 233.

9. Angela Collet, "Interrogating 'Sexualities' at Beijing +10," SPW Working Papers No. 3 (Rio de Janeiro: Sexuality Policy Watch, 2006), 6–8; Dearham, "NGOs and Queer Women's Activism," 192–93.

10. The distinction was usually spelled out in supranational forums. In practice, the two terms were often used interchangeably, and I use them interchangeably throughout this book.

11. This strategy is best embodied in the Yogyakarta Principles on the Application of International Human Rights Law in Relation to Sexual Orientation and Gender Identity, which take the most basic obligations of states under international human rights law and insist that these must be observed regardless of SOGI. See Ryan Richard Thoreson, "Queering Human Rights: The Yogyakarta Principles and the Norm That Dare Not Speak Its Name," *Journal of Human Rights* 8, no. 4 (2009): 323–39.

12. Mutua, "Sexual Orientation and Human Rights," 456.

13. Notably, same-sex marriage is not included in the Yogyakarta Principles, as the authors concluded the scope of the right to marry and found a family of one's choosing is only tentatively defined in international law. See Thoreson, "Queering Human Rights," 328.

14. Charles T. Call, "A Human Rights Practitioner's Perspective," in *Restructuring World Politics: Transnational Social Movements, Networks, and Norms,* ed. Sanjeev Khagram, James V. Riker, and Kathryn Sikkink (Minneapolis: University of Minnesota Press, 2002), 127.

15. UN Economic and Social Council, "Siracusa Principles on the Limitation and Derogation Provisions in the International Covenant on Civil and Political Rights," UN Doc. E/CN.4/1985/4 (1984).

16. International Covenant on Civil and Political Rights (ICCPR), Dec. 16, 1966, 999 U.N.T.S. 171; Organization of African Unity, African Charter on Human and Peoples' Rights, June 27, 1981, O.A.U. Doc. CAB/LEG/67/3 rev. 5.

17. Thom Khanje, "Donors Speak on Gay Rights," *Daily Times* (Malawi), March 17, 2010, http://www.bnltimes.com/index.php?option=com_content&task=view&id=2680 &Itemid=26.

18. Kate Sheill, "Human Rights, Sexual Orientation, and Gender Identity at the UN General Assembly," *Journal of Human Rights Practice* 1, no. 2 (2009): 315–19.

19. As Clarke recalled, many communications and program staff during her tenure at IGLHRC discouraged the use of the term "LGBT." They recognized that "LGBT" might be more recognizable to American audiences, but preferred longer constructions using "SOGI" or, at times, used "sexual minorities." In the LAC region, "LGBTTI" was used if an acronym was absolutely necessary.

20. Jaya Sharma, "The Language of Rights," in Cornwall, Corrêa, and Jolly, *Development with a Body*, 68.

21. Aeyal Gross, "Queer Theory and International Human Rights Law: Does Each Person Have a Sexual Orientation?," *American Society of International Law Proceedings* 101 (2007): 129–32; Waites, "Critique of 'Sexual Orientation.'"

22. Sean Chabot and Jan Willem Duyvendak, "Globalization and Transnational Diffusion between Social Movements: Reconceptualizing the Dissemination of the Gandhian Repertoire and the 'Coming Out' Routine," *Theory and Society* 31, no. 6 (2002): 711–14; Wright, "The Case of Bolivia," 92–96; Chao, "Global Metaphors and Local Strategies," 382; Murray, "Rock and a Hard Place," 263–64; J. Neil C. Garcia, "Unfurling Lives: An Introduction," in *Ladlad: An Anthology of Philippine Gay Writing*, ed. J. Neil C. Garcia and Danton Remoto (Pasig: Anvil, 1994), xv.

23. Altman, "On Global Queering."

24. Massad, "Re-orienting Desire"; Long, "Unbearable Witness."

25. See Suzanne LaFont, "Not Quite Redemption Song: LGBT-Hate in Jamaica," in *Homophobias: Lust and Loathing across Time and Space*, ed. David A. B. Murray (Durham, N.C.: Duke University Press, 2009), 118–21.

26. Sylvia Rivera Law Project (SRLP), "SRLP on Hate Crime Laws," n.d., http://srlp.org/our-strategy/policy-advocacy/hate-crimes.

27. Donnelly, *Universal Human Rights*, 229.

28. Eve Kosofsky Sedgwick, *Epistemology of the Closet* (Berkeley: University of California Press, 1990), 34–35.

29. Traditional Values Coalition, "What Is a 'Sexual Orientation'?," n.d.

30. Sonia Katyal, "Exporting Identity," *Yale Journal of Law and Feminism* 14 (2002): 97–176.

31. For a critical interrogation of the term "MSM," see Andil Gosine, "'Race,' Culture, Power, Sex, Desire, Love: Writing in 'Men Who Have Sex with Men,'" *IDS Bulletin* 37, no. 5 (2006): 27–33.

32. Rebecca M. Young and Ilan H. Meyer, "The Trouble With 'MSM' and 'WSW': Erasure of the Sexual-Minority Person in Public Health Discourse," *American Journal of Public Health* 95, no. 7 (2005): 1144–49.

33. Marc Epprecht, "Sexual Minorities, Human Rights and Public Health Strategies in Africa," *African Affairs* 111, no. 443 (2012): 223–43.

34. Thoreson, "Realizing Rights in Manila," 532.

35. Petchesky, "Sexual Rights"; Armas, "A Democracy of Sexuality"; Epprecht, *Sexuality and Social Justice in Africa*, 160–64.

36. See Budhiraja, Fried, and Teixeira, "Spelling It Out," 141.

37. Julia Serano defines "cissexual" as "people who are not transsexual and who have only ever experienced their subconscious and physical sexes as being aligned." Julia Serano, *Whipping Girl: A Transsexual Woman on Sexism and the Scapegoating of Femininity* (Berkeley, Calif.: Seal Press, 2007), 12.

38. IGLHRC, "Indonesia: Activists Fight to Overturn Oppressive Law in Aceh," September 25, 2009, http://www.iglhrc.org/cgi-bin/iowa/article/takeaction/resource center/975.html.

39. After my fieldwork, IGLHRC adopted a new strategic plan. As Poore pointed out, this went a long way in foregrounding intersectionality and the interconnectedness of human rights. I note this strategic plan, and other post–fieldwork developments, in the conclusion.

40. IGLHRC, "Protests against Ban of Sex Worker Rights Meeting in Kampala," November 19, 2010, http://www.iglhrc.org/cgi-bin/iowa/article/takeaction/partners/1273.html.

41. This was not uncommon; IGLHRC cited one survey by the Buenos Aires Ombudsman's Office and Asociación Lucha por la Identitdad Travesti y Transexual (ALITT) in which 89 percent of transvestite respondents in Buenos Aires were engaging in sex work. IGLHRC, *The Rights of Transvestites in Argentina*, n.d. (ca. 2001), http://www.iglhrc.org/sites/default/files/184-1.pdf; Sonia Corrêa and Susie Jolly, "Development's Encounter with Sexuality: Essentialism and Beyond," in Cornwall, Corrêa, and Jolly, *Development with a Body*, 36.

42. Phillips, "Blackmail in Zimbabwe," 357–59; Alice M. Miller, "Sexuality, Violence against Women, and Human Rights: Women Make Demands and Ladies Get Protection," *Health and Human Rights* 7, no. 2 (2004): 17–47.

43. Gayle Rubin, "Thinking Sex: Notes for a Radical Theory of the Politics of Sexuality," in Vance, *Pleasure and Danger*, 280.

44. The fact that work on Senegal was being primarily coordinated from New York rather than the Africa Program might also have shaped how aggressively incidents like these were investigated.

45. Stefan Baral et al., "HIV Prevalence, Risks for HIV Infection, and Human Rights among Men Who Have Sex with Men (MSM) in Malawi, Namibia, and Botswana," *PLoS ONE* 4, no. 3 (2009): 4.

46. Ibid.

47. Stefan Baral, e-mail message to author, September 28, 2010.

48. Stefan Baral et al., "Bisexual Practices and Bisexual Concurrency among Men Who Have Sex with Men (MSM) in Peri-Urban Cape Town, South Africa" (presented

at the Fifth International AIDS Society Conference on HIV Pathogenesis, Treatment and Prevention, Cape Town, South Africa, July 19–22, 2009).

49. For a list of various treaty bodies' references to extortion, see Ryan Richard Thoreson, "Responding to Blackmail and Extortion as Human Rights Violations," in *Nowhere to Turn: Blackmail and Extortion of LGBT People in Sub-Saharan Africa,* ed. Ryan Thoreson and Sam Cook (New York: IGLHRC, 2011), 134 n2.

50. Ibid.

51. Ibid., 135–39.

52. Rhonda Copelon, "Recognizing the Egregious in the Everyday: Domestic Violence as Torture," *Columbia Human Rights Law Review* 25 (1994): 291–367; Rhonda Copelon, "Intimate Terror: Understanding Domestic Violence as Torture," in Cook, *Human Rights of Women,* 116–52; Radhika Coomaraswamy, "Combating Domestic Violence: Obligations of the State," *Innocenti Digest* 6 (2000): 10–11.

53. Copelon, "Intimate Terror," 127, 139; Katrina Crew, "Campaigning for an End to Domestic Violence: The Need for Multilateral Approaches," *Essex Human Rights Review* 4, no. 2 (2007): 12–13.

54. Inter-American Convention to Prevent and Punish Torture, December 9, 1985, O.A.S.T.S. 67.

55. Convention against Torture and Other Cruel, Inhuman, or Degrading Treatment or Punishment, December 10, 1984, 1465 U.N.T.S. 85.

56. Notably, many mainstream human rights organizations distinguish humanitarianism and human rights, and deliberately avoid giving material goods to grassroots groups and individuals to avoid later allegations that their accounts of human rights violations were purchased from victims. At IGLHRC, where brokers were not solely in the business of human rights reporting, an emphasis on lasting, substantive partnerships gave brokers greater flexibility to respond to immediate needs.

4. LGBT HUMAN RIGHTS ADVOCACY AND THE PARTNERSHIP PRINCIPLE

1. Manuel Castells, *The Power of Identity* (Oxford: Blackwell, 1997), 106; Margaret E. Keck and Kathryn Sikkink, *Activists beyond Borders: Advocacy Networks in International Politics* (Ithaca, N.Y.: Cornell University Press, 1998), 121–64; Mimi Sheller and John Urry, "Mobile Transformations of 'Public' and 'Private' Life," *Theory, Culture and Society* 20, no. 3 (2003): 107–25; Sanjeev Khagram, "Restructuring the Global Politics of Development: The Case of India's Narmada Valley Dams," in Khagram, Riker, and Sikkink, *Restructuring World Politics,* 206–30; Smitu Kothari, "Globalization, Global Alliances, and the Narmada Movement," in Khagram, Riker, and Sikkink, *Restructuring World Politics,* 231–41.

2. Alan Hudson, "NGOs' Transnational Advocacy Networks: From 'Legitimacy' to 'Political Responsibility'?" *Global Networks* 1, no. 4 (2001): 335.

3. Alan F. Fowler, "Authentic NGDO Partnerships in the New Policy Agenda for International Aid: Dead End or Light Ahead?," *Development and Change* 29 (1998):

137–59; Lisa Jordan and Peter Van Tuijl, "Political Responsibility in Transnational NGO Advocacy," *World Development* 28, no. 12 (2000): 2051–54; Jeremy Gould, "Timing, Scale and Style: Capacity as Governmentality in Tanzania," in *The Aid Effect: Giving and Governing in International Development,* ed. David Mosse and David Lewis (London: Pluto Press, 2005), 61; Lewis, *Management of Non-governmental Development Organizations,* 22.

4. Fowler, "Authentic NGDO Partnerships," 140; Bedford, *Developing Partnerships,* xiv; Lewis, *Management of Non-governmental Development Organizations,* 77–78; David Mosse, "Global Governance and the Ethnography of International Aid," in Mosse and Lewis, *Aid Effect,* 4–5.

5. Hudson, "From 'Legitimacy' to 'Political Responsibility'?," 332.

6. Gordon Crawford, "Partnership or Power? Deconstructing the 'Partnership for Governance Reform' in Indonesia," *Third World Quarterly* 24, no. 1 (2003): 139–59; Heiko Henkel and Roderick Stirrat, "Participation as Spiritual Duty; Empowerment as Secular Subjection," in *Participation: The New Tyranny?,* ed. Bill Cooke and Uma Kothari (London: Zed, 2001), 168–84.

7. Andi Mallarangeng and Peter Van Tuijl, "Breaking New Ground or Dressing-Up in the Emperor's New Clothes? A Response to a Critical Review," *Third World Quarterly* 25, no. 5 (2004): 919–33. See also William J. Spurlin, *Imperialism within the Margins: Queer Representation and the Politics of Culture in Southern Africa* (New York: Palgrave Macmillan, 2006), 110–15.

8. Mosse, "Ethnography of International Aid," 10.

9. Chandra Talpade Mohanty, "Under Western Eyes: Feminist Scholarship and Colonial Discourses," *Boundary 2* 12/13 (1984): 333–58.

10. Massad, "Re-orienting Desire"; Hoad, *African Intimacies,* 60–67; Haritaworn, Tauqir, and Erdem, "Gay Imperialism."

11. Elizabeth Weill-Greenberg, "Int'l Gay Group Loses Staff amid Criticism," *New York Blade,* March 15, 2006.

12. Andrés Duque, "Alejandra Sarda Leaves IGLHRC," *Blabbeando* (blog), August 1, 2006, http://blabbeando.blogspot.com/2006/08/alejandra-sarda-leaves-iglhrc.html.

13. The fact that brokers at IGLHRC typically referred to their significant others as "partners" also gave partnership a unique valence in LGBT advocacy. In development anthropology, "partner" has a more contractual, businesslike connotation; for LGBT activists, "partner" carried strong connotations of intimacy, trust, and commitment.

14. Lewis, *Management of Non-governmental Development Organizations,* 206–7.

15. Thomas Bierschenk, "Development Projects as Arenas of Negotiation for Strategic Groups: A Case Study from Bénin," *Sociologia Ruralis* 28, nos. 2/3 (1988): 146; Mosse, "Social Research in Rural Development," 160–61.

16. Jordan and Van Tuijl, "Political Responsibility."

17. Aet Annist, "The Worshippers of Rules? Defining Right and Wrong in Local Participatory Project Applications in South-Eastern Estonia," in Mosse and Lewis, *Aid Effect,* 150–70; Pieter Glasbergen, "Setting the Scene: The Partnership Paradigm in

the Making," in *Partnerships, Governance and Sustainable Development: Reflections on Theory and Practice,* ed. Pieter Glasbergen, Frank Biermann, and Arthur P. J. Mol (Cheltenham: Edward Elgar, 2007), 7–9.

18. This was not uncommon for groups working on LGBT issues. Epprecht, *Sexuality and Social Justice in Africa,* 167–68.

19. See Thomas Carothers and Marina Ottaway, "The Burgeoning World of Civil Society Aid," in *Funding Virtue: Civil Society Aid and Democracy Promotion,* ed. Marina Ottaway and Thomas Carothers (Washington, D.C.: Carnegie Endowment for International Peace, 2000), 13; Kathryn Sikkink, "Restructuring World Politics: The Limits and Asymmetries of Soft Power," in Khagram, Riker, and Sikkink, *Restructuring World Politics,* 308–9. For a critical take on how this can distort Southern LGBT movements, see Gathoni Blessol, "LGBTI-Queer Struggles Like Other Struggles in Africa," in Ekine and Abbas, *Queer Studies Reader,* 223.

20. As discussed in chapter 2, IGLHRC was not a funder, but did help facilitate projects and travel for activists.

21. Sardá, "Discrimination against Lesbians," 111, 119.

22. Mouhamadou Tidiane Kassé, "Mounting Homophobic Violence in Senegal," in Ekine and Abbas, *Queer African Reader,* 262–72.

23. Ibid., 265–66.

24. Ibid., 266.

25. Codou Bop (panel discussion, "Policing Sexuality: Law, Society, and Homosexuality in Sub-Saharan Africa," NYU School of Law, New York, February 17, 2010).

26. HRW released its report in October 2010, without any major repercussions that I am aware of reported in Senegal. The report was developed with some of the same stakeholders, although it deals exclusively with men who are gay or perceived to be gay. HRW, *Fear for Life: Violence against Gay Men and Men Perceived as Gay in Senegal* (New York: HRW, 2010).

27. An account of this episode is also offered by Mouhamadou Tidiane Kassé, who suggests that IGLHRC and HRW could still have used the reports for advocacy with government officials, human rights groups, and HIV/AIDS organizations in Senegal. At the time of the report's embargo, my understanding was that IGLHRC should not use the reports at all, and certainly not with government officials. Although IGLHRC never publicly released the report, the crisis committee apparently has used it for advocacy and training. Kassé, "Mounting Homophobic Violence," 267–68.

28. Keck and Sikkink, *Activists beyond Borders,* 12–13.

29. Ibid., 207–9.

30. Massad, *Desiring Arabs,* 160–90; Long, "Unbearable Witness." This has been a concern since human rights entered the foreign policy arena in a robust way. See Daniel C. Thomas, "Human Rights in U.S. Foreign Policy," in Khagram, Riker, and Sikkink, *Restructuring World Politics,* 84–85.

31. Richard Morgan, "Industrial Porn and Magic," *Out,* August 1, 2010, 56.

32. CEDEP, "Welcome to CEDEP," 2009, http://www.cedepmalawi.org.

33. Secrecy is not unique to LGBT advocacy; at times, AI and other groups have had to adapt their solidarity model to protect prisoners who were likely to be punished as a result of transnational interventions. Jonathan Power, *Like Water on Stone: The Story of Amnesty International* (London: Penguin Press, 2001), 144.

34. Armas, "A Democracy of Sexuality," 220–21.

35. Ellen Messer, "Pluralist Approaches to Human Rights," *Journal of Anthropological Research* 53, no. 3 (1997): 304–5; Susan Moller Okin et al., eds., *Is Multiculturalism Bad for Women?* (Princeton, N.J.: Princeton University Press, 1999); Will Kymlicka, *Multicultural Citizenship: A Liberal Theory of Minority Rights* (Oxford: Oxford University Press, 1995).

36. The message to IGLHRC was reprinted widely in the LGBT press. See "Fourteen from Haiti AIDS Group Among Dead," *Advocate*, January 18, 2010, http//www.advocate.com/news/daily-news/2010/01/18/fourteen-haiti-aids-group-among-dead.

37. IGLHRC and SEROvie, "The Impact of the Earthquake, and Relief and Recovery Programs on Haitian LGBT People," Briefing Paper (New York: IGLHRC, 2011).

38. See Gerhard Anders, "Good Governance as Technology: Towards an Ethnography of the Bretton Woods Institutions," in Mosse and Lewis, *Aid Effect*, 37; Jennifer M. Brinkerhoff, "Partnership as a Means to Good Governance: Towards an Evaluation Framework," in Glasbergen, Biermann, and Mol, *Partnerships, Governance, and Sustainable Development*, 76.

39. See Currier, "Behind the Mask," 164–67.

40. Bedford, *Developing Partnerships*, xx.

41. Rosalind Eyben and Rosario León, "Whose Aid? The Case of the Bolivian Elections Project," in Mosse and Lewis, *Aid Effect*, 106–25.

42. HRW, *This Alien Legacy: The Origins of "Sodomy" Laws in British Colonialism* (New York: HRW, 2008); Corinne Lennox and Matthew Waites, eds., *Human Rights, Sexual Orientation and Gender Identity in the Commonwealth: Struggles for Decriminalisation and Change* (London: Institute of Commonwealth Studies, 2013). In England and Wales, laws against "gross indecency" remained on the books until 1967, when the Sexual Offences Act decriminalized same-sex activity in private between two men over the age of twenty-one.

43. "The Anti-Homosexuality Bill of 2009," *Uganda Gazette* 102, no. 47, September 25, 2009.

44. After years of debate and discussion, a revised version of the Anti-Homosexuality Bill was passed by Parliament in late 2013 and signed by President Museveni in early 2014. For the text of the Anti-Homosexuality Act of 2014, see "The Anti-Homosexuality Act of 2014," *Uganda Gazette* 107, no. 14, March 10, 2014.

45. IGLHRC and SMUG, "Uganda: The U.S. Religious Right Exports Homophobia to Africa," March 4, 2009, http://www.iglhrc.org/cgi-bin/iowa/article/takeaction/partners/868.html.

46. IGLHRC and CEDEP, "IGLHRC and CEDEP Commend Presidential Pardon in Malawi," May 29, 2010, http://www.iglhrc.org/cgi-bin/iowa/article/pressroom/pressrelease/1137.html.

47. IGLHRC, "Kenya: IGLHRC Monitors Reports of Violence and Arrests," February 12, 2010, http://www.iglhrc.org/cgi-bin/iowa/article/takeaction/resourcecenter/1092.html.

48. Fowler, "Authentic NGDO Partnerships," 139–40; Jordan and Van Tuijl, "Political Responsibility," 2053–54.

5. Knowledge as Power

1. Julie Bolcer, "Uganda LGBT Volunteer Beheaded," *Advocate,* July 6, 2010.

2. Tabu Butagira, "Man Beheaded at Electoral Commission Boss' Farm," *Daily Monitor* (Uganda), July 4, 2010.

3. Boellstorff, "Dubbing Culture"; Chao, "Global Metaphors and Local Strategies"; Carlos Ulises Decena, "Tacit Subjects," *GLQ* 14, nos. 2/3 (2008): 339–59; Donham, "Freeing South Africa"; Peter A. Jackson, "An Explosion of Thai Identities: Global Queering and Re-imagining Queer Theory," *Culture, Health and Sexuality* 2, no. 4 (2000): 405–24; Peter A. Jackson, *"Kathoey >< Gay >< Man: The Historical Emergence of Gay Male Identity in Thailand," in Sites of Desire, Economies of Pleasure: Sexualities in Asia and the Pacific,* ed. Lenore Manderson and Margaret Jolly (Chicago: University of Chicago Press, 1997), 166–90; Don Kulick, *Travesti: Sex, Gender, and Culture among Brazilian Transgendered Prostitutes* (Chicago: University of Chicago Press, 1998); Mark McLelland, "Is There a Japanese 'Gay Identity'?," *Culture, Health and Sexuality* 2, no. 4 (2000): 459–72; Murray, "Rock and a Hard Place"; Patton, "Stealth Bombers of Desire"; Denis M. Provencher, "Coming out à l'oriental: Maghrebi-French Performances of Gender, Sexuality, and Religion," *Journal of Homosexuality* 58, nos. 6/7 (2011): 812–33; Chris K. K. Tan, "Go Home, Gay Boy! Or, Why Do Singaporean Gay Men Prefer to 'Go Home' and Not 'Come Out'?," *Journal of Homosexuality* 58, nos. 6/7 (2011): 865–82; Michael L. Tan, "From *Bakla* to Gay: Shifting Gender Identities and Sexual Behaviors in the Philippines," in *Conceiving Sexuality: Approaches to Sex Research in a Postmodern World,* ed. Richard G. Parker and John H. Gagnon (New York: Routledge, 1995), 85–96; Thoreson, "Realizing Rights in Manila"; Wright, "The Case of Bolivia."

4. Altman, "On Global Queering"; Dennis Altman, *Global Sex* (Chicago: University of Chicago Press, 2001), 86–105; Dennis Altman, "Global Gaze/Global Gays," in Blasius, *Sexual Identities/Queer Politics,* 96–117; Arnaldo Cruz-Malavé and Martin F. Manalansan IV, "Introduction: Dissident Sexualities/Alternative Globalisms," in Cruz-Malavé and Manalansan, *Queer Globalizations,* 1–10; Katie King, "'There Are No Lesbians Here': Lesbianisms, Feminisms, and Global Gay Formations," in Cruz-Malavé and Manalansan, *Queer Globalizations,* 33–45; Massad, *Desiring Arabs,* 160–90.

5. Boellstorff and Leap, "Globalization and 'New' Articulations," 2.

6. Goodale, "Locating Rights, Envisioning Law," 10–24; Riles, *Network Inside Out*; Keck and Sikkink, *Activists beyond Borders*.

7. Sanjeev Khagram, James V. Riker, and Kathryn Sikkink, "From Santiago to Seattle: Transnational Advocacy Groups Restructuring World Politics," in Khagram, Riker, and Sikkink, *Restructuring World Politics*, 6–15; Sikkink, "Limits and Asymmetries of Soft Power," 303–6.

8. Wilson, "Representing Human Rights Violations"; Hastrup, "The Limits of Legal Language"; Merry, "Mapping the Middle," 49.

9. Altman, *Global Sex*, 73–78.

10. Mosse and Lewis, "Theoretical Approaches to Brokerage," 15–16; Anthony Pagden, "The Genesis of 'Governance' and Enlightenment Conceptions of the Cosmopolitan World Order," *International Social Science Journal* 50, no. 155 (1998): 7–15; Matthew Eagleton-Pierce, "Unravelling the Received Idea of 'Governance'" (paper presented at "Regional and Global Institutions in the 21st Century," Oxford University, Oxford, April 30–May 1, 2008); Michael Herzfeld, *The Social Production of Indifference: Exploring the Symbolic Roots of Western Bureaucracy* (Oxford: Berg, 1992), 115.

11. For a rich discussion of strategies to enhance NGO credibility, see Peter A. Gourevitch and David A. Lake, "Beyond Virtue: Evaluating and Enhancing the Credibility of Non-governmental Organizations," in *The Credibility of Transnational NGOs: When Virtue Is Not Enough*, ed. Peter A. Gourevitch, David A. Lake, and Janice Gross Stein (Cambridge: Cambridge University Press, 2012).

12. Jodi Dean, Jon W. Anderson, and Geert Lovink, "Introduction: The Postdemocratic Governmentality of Networked Societies," in *Reformatting Politics: Information Technology and Global Civil Society*, ed. Jodi Dean, Jon W. Anderson, and Geert Lovink (New York: Routledge, 2006), xxvi.

13. Michel Foucault, "Two Lectures," in *Power/Knowledge: Selected Interviews and Other Writings, 1972–1977*, ed. Colin Gordon, trans. Colin Gordon et al. (New York: Pantheon, 1980), 93.

14. Chao, "Global Metaphors and Local Strategies," 383–88; Pigg, "Globalizing the Facts of Life"; Goldstein, "Human Rights as Culprit."

15. Daniel Ottosson, *State-Sponsored Homophobia: A World Survey of Laws Prohibiting Same Sex Activity between Consenting Adults* (Brussels: ILGA, 2010).

16. As one former IGLHRC employee has commented, "In the context of human rights advocacy, the people whose rights are being advocated for are cast as the content providers (African LGBT victims) and the advocates are cast as the authoritative producers of knowledge from that content (white and/or male citizens of the US or Europe)." Makahamadze and Murungi, "*Nhorondo—Mawazo Yetu*," 295.

17. Sperling, Ferree, and Risman, "Constructing Global Feminism," 1176.

18. Arjun Appadurai, "Disjuncture and Difference in the Global Cultural Economy," in Inda and Rosaldo, *Anthropology of Globalization*, 60–62; Chabot and Duyvendak, "Globalization and Transnational Diffusion," 701–8.

19. Doug McAdam and Dieter Rucht, "The Cross-National Diffusion of Movement Ideas," *Annals of the American Academy of Political and Social Science* 528 (1993): 59. Manuel Castells distinguishes "the space of places" and "the space of flows," while Sean Chabot and Jan Willem Duyvendak differentiate "interpersonal" from "media" channels. Castells, *Information Age*, 123–24; Chabot and Duyvendak, "Globalization and Transnational Diffusion," 706. In slightly different registers, each framework distinguishes relational and nonrelational channels of diffusion.

20. Notably, this was not true of IGLHRC's partners in the LAC region, who worked with staff in Buenos Aires who were Argentinean and fluent in Spanish.

21. Brokers were frank about this point; Cook called English "the lingua franca of this organization."

22. One example of a Lusophone initiative was IGLHRC's transgender training in Mozambique in 2010.

23. Dean, Anderson, and Lovink, "Postdemocratic Governmentality," xv.

24. Martha McCaughey and Michael D. Ayers, "Introduction," in *Cyberactivism: Online Activism in Theory and Practice*, ed. Martha McCaughey and Michael D. Ayers (New York: Routledge, 2003), 6; Joanne Lebert, "Wiring Human Rights Activism: Amnesty International and the Challenges of Information and Communication Technologies," in McCaughey and Ayers, *Cyberactivism*, 216; Sandip Roy, "From Khush List to Gay Bombay: Virtual Webs of Real People," in Berry, Martin, and Yue, *Mobile Cultures*, 189.

25. Okoth Fred Mudhai, "Exploring the Potential for More Strategic Civil Society Use of Mobile Phones," in Dean, Anderson, and Lovink, *Reformatting Politics*, 109.

26. The concept of "good enough" knowledge is akin to "good enough" ethnography, a concept developed by Nancy Scheper-Hughes in her fieldwork in Bom Jesus da Mata. Nancy Scheper-Hughes, *Death without Weeping: The Violence of Everyday Life in Brazil* (Berkeley: University of California Press, 1992), 28. Both hint at a kind of functional compromise that recognizes inevitable imperfections but allows the larger project to proceed.

27. Even Behind the Mask, an NGO that collected and reported stories about sex, gender, and sexuality across Africa, struggled with this problem. Currier, "Behind the Mask," 163.

28. Currier, *Out in Africa*, 132–39.

29. Cowan, "Uncertain Political Limits," 141; David N. Gellner, "Making Civil Society in South Asia," in *Varieties of Activist Experience: Civil Society in South Asia*, ed. David N. Gellner (London: Sage, 2010), 12.

30. Ryan Richard Thoreson, "Troubling the Waters of a 'Wave of Homophobia': Political Economies of Anti-queer Animus in Sub-Saharan Africa," *Sexualities* 17, nos. 1/2 (2014): 23–42; Sibongile Ndashe, "The Single Story of 'African Homophobia' is Dangerous for LGBTI Activism," in Ekine and Abbas, *Queer African Reader*, 155–64; Patrick Awondo, Peter Geschiere, and Graeme Reid, "Homophobic Africa? Toward a More Nuanced View," *African Studies Review* 55, no. 3 (2012): 145–68.

6. Demanding Rights, Compelling Recognition

1. Karen Brown Thompson, "Women's Rights Are Human Rights," in Khagram, Riker, and Sikkink, *Restructuring World Politics,* 96–122.

2. Kristen L. Walker, "Evolving Human Rights Norms around Sexuality," *ILSA Journal of International and Comparative Law* 6 (2000): 346–48; Kate Sheill, "Sexual Rights Are Human Rights," in Cornwall, Corrêa, and Jolly, *Development with a Body,* 46.

3. Duncan Osborne, "Ill Will toward ILGA," *Advocate,* March 8, 1994, 27; Joshua Gamson, "Messages of Exclusion: Gender, Movements, and Symbolic Boundaries," *Gender and Society* 11, no. 2 (1997): 178–99.

4. Ruth S. Limjuco, chairperson of the Committee on NGOs, to Hans Hjorpe-kjon, secretary-general of ILGA, "Questionnaire for Member Organizations and Subsidiaries of the International Lesbian and Gay Association," June 9, 1995.

5. Ibid.

6. IGLHRC's own lengthy but ultimately successful efforts to win consultative status are described later in this chapter.

7. Arvind Narrain, "Brazil Resolution on Sexual Orientation: Challenges in Articulating a Sexual Rights Framework from the Viewpoint of the Global South," (paper presented at "Sexualities, Genders and Rights in Asia: First International Conference of Asian Queer Studies," Mahidol University, Bangkok, Thailand, July 2005).

8. Daniel Fischlin and Martha Nandorfy, *The Concise Guide to Global Human Rights* (New York: Black Rose, 2007), 91.

9. United Nations High Commissioner for Human Rights, "Postponement of Draft Resolution E/CN.4/2003/L.92 and the Proposed Amendments Thereto E/CN.4/2003/L.106–110," 2003, http://ap.ohchr.org/documents/E/CHR/decisions/E-CN_4 -DEC-2003-118. doc.

10. Donnelly, *Universal Human Rights,* 238.

11. France's announcement that it would seek universal decriminalization at the UN initially came as a surprise to many brokers, who worried the effort would backfire and entrench opposition to LGBT human rights. Sheill, "UN General Assembly," 315–16.

12. See HRW, "UN: General Assembly Statement Affirms Rights for All," December 19, 2008, http://www.hrw.org/en/news/2008/12/18/un-general-assembly-state ment-affirms-rights-all.

13. It has been suggested that new norms come into being when they are supported by one-fourth to one-third of state actors. Khagram, Riker, and Sikkink, "From Santiago to Seattle," 15. Under this operational definition, these victories at the UN over the past three years do mark a turning point for the normative recognition of human rights regardless of SOGI.

14. The documents released by Wikileaks also show U.S. engagement with governments and sexual rights advocates in various countries. Epprecht, *Sexuality and Social Justice in Africa,* 142.

15. Lyn Ossome, "Postcolonial Discourses of Queer Activism and Class in Africa," in Ekine and Abbas, *Queer African Reader,* 38.

16. A notable abstention from the resolution was the United States itself, which regularly abstains from the resolution on extrajudicial, summary, or arbitrary executions.

17. The incorporation of LGBT human rights into a host of other diplomatic and foreign policy initiatives is itself a strong sign of a growing norm. Oona Hathaway and Scott J. Shapiro, "Outcasting: Enforcement in Domestic and International Law," *Yale Law Journal* 121 (2011): 252–349; Anthony D'Amato, "Is International Law Really 'Law'?," *Northwestern University Law Review* 79 (1985): 1293–314.

18. IGLHRC, "Belize: Protect Students from Discrimination and Expulsion," December 3, 2009, http://www.iglhrc.org/cgi-bin/iowa/article/takeaction/globalactionalerts/1032.html.

19. Keebet von Benda-Beckmann, *The Broken Stairways to Consensus: Village Justice and State Courts in Minangkabau* (Dordrecht: Foris, 1984), 37.

20. IGLHRC, HRW, ILGA-Europe, Global Advocates for Trans Equality (GATE) and COC Netherlands, "Turkey: Drop Charges against Transgender Rights Defenders," October 18, 2010, http://www.iglhrc.org/cgi-bin/iowa/article/pressroom/pressrelease/1222.html.

21. The Special Rapporteur on Freedom of Expression was deemed a more difficult sell in this instance, for example, since the person occupying the position focused almost exclusively on political expression and eschewed more expansive interpretations that might have included gender expression.

22. Special Rapporteur on the Promotion and Protection of Human Rights and Fundamental Freedoms While Countering Terrorism, Martin Scheinin, "Report of the Special Rapporteur on the Promotion and Protection of Human Rights and Fundamental Freedoms While Countering Terrorism," UN Doc. A/64/211 (August 3, 2009), 19–20. (Hereinafter Scheinin Report.)

23. Scheinin Report, 20, 48. For reactions, see Joseph Abrams, "U.N. Report Demands Repeal of Counterterrorism Laws to Promote 'Gender Equality,'" *Fox News*, October 21, 2009, http://www.foxnews.com/world/2009/10/21/report-demands-repeal-counterterrorism-laws-promote-gender-equality; Kilian Melloy, "U.N. Terrorism Report Cites Transgender Prejudice," *Edge News*, October 20, 2009, http://www.edgeboston.com/news.//reviews//97918/un_terrorism_report_cites_transgender_prejudice.

24. Office of the High Commissioner for Human Rights, "Monitoring the Core International Human Rights Treaties," 2010, http://www2.ohchr.org/english/bodies/treaty/index.htm.

25. Andrew Byrnes, "Toward More Effective Enforcement of Women's Human Rights through the Use of International Human Rights Law and Procedures," in Cook, *Human Rights of Women*, 207–8; Rebecca J. Cook, "State Accountability under the Convention on the Elimination of All Forms of Discrimination against Women," in Cook, *Human Rights of Women*, 253.

26. IGLHRC, *Equal and Indivisible: Crafting Inclusive Shadow Reports for CEDAW* (New York: IGLHRC, 2009).

27. IGLHRC, "Successful Launch of *Equal and Indivisible* at CEDAW," July 29, 2009, http://www.iglhrc.org/cgi-bin/iowa/article/takeaction/resourcecenter/952.html.

28. ICJ, "International Human Rights Law," 7.

29. Committee on the Elimination of Discrimination against Women, "General Recommendation No. 27 on Older Women and Protection of Their Human Rights," UN Doc. CEDAW/C/GC/27 (December 16, 2010), 13.

30. Committee on the Elimination of Discrimination against Women, "General Recommendation No. 28 on the Core Obligations of States Parties under Article 2 of the Convention on the Elimination of All Forms of Discrimination Against Women," UN Doc. CEDAW/C/GC/28 (December 16, 2010), 18.

31. Ibid., 31.

32. International Women's Rights Action Watch Asia Pacific, "State Parties to CEDAW," *CEDAW Knowledge Resource,* May 5, 2009, http://www.iwraw-ap.org/convention/parties.htm.

33. Merry, *Human Rights and Gender Violence,* 36–71.

34. Marybeth Herald, "Explaining the Differences: Transgender Theories and Court Practice," in Barclay, Bernstein, and Marshall, *Queer Mobilizations,* 187.

35. Marie-Bénédicte Dembour, "Human Rights Talk and Anthropological Ambivalence: The Particular Context of Universal Claims," in *Inside and Outside the Law: Anthropological Studies of Authority and Ambiguity,* ed. Olivia Harris (London: Routledge, 1996), 19–40.

36. United States Mission to the United Nations, "Remarks by Ambassador Rosemary A. DiCarlo, U.S. Deputy Permanent Representative to the United Nations, during an Economic and Social Council Debate on the Accreditation of the International Gay and Lesbian Human Rights Commission," July 19, 2010, http://usun.state.gov/briefing/statements/2010/144833.htm.

37. Edith M. Lederer, "New HIV Infections Increasing among Homosexuals," *AEGiS,* March 16, 2010, http://www.aegis.org/DisplayContent/?SectionID=147230.

38. IGLHRC, "Iraq: IGLHRC Asks the Iraqi Government to Protect LGBT People," April 17, 2009, http://www.iglhrc.org/cgi-bin/iowa/article/takeaction/partners/889.html.

39. Didde Margrethe Nielsen, *Handbook concerning UN Accreditation for LGBT Organizations* (Copenhagen: Landsforeningen for Bøsser og Lesbiske, 2007).

40. IGLHRC, "Application for Consultative Status with the Economic and Social Council," May 10, 2007, 2.

41. Ibid., 2–3.

42. Cary Alan Johnson, executive director of IGLHRC, to Joop Theunissen, deputy chief, NGO Section, Department of Economic and Social Affairs, "Re: Application for Consultative Status with ECOSOC," May 12, 2009, 1–8.

43. IGLHRC, "Answers to Questions Posed on May 19, 2009 during Q&As with NGOs," May 19, 2009, 1–2.

44. Cary Alan Johnson, executive director of IGLHRC, to Andrei Abramov, chief of the Office of ECOSOC Support and Coordination—NGO Branch, Department of Economic and Social Affairs, "Re: IGLHRC Application for Consultative Status with the United Nations Economic and Social Council (ECOSOC)," February 2, 2010, 1–7.

45. Rebecca J. Cook, "Women's International Human Rights Law: The Way Forward," in Cook, *Human Rights of Women*, 10.

46. Rachel Murray and Franz Viljoen, "Towards Non-Discrimination on the Basis of Sexual Orientation: The Normative Basis and Procedural Possibilities before the African Commission on Human and Peoples' Rights and the African Union," *Human Rights Quarterly* 29 (2007): 102–5.

47. ACHPR, *Zimbabwe Human Rights NGO Forum v. Zimbabwe*, Comm. No. 245/2002 (2006), 169.

48. See Peter Evans, "Fighting Marginalization with Transnational Networks: Counter-Hegemonic Globalization," *Contemporary Sociology* 29, no. 1 (2000): 230–41.

49. Keck and Sikkink, *Activists beyond Borders*, 12–13.

Conclusion

1. Wilson, "Introduction," 10–14; Goodale, "Locating Rights, Envisioning Law," 24; Mark Goodale, *Surrendering to Utopia: An Anthropology of Human Rights* (Stanford, Calif.: Stanford University Press, 2009), 14–16.

2. Olivia Harris, "Introduction: Inside and Outside the Law," in Harris, *Inside and Outside the Law*, 2.

3. Ishay, *History of Human Rights*, 107–16.

4. Ibid., 293–311.

5. Cynthia Rothschild, "Not Your Average Sex Story: Critical Issues in Recent Human Rights Reporting Related to Sexuality," *Health and Human Rights* 7, no. 2 (2004): 168–69.

6. Budhiraja, Fried, and Teixeira, "Spelling It Out," 133; Cornwall, Corrêa, and Jolly, "Development with a Body," 9.

7. Tom Hall and Heather Montgomery, "Home and Away: 'Childhood,' 'Youth,' and Young People," *Anthropology Today* 16, no. 3 (2000): 13–15; Heather Montgomery, "Imposing Rights? A Case Study of Child Prostitution in Thailand," in *Culture and Rights: Anthropological Perspectives*, ed. Jane K. Cowan, Marie-Bénédicte Dembour, and Richard A. Wilson (Cambridge: Cambridge University Press, 2001), 80–101; Judith Ennew, "Future Generations and Global Standards: Children's Rights at the Start of the Millennium," in *Exotic No More: Anthropology on the Front Lines*, ed. Jeremy Mac-Clancy (Chicago: University of Chicago Press, 2002), 338–50.

8. Ruth O'Brien, "From a Doctor's to a Judge's Gaze: Epistemic Communities and the History of Disability Rights Policy in the Workplace," *Polity* 35, no. 3 (2003): 325–46; Michael Ashley Stein, "Disability Human Rights," *California Law Review* 95, no. 1 (2007): 75–121.

9. John Gledhill, "Rights and the Poor," in Wilson and Mitchell, *Human Rights in Global Perspective*, 211; Jackson, "Rights to Indigenous Culture."

10. Manisha Desai, "Transnational Solidarity: Women's Agency, Structural Adjustment, and Globalization," in *Women's Activism and Globalization: Linking Local Struggles and Transnational Politics*, ed. Nancy A. Naples and Manisha Desai (New York: Routledge, 2002), 15–33.

11. Rothschild, "Not Your Average Sex Story," 167–68.

12. American Civil Liberties Union, "Jessica Gonzales v. U.S.A.," August 7, 2013, http://www.aclu.org/human-rights-womens-rights/jessica-gonzales-v-usa.

13. Kymlicka, *Multicultural Citizenship*; Donnelly, *Universal Human Rights*, 204–21; Goodale, *Surrendering to Utopia*, 33, 111–27; Cowan, "Culture and Rights," 12–15.

14. Khagram, Riker, and Sikkink, "From Santiago to Seattle," 13.

15. Messer, "Pluralist Approaches," 310–11. See Dembour, "Human Rights Talk and Anthropological Ambivalence," 32–33.

16. Arendt, *Origins of Totalitarianism*, 296–97.

17. Ibid.; Seyla Benhabib, *The Rights of Others: Aliens, Residents, and Citizens* (Cambridge: Cambridge University Press, 2004), 68.

18. Benhabib, *Rights of Others*, 56–57.

19. Richard Rorty, "Human Rights, Rationality, and Sentimentality," in *On Human Rights: The Oxford Amnesty Lectures, 1993*, ed. Stephen Shute and Susan Hurley (New York: Basic, 1993), 111–34.

20. Stein, "Disability Human Rights," 121. The emphasis on ontological claims is evident, for example, in HRW's report on the rights of persons with disabilities in Northern Uganda. See HRW, *"As If We Weren't Human": Discrimination and Violence against Women with Disabilities in Northern Uganda* (New York: HRW, 2010). Of course, attempts at inclusion also produce particular kinds of subjects. As they seek recognition as human, marginalized groups not only locate themselves within fixed juridical categories, but often foreground their most normatively respectable characteristics, and make respectable demands, to demonstrate they are deserving of human rights. Miller, "Women Make Demands."

21. Sonia Corrêa, Rosalind Petchesky, and Richard Parker, *Sexuality, Health, and Human Rights* (New York: Routledge, 2008), 152.

22. Elizabeth A. Donnelly, "Proclaiming Jubilee: The Debt and Structural Adjustment Network," in Khagram, Riker, and Sikkink, *Restructuring World Politics*, 155–80.

23. Cynthia Rothschild, *Written Out: How Sexuality Is Used to Attack Women's Organizing*, 2nd ed. (New York: IGLHRC, 2005).

24. Michael O'Flaherty and John Fisher, "Sexual Orientation, Gender Identity and International Human Rights Law: Contextualising the Yogyakarta Principles," *Human Rights Law Review* 8, no. 2 (2008): 207–48; Thoreson, "Queering Human Rights."

25. Hall and Montgomery, "Home and Away."

26. Awino Okech, "'In Sisterhood and Solidarity': Queering African Feminist Spaces," in Ekine and Abbas, *Queer African Reader*, 10.

27. During most of the 2000s, the U.S. delegation to the UN routinely framed sexual rights as "new." See Sheill, "Sexual Rights Are Human Rights," 48.

28. Stein, "Disability Human Rights."

29. M. Jean Heriot, "Fetal Rights versus the Female Body: Contested Domains," *Medical Anthropology Quarterly* 10, no. 2 (1996): 176–94; Michael Lim Tan, "Fetal Discourses and the Politics of the Womb," *Reproductive Health Matters* 12, no. 24 (2004): 157–66.

30. Massad, "Re-orienting Desire."

31. Long, "Unbearable Witness."

32. ICJ, "International Human Rights Law," 7.

33. Marie-Bénédicte Dembour, "Following the Movement of a Pendulum: Between Universalism and Relativism," in Cowan, Dembour, and Wilson, *Culture and Rights,* 56–79.

34. Sherry B. Ortner, "Is Female to Male as Nature Is to Culture?" in *Woman, Culture and Society,* ed. Michelle Zimbalist Rosaldo and Louise Lamphere (Stanford, Calif.: Stanford University Press, 1974), 67–88.

35. Ndashe, "Single Story of 'African Homophobia,'" 161. Makau Mutua echoes this assessment, noting, "In no other identity issue is this truer than with respect to sexual orientation. In a sense, sexual orientation claims might be among the last impenetrable frontiers." Mutua, "Sexual Orientation and Human Rights," 453.

36. Geertz, "Local Knowledge"; Hastrup, "The Limits of Legal Language."

37. Waites, "Critique of 'Sexual Orientation.'"

38. Jane K. Cowan, Marie-Bénédicte Dembour, and Richard A. Wilson, "Introduction," in Cowan, Dembour, and Wilson, *Culture and Rights,* 5–6.

Index

Abzug, Bella, 34
action alerts, 80–82
Activist Institutes, 46, 78–79; hybridity of LGBT-human rights advocacy and, 112–13; sexual identity politics in, 103
activists: brokers as, 61–90, 243n.13; globalized movement building partnerships and importance of, 131–33
ACT-UP Philadelphia, 146
Adams, Jennifer, 65–66
adultery laws, LGBT human rights and, 103–11
Advocate magazine, 153
Afghanistan, IGLHRC opposition to U.S. bombing of, 42, 117–18
Africa: collaboration and trust building by IGLHRC in, 126–28; emergency response and movement building in, 77–80; facticity and ambiguity in advocacy programs in, 168–72; globalized movement building partnerships in, 129–33; IGLHRC human rights advocacy in, 40–50, 62–72, 74–75, 113, 196, 225; LGBT rights contestability in, 5–8, 15–20; linguistic limits of advocacy in, 162–65; motives and politics of

transnational advocacy networks in, 172–73; network politics and information production in, 161–62; reports on activities in, 85–89; resistance to Brazil Resolution in, 184–85; self-sufficient organizations' partnerships with IGLHRC in, 149–51; sexual identity politics in, 102–3; sex workers' rights in, 108–11
African Charter, 94–95
African Commission on Human and Peoples' Rights (ACHPR), 29, 46, 75, 78, 126, 140, 196, 208–9
African Human Rights Organization (AFHRO), 47
African Men for Sexual Health and Rights (AMSHeR), 52, 64, 127
African Services Committee, 146
African Union (AU), 83, 126
African Women's Leadership Institute, 107
Africare, 49
Ahmadinejad, Mahmoud, 5
AIDS Coalition to Unleash Power (ACT-UP), 31
AIDS epidemic, queer politics and, 31–38
Akina Mama wa Afrika, 107, 146

261

Ryan R. Thoreson has a JD from the Yale Law School and a DPhil in anthropology from Oxford University.